ROAD ANGELS

Bridge of the Gods

ROAD ANGELS

Searching for Home
on America's Coast of Dreams

KENT NERBURN

HarperSanFrancisco
A Division of HarperCollins*Publishers*

HarperCollins books may be purchased for educational, business, or sales promotional use. For information please write: Special Markets Department, HarperCollins Publishers Inc., 10 East 53rd Street, New York, NY 10022.

HarperCollins Web site: http://www.harpercollins.com
HarperCollins®, 📖®, and HarperSanFrancisco™ are
trademarks of HarperCollins Publishers Inc.

Designed by Joseph Rutt
FIRST EDITION

Library of Congress Cataloging-in-Publication Data
Nerburn, Kent
Road angels : searching for home on America's coast of dreams /
Kent Nerburn.— 1st ed.
p. cm.
ISBN 0–06–0698683 (cloth)
1. Pacific Coast (U.S.)—Description and travel. 2. Pacific States—Description and travel. 3. Pacific Coast (U.S.)—Social life and customs. 4. Pacific States—Social life and customs. 5. Nerburn, Kent, 1946—Journeys—Pacific Coast (U.S.) 6. Nerburn, Kent, 1946—Journeys—Pacific States. 7. Nerburn, Kent, 1946—Philosophy.
I. Title.
F852.3 .N46 2001
917.9—dc21
2001024222
01 02 03 04 05 ❖/RRD 10 9 8 7 6 5 4 3 2 1

To my mother, Virginia Nerburn,
who put the hunger for distances in my heart.

CONTENTS

ONE

GOOD BULBS

Hell, there ain't no one beginning. A couple of creeks, some lakes and streams, water running in from some swamps. It all just adds up. Pretty soon there's a river.

—An old Ojibwe man discussing the source
of the Mississippi here in northern Minnesota

Sometimes big events have small origins.

There was no divorce, no loss of job, no dramatic crisis of faith and self-confidence. It was, at heart, the accretion of little things, like a deepening blanket of snow, that finally caused the branch to snap and sent me careening back to the West Coast from my comfortable home in the woods of northern Minnesota.

Let me tell you how it happened.

I have always had the firm conviction—and it has only strengthened as I've gotten older—that we're shaped by the land on which we live. I mean this in the profoundest sense. The monumental forces—the weather, the quality of light and the quantity of darkness, the sense of distance or possibility or enclosure in the terrain—all of these shape our spirits and become our point of contact with the gods. In ways we can only dimly understand, they make us who we are.

I was born into the long cold flatness of the Midwestern North, where justice speaks in the voice of thunder, forgiveness falls like a mantle of snow, and the endless turning of the seasons weaves humility and caution into the very fabric of our lives. Without knowing it, we become watchers and distant observers, valuing objectivity over passionate involvement, because we sense in our bones that the wheel of life, like the seasons, is always turning and will leave us grasping at something ephemeral and fleeting if we invest too strongly in any passing emotion or passion.

At our best this makes us clear-eyed and fair-minded, with an unerring instinct for the essential. At our worst we become cynical and retrograde, holding life at a distance and making a virtue of intractability. But in either case, gradually and unwittingly, we take on the face of American Gothic, full of stolid honesty and spiritual severity, bound to the earth and its hard lessons, aware in our bones that the wheel of fate, more than the trajectory of progress, is the light by which our lives must be lived.

In my youth this was just fine. I was surrounded by people who shared the same worldview, and I knew no other way. It was quite enough to be the laconic watcher, the ironist, the cautious skeptic who held the world at arm's length, putting it in context and parsing its deficiencies. But as I grew, this critical distance became stultifying. Irony casts out love, and I, like everyone else, wanted love. Not just love of another person, but love of life. I wanted to embrace, not analyze. Kerouac-crazy midnight drives, paper-bag cheap-whiskey drunks, and Woody Guthrie walking the railroad tracks with collar up almost sufficed. But that was drunken love—an embrace of disengagement, a cloaked celebration of detachment from something larger.

I wanted something else. I wanted union, oneness, wholeness.

I wanted belief.

Eventually, like so many before me, I heard the siren song of California. I packed a few belongings in my rusty Minnesota car and undertook that time-honored, mythic American journey toward freedom and possibility. It was an exhilarating liberation. Even now I remember that first moment, driving in on I–80, just past Reno at the edge of the Sierras, when I pulled over and stepped out into the mountain-sweet amber morning light. The air intoxicated me. The scale overwhelmed me. I stood on a fallen fir as big around as my car and thrust my arms in the air, like Moses thanking God for the tablets or Jesus telling the waters, "Peace. Be still."

And, indeed, the waters were beginning to still. Some tablets were being handed down. Whatever it was that had made the Pomo and the Miwok trade with each other rather than cut off each other's feet, like the Ojibwe and Dakota of my native North, was softening my spirit as well. I was moving inside myself, becoming the participant rather than the observer. The man with his hands in his pockets and his James Dean hunch was fading into the past. For the first time in my life, I was losing the distance of irony and replacing it with the fullness of belief.

Over time, I fell completely under the spell. And it wasn't just California; it was the entire West Coast. I rambled about from border to border, sleeping on beaches, waking under the redwoods, living in cabins and cities, and falling in and out of love. It was an intoxicating time in an intoxicating land, where the gods that shaped the spirit were not the gods of ice and thunder, but the gods of Pacific vistas and the susurrations of the sea. Meaning was not something glacial and ground out; it was eruptive, epiphanic. One could dream of change, of metanoia, of conversion.

From every corner, life was shouting "Yes!" It was a great embrace, a great affirmation. I flowed with the waters, rolled with the hills, lived the life of easy grace in which judgment, by God or man, receded like a distant whisper. For the first time I was not apart from my life; I was in it.

I had slipped the bonds of European thought. T. S. Eliot and Hegel and Aquinas and Augustine were left behind. I was part of hope, of future, of discovery. There was wisdom to the East and worlds to explore, where the past was not a weight and an obligation, but an illusion of my own devise. I could cast it off, like everything else—shed my existential slouch like a chrysalis—and fly free into a world limited only by the shackles of my own consciousness.

Was I naive? I don't think so. I was simply intoxicated by discovery. There were magical places of both the spirit and the intellect that had not been touched by the forces that had formed me, and I was exploring them with my entire being.

But eventually the intoxication wore off. I began to see the dark side to this reality. I found myself party to a kind of cultural amnesia, an obsession with the self, an overvaluation of newness, a deification of possibility at the expense of responsibility. Here, in the land where one could breathe free, one could also simply walk free of entanglements. Moral ambiguity was too easily dismissed as negativity, and the long, slow winnowing of history—the patient clarification of incremental progress—was too readily disregarded.

At its best, it was a shucking of the husks of old paradigms. At its worst, it was a selfish joyride, pedal to the metal, and no one was stopping to check the oil.

Finally, for me, the wheels came off. I became agitated, unhappy, a man without a center. I longed for the grounding values of hard work and family and meaningful social context. I wanted to go back to a place where everyone wasn't from somewhere else, and movement—both physical and spiritual—wasn't a panacea for all ills.

I wanted solidity, not fluidity. I was sick of change as a value.

I wanted to go home.

So I did.

I worked my way north, from the Bay Area through Oregon and British Columbia. It was a slow backward waltz, several years in the making, and along the way I found good lives I could have claimed. But, somehow, the die had been cast. I was going home, and until I touched that holy ground of my birth again and found some sense of spiritual center, all stops along the way were only detours. I needed to regroup, rethink, reconnect. Then I would set out again.

Funny thing, life.

Fifteen years after that return to the landscape of my birth—a return that was intended to be nothing more than a packing and regrouping stop on my way back west—I found myself living not in the exuberant craziness of the Bay Area or the mystical melancholic greyness of the Oregon forests or the Olympic Peninsula, but in this forgotten corner of northwestern Minnesota, hard against the Canadian border, a mere two hundred miles from the place of my birth and fifteen hundred miles from the rhythmic washings of any sea.

I'm not quite sure how it happened. Nothing conspired to hold me here. No great event froze me in my tracks and made it impossible for me to return to the West. It was simply something incremental and centripetal, a gravitational force made up of aging parents, old friends, and the lure of the deep familiar. Day by day, and quite unnoticed, the webbings of interconnections and responsibilities wove themselves more tightly around me, my dissatisfactions became more blunted, and I sank back into the comfortable shape of my Midwestern self like a man sinks into the familiar shape of a comfortable chair.

But if it was comfortable, it was also a kind of drowning. Quietly, and almost unnoticed, the accursed objectivity returned. My jaw became set, my eyes became distant. My manner, which out west had become loose-limbed, mirthful, and jangly, became clear-eyed, taciturn, and restrictive. I was once again a man of the center, full of skepticism and intellectual wariness, living life with my elbows at my side. For better or for worse, I had tumbled backward into the dour righteousness of American Gothic, where I stood, pitchfork at the ready, intent upon defending the small but well-tilled boundaries of the tiny plot of life I had carved out for myself.

Perhaps I should have seen this coming and bolted. But things aren't always that easy or simple. This may be the land of American Gothic, but it is also the land of Abe Lincoln honesty. There is a goodheartedness in people who know they will be neighbors forever, and a comfort in knowing that your children are watched by caring eyes as they run outside to play. It is only at great peril that one abandons a place where you can leave your keys in your car and your doors unlocked, and children can trick-or-treat unchaperoned in wide-eyed innocence.

And then there was the fact that the shadow side of the West Coast never left my mind. Every time I cursed the dark-robed Minnesota fatalism and spiritual breast-beating, I thought of the glazed-eyed breathiness of so many of my West Coast friends as they buttonholed me to exult about the deep wisdom of Sri so-and-so or the new seven-step technique they had discovered to clear their consciousness of negative energy.

Rail though I might against the visionless plodding and self-deprecation of my sodden Midwestern compatriots, I could not shake the memory of the week when I counted twenty-two instances where the *San Francisco Chronicle* had described different people as "geniuses."

No, it was not completely by accident that I ended up back on these hardscrabble margins of the American Midwest. And I am not completely unhappy that I have done so.

Still, the memory of the Pacific sunsets lingers. Around the edges of my life, I hear the lapping of distant seas.

The town where I have made my home is an unlikely place indeed. It's a small community of ten thousand, huddled among the lakes and rivers of northern Minnesota, just at the point where the deep pine forests of the North begin to give way to the cold, lonely emptiness of the North Dakota prairies.

To say we're off the beaten track is generous. We're not quite the equivalent of some "beard to the knees" militiamen enclave in the panhandle of northern Idaho, but we're close. The nearest freeway is a hundred miles away, as is the next nearest town our size. To anyone flying over at night we're a tiny island of lights in an unrelenting sea of darkness.

The area was settled by people who were primarily trying to get away from something—misfits, miscreants, steel-jawed Finlanders and Norwegians who dragged wide-eyed, hysterical wives across the frozen northern wastes in order to claim a chunk of this rocky, unfertile soil for their own. They sheared trees, pushed boulders into piles, planted scrubby crops, and alternately shot at and mated with the

Ojibwe Indians (wives notwithstanding), whose land it had been before they had so summarily taken it for their own. "Leave me alone" was their motto, "Pull out an infected tooth with a pliers" was their *modus operandi,* and "Anything I don't know I don't like" was their basic intellectual stance toward the world. Their heirs still run this town.

The terrain on which we sit is almost more water than land—an endless maze of lakes, rivers, creeks, and swamps that was left in the wake of the glacier's retreat. In winter, the temperature dips to forty below and holds us in a death grip for weeks at a time. Cars freeze solid. Icebound lakes crack and thunder. People fray around the edges and lapse into a kind of cryogenic hysteria. On the local news several years ago, a man was shown pounding a nail into a board with a frozen banana. It was something to do.

Few people visit us. Other than the occasional fisherman or resorter, and Canadians on their way to the bejeweled wealth of American cities to the south, travelers bypass this empty quadrant of the state. With the possible exception of the origin of the Mississippi River, there is little here to draw them.

Population is sparse and scattered. A few small towns struggle gamely to hang on, but that generally means only the procurement of a convenience store and gas station to compete with, and eventually kill, the little two-story main street that thrived in the halcyon days when the railroad shaped the settlement patterns and city people seeking vacation destinations had to keep their trips close to home. Once outside these towns, the nights are dark and the roads are lonely.

It's a hard and bitter reality, set against a backdrop of lakes and pines and loon calls on summer nights. But few who live here would move; their lives would only get worse. And for what they have in privacy and natural beauty, they're willing to suffer what they lack. After several generations, it becomes second nature to assume that incremental progress—a new pickup truck every dozen years, a better chain saw, getting the wood in earlier in the season—is enough.

Dreams scale down; hope is seen as a luxury; the outside world becomes a threat coming in like a juggernaut to rip from their grasp what little they have managed to accumulate over the years, the decades, the generations.

In all fairness, it's not a bad life. In fact, there's much to recommend it. You can listen to the seasons, feel the presence of the waters, revel in the shift in spirit that takes place as the vast blanket of pine forest gives way to the holy space of the western plains. The heartbeat of the native Ojibwe is always just beneath the surface, and we wake daily to birdsong and fall asleep each night beneath star-drenched skies. Truly, one could do worse.

But occasionally it all becomes too much. The weather, the isolation, a life defined by gods of ice and thunder rather than gods of ocean vistas and sunsets, and the suffocating sense of being half a continent away from the healing balm of the whispering surf, all align in a heartbeat, and something in us snaps.

It was just such a snap I felt on the cold November day when my journey back west really began.

I had driven to the local supermarket to pick up a few things for supper. My eyes were fixed on the ominous, brooding sky. Something big was blowing in from the prairies, the radio announcer was saying. They were tracking it. Two feet of snow in Moosejaw; sixty below windchill in Minot. The winter gods were marching, and they were coming our way.

Sleet pummeled my windshield as I pulled into the supermarket parking lot. Cars had their headlights on, though it was only three in the afternoon. Just a week before, autumn's tawny days had stretched like a lazy house cat across the landscape. Trees had been exploding matchheads of reds and oranges and yellows. Children could be seen playing knee-deep in tapestries of leaves, while fathers in T-shirts drank beer, raked lawns, and listened to football games on the radio. A smoky indolence had hung in the air, and every day had felt like fine wine.

But a few nights of frigid November rain had changed everything. The multicolored foliage now lay sodden and dying on frost-covered ground. The wind had taken on a cruel and malicious edge, and those same trees that had only days before been firestorms of color now stood naked and shivering against the gunmetal sky.

There was a strange electricity among the shoppers as I entered the store—a combination of deep foreboding and manic intensity. The memory of last winter—the worst on record—was still fresh in everyone's minds. On the prairies, not too many miles from here, houses had been buried beneath thirty-foot snowdrifts, and families had been trapped inside their homes for days at a time until crews could come and dig them out. Ordinary drives to town had become dangerous journeys through drifting, heartless desolation. And despite emergency packs with candles, sleeping bags, candy bars, and red flags to tie on antennas, simple shopping trips and family visits had turned to tragedy. Bodies had been found huddled inside of cars, victims of a faulty battery or a broken fan belt or the simple need to pull to the side of the road to let the snows subside. Farmers had strung ropes from their houses to their barns so they wouldn't get lost trying to make their way out to feed the cattle. One man had been found a mere hundred yards from his house, his hand protruding from the snows, as if beckoning, or waving.

Such terrors, if they were to come at all, were still weeks away. But this first snow had awakened dark memories. People were laying in stores.

I had stopped in front of the bulletin board to get my bearings. I wanted to disappear into the small concerns of the domestic and get my mind off the approaching six-month winter.

My eye moved slowly across the torn slips of paper and three-by-five note cards.

Kittens. $1. Cute.
Wood. 3 Cord. Cheap. Must sell.

The shorthand of stolid, wordless people; the haiku of poverty and desperation.

One card, in particular, caught my eye. It was written in the unsteady hand of the aged. They're easy to spot, these cards of the elderly. Palmer Method scrolls and curls grace the letters; the struggling attempt to keep the lines straight is palpable. It's the writing of a perfect hand gone weak. Not like the cards written by younger hands, where rude scrawls and harsh block letters speak of lessons never learned and skills never mastered.

No, these cards speak of a passing generation. Images are conjured up of small country schoolhouses and horse-drawn sleighs, of learning subtraction with kernels of corn, of going to school tattered but well scrubbed—making a statement with your hygiene that you could not afford to make with your clothes.

When such hands place a note on a bulletin board, they do not do so lightly, for theirs is not a generation that easily parts with possessions. Something of life is being abandoned or reluctantly handed on. Overvalued or undervalued, history is being passed along. Someone's story is being revealed.

I step up close and examine the card that has fascinated me.

For Sale. Table lamps. $3 each. Good bulbs.

That's when I felt the snap. All the honesty and poverty and virtue and futility, all the hopeless tomorrows and tomorrows and tomorrows of this life on the margins came cascading over me.

I snatch the woman's card—it is a woman's hand, I'm sure—and run to the pay phone.

"Yes," she says, "the lamps are still available. Oh, yes, they're very nice. You could come over now if you like. I'm not busy."

I drive through the deepening snow to the woman's house. She's peering from behind a curtain, waiting. She opens the door willingly and lets me in.

She is elderly and frail, probably nearing eighty. The house is spotless, and done in the pink and aqua plastic tile and Formica of the 1960s. It smells of Lysol and furniture polish.

Some soup is on the stove. Would I like some?

"No, thank you," I say. "I have to meet my wife."

It's a lie, but it is the accepted code: I'm not there for social purposes; let us do our business and be done with it.

But the woman is lonely. She lifts a photo album from an end table. Would I like to see pictures of her son? He lives in Denver now. And here is her daughter and her children. She'll visit them at Christmas, if her surgery allows her to travel.

The tragic intimacies of her life are showered upon me, keyed by the photographs in the album she won't put down. That was her husband. He worked for the sawmill until he caught the cancer. They thought they got it all, but there must have been some left. He died in Fargo, at the hospital. The doctors were all so nice.

The closeness is stultifying, the loneliness heartbreaking. All I want to do is get out.

I ask to see the lamps. She goes into the bedroom and brings them out one at a time.

There are two of them. They're grotesque, with unpainted plaster bases and beige crenelated, old-lady lampshades.

"They've hardly been used at all," she says, "especially the one that was on my husband's side of the bed."

Would I like to test them to see if the bulbs work?

"No," I say, "I trust you."

I give her six dollars. She beams. "I have extra bulbs if you need them," she says.

"No," I respond, "I'm sure these are fine."

"I hope you enjoy them," she calls after me as I carry the lamps through the pelting snow toward the car. "Come back and visit if you like. The only visitor I ever get is the mailman."

It's strange how the fragments of our lives come together. One minute they're pieces of a puzzle scattered on the floor. The next, a pattern emerges, and we reach down and from the jumble grab two or three that fit together, and everything begins to make sense.

I back out of the driveway with my mind racing. The woman is standing at the window, waving.

I wave. She waves back.

I wave again, try not to look.

As I turn into the street I can see her out of the corner of my eye, just standing there, at the window, behind the curtain, waving.

The image fades and is replaced by another. It's a sad-eyed young man with shoulder-length hair and a lonely, hopeful look on his face. He's standing at the window of a broken-down cabin, staring out onto the misted Oregon hillsides through a relentless winter rain.

The year is 1973, and the young man is me.

I had arrived at this cabin under the most capricious of circumstances. Wounded by a dying love affair, I had bolted from a prestigious graduate program in religious studies at Stanford University, in Palo Alto, California. Awash in my own spiritual anguish, I had stomped into my advisor's office, where I announced that true faith was not to be found in the academic study of other people's belief, and demanded, with transparent brittleness, that I be given a year off to seek some version of truth that was more hot-blooded and immediate than the cold academic analysis that the institution was foisting upon me.

They had taken one look at the fragile and adamant young man frothing before them and sent me packing, convinced that someone on the edge of a nervous breakdown was not likely to do himself or their program any good by twitching in a classroom and raging against Descartes and Pascal as men deficient in unfiltered spiritual experience.

So I had thrown off my perceived shackles and made my way north along the California coast. It was one more Kerouac wild-man's drive. I had, if memory serves me, twenty-three dollars, some peanut-butter-and-jelly sandwiches, and a few cardboard boxes of possessions jammed in the back of my de rigueur Volkswagen bus. With the pocket-change assistance of various hitchhikers, I had made it all the way to Puget Sound, where I had camped for several weeks at the base of Mt. Rainier, subsisting on Spam and day-old doughnuts and trying to figure out what to do with the rest of my life. Eventually, for reasons I no longer remember, I had determined that I should find a place somewhere in the Trinity Alps of northern California and undertake the writing and carving projects that I was convinced academic life had denied me.

I was gradually working my way back south when one of my treadbare tires gave up the ghost and left me stranded on a roadside in central Oregon with five or six dollars in my pocket. Lacking any better intellectual alternative, I determined it was part of the universe's mysterious but inevitable unfolding, and that this was where I was meant to be.

Through a bit of dumb luck and a few chance encounters, I had managed to find this leaky, clapboard cabin in which I was now living. It had been discarded by a peripatetic local who had lit out for the territories to seek his fortune in the even deeper dark and isolation of the Alaskan interior.

The cabin was in a forgotten, forested valley about sixty miles from the coast. A single road wound its way back into the valley, hugging the side of a meandering creek that coursed and brooded its way from some distant origin out to a wider river and finally to the sea. But that was all miles away. In my valley, it was still only "creek," torpid and puddling in the summer, raging and dangerous when filled with winter rains.

The houses along the road were scattered and ramshackle, with junk cars in the yards and spinal dogs sleeping under stoops. The hills were so steep and tight that on bitter winter days they shut out the sunlight shortly after noon, leaving those of us who lived in the valley in a state of almost perpetual drear and shadow.

Armed with commodity foodstuffs, wood chisels, typewriter, and books, I had settled into my own private *Götterdämmerung* among the dripping dank of a shapeless Oregon winter. I passed my days in silent brooding, tearful reminiscing, and spasms of desperate effort to create some work of art that would give meaning to my life.

My only friend was the mailman. He came once a day, shortly after noon, in his battered blue Ford Econoline and slid the mail into a dented metal box that sat canted on a rotting, tottering post across the creek from my cabin. Even in the heavy rain I could hear him coming, for his engine was loud and his muffler was punctured.

I would wait like a dog for his arrival, hoping that some manuscript I had sent off would return to me with opportunities, or perhaps that someone I had reached out to in my turgid, frenzied prose of isolation would write me with some knowledge that would buoy up this life I had chosen but could hardly endure.

The mailman was a rugged sort. His accent was rural, betraying the Oklahoma origins from which his parents and grandparents had sprung. He wore his hair short and flat, and his voice boomed as he handed me the mail through the window of his faded blue van. He knew everyone, and could construct their secret lives and dreams from the envelopes that came and went through their mailboxes. He was older than I, well into his fifties. But he lived alone, and he knew a young man's demons. He could see my desperation and determination as I waited behind the curtain, trying to look casual as I breathlessly stared out in anticipation of his noontime arrival.

Gradually, from a few simple nods, we became friends. When he had a package he would honk, I would cross the rickety suspension bridge that hung swaybacked over the creek, and we would pass the time for a few minutes while he organized the mail on the seat beside him. He would never probe, but I was anxious to talk. The few letters I received or those I was sending were more than enough incentive for me to begin sharing stories of my life with him.

He listened attentively. The locals, who were insular and suspicious, wanted to know more about me, and he knew he was assigned to be the bearer of information and insight.

Soon, without ever telling me, he became my protector. People along our road were asking questions about the young man in the cabin who seemed never to work, wore odd clothes, and had long hair. Rumors of Satanism and midnight animal slaughters had begun to circulate among the most ill-educated, and drunken rumblings about vigilante action had been heard in bars and around kitchen tables. All this the mailman took in and processed and measured against the sad-eyed, lonely young man who waited daily behind the curtains of his cabin window.

"You've got to get to know them," he said, without ever telling me why. "It's important."

He offered to take me along on his delivery. So I took to riding with him on his route and exchanging pleasantries with the old women who stood in the rain near their mailboxes waiting for their Social Security checks or letters from their children in faraway cities. Some responded when I spoke. Others turned away and refused to talk; the mailman was the one moment of intimacy in their solitary lives, and they did not wish to share that intimacy with the strange young man.

The mailman began to confide in me. His name was Don. He lived alone now. His first wife had died; his second had left "for a while" because they were not getting along. She had taken with her his only daughter, the light of his life. They lived in Sacramento. He had not seen them since they had left. He had wanted to, but he couldn't leave. In fact, in twenty years he had never let himself have a vacation—only Sundays off. He dared not have his route delivered by someone else.

"This is a contract route," he said. "It's the only steady job around. I have to bid for it every year. A lot of people want it, but they know it's mine. They won't bid against me, because they won't take bread from my mouth. But times are getting tougher. If I take a vacation, and something goes wrong, even for one day . . ." His voice trailed off.

On some days he was expansive. He would tell me about the people who had lived in our valley years ago, point out the cemetery no one knew about far up on the mist-shrouded hill, show me the foundations of a town that no longer existed anywhere but on a few old plat maps. His hand swept lyrically over the grey, misty hillsides as he talked.

On other days he was morose and withdrawn, and we rode in silence. The roads were gravel, the forests dense.

Occasionally, he would have me read to him from an old brown hardbound copy of *The Grapes of Wrath.* That was just the way his parents' lives had been, he said, when they came west to work in the fields in the Salinas Valley. He would have read it himself, but he had been forced to quit school in the eighth grade and, anyway, he liked it better when he heard me say the sentences out loud, because they seemed like pictures, not like words. He saved his own reading "to make sure he got the names on the envelopes right."

Sometimes, in the afternoons after the route was over, we would work on his van together. He was a good mechanic in that way that country people are, where ingenuity and wire and bolts and a few hand tools can keep a vehicle running against all odds. He was forever shaping pieces of cork into gaskets, or making return springs for his brake shoes from parts of an old abandoned tractor. I watched in amazement and offered my suggestions, for I was good with theory, though short on patience and sloppy with my hands.

Eventually he came to trust me. He showed me pictures of his first wife. He showed me pictures of their son, who was in the military. He showed me where the keys to the shed were, where he kept his tools. "If you need anything, you just go right in and take it," he told me. He even showed me an old atlas he kept in a drawer. "Someday I'm going to see these places," he confided, pointing to a series of towns he had circled throughout California. "These are where my folks worked. And Big Sur, that sounds like a hell of a place. That's one spot I'd really like to see."

One day he stopped at my house before sunup. "Want to go with me?" he asked. He never did this unless he needed company. Sensing something important, I went.

All through the day he seemed agitated and distracted. As we got to the last part of the route, he began telling me the stories of the people who lived at each mailbox, as if it were important that I understand. The winter light was waning, though it was barely two in the afternoon, and we were far up a forest road that was gradually reducing to ruts.

"My son's coming in from overseas," he said. "He's going to be in Sacramento, where my daughter is. What would you think about taking the route for a week or so?"

Fingers of fog were poking over the darkening hills. There was a winter chill in the air. His wipers slapped away globs of mushy snow that pelted the windshield.

"I'd be proud to," I said.

"I've never done this before," he responded. There was challenge, threat, and fear in his voice.

"I'll do it right," I said.

For months he had been giving me labored explanations of how the job was so fragile, about how he had gotten it from his father and about all the people who wanted it; about people who were actually waiting for him to die so they could get it; about how he had sometimes worked on his van until three in the morning, then gone directly to sort the mail, without a moment of sleep, because if he missed a day of delivery he could be reported and someone else could lay claim to the job.

Now he said simply, "You can use the van. She's running good."

The week he was to leave, a violent Pacific storm blew in. The Douglas fir were lost in the lashing of the wind, and the creeks and rivers were churned into rushing foam by the hammering of the rain. On the day he was to leave I drove him to the bus. He stood outside the cafe where the Greyhound would stop and gave me a long list of instructions on how to sort and how to deliver, who needed the mail wrapped in a rubber band because of arthritis, who wanted me to honk as I drove up. He wore a polyester sport coat that was worn and ragged and smelled of wood smoke. His suitcase was an old pigskin rectangle with one corner worn away.

As the Greyhound groaned its way through the rain, he took my hand and held it. "Keep the radio off," he said. "If you're on one of the back roads and you hear the gears of a log truck, just drive into the ditch. Those guys can't stop, and they don't want to. They get paid by the load." He dropped my hand and made his way onto the waiting bus.

I did the route for five days. There were no incidents with log trucks. The people in the post office in town were good to me and helped sort the route so I would make no mistakes. I would rise at three, drive in darkness to the town, and be on the road before dawn. The delivery covered over eighty-five miles each day on rain-soaked, curving back roads and rutted logging paths. Each day finished as it began, in darkness. The old women waiting for their checks clucked and laughed and made bitter jokes about the mailman's high style of living and how he could afford a vacation. But I made no mistakes.

When he returned, the post-office people told him I had done well. Don was happy and proud. He had seen his son and spent time with his daughter. He had even taken her to a restaurant. He showed me a postcard with its picture. It was a Highway Host. He had ordered Salisbury steak and his daughter had ordered fried chicken. He had written what they had ordered on the back, along with the date.

While he was gone, the post-office people told him, five people had quit the route. From now on they would drive to town to pick up their mail, they said. They didn't want their letters touched by a hippie. Don said nothing. He fingered the postcard in his breast pocket.

Four months later, as my birthday approached, I decided to give up. I had been robbed twice. Nothing I had written had received any response. I had not been able to create a carving. Someone had placed a dead rat in the holding tank of my well.

On the day of my departure, Don stopped by on his noon break. I was shoving a last bag of clothing into the packed car. He helped me check my oil and listened to the engine. "She's running good," he said. "She'll make it."

He took my hand one final time in that firm and motionless grip.

"I'll make sure your mail gets forwarded," he said. "You can be damn sure of that." Our eyes met fleetingly, then we both looked away.

I drove off down the curving six-mile road to the main highway. He followed behind at a respectful distance, like a concerned father or a mourner in a funeral cortege.

At the junction he pulled up beside me. He leaned over and reached out the window with his heavy, gnarled hand. I reached up and grasped it one last time. We sat there, our cars at idle, our eyes averted, our hands locked in a motionless grip.

"Well . . . ," I said, finally, "I guess I better get going."

He started to say something, then stopped.

Finally, he spoke. His voice was little more than a whisper.

"You did a hell of a job delivering the mail," he said. "A hell of a job."

Then he released his grip and slid back into the driver's seat.

I turned right. He turned left.

I never saw him again.

The snow is blowing. The streets are icing over. Down the strip the neon franchise signs are almost obscured by the whirling snow. Men with baseball caps and bad teeth and long, untrimmed beards are roaring by me in big, growling pickups, kicking snow onto my windshield like bullies on the beach kicking sand in my face. A mother with four ragged kids in tow makes her way along the sidewalk. They're all wearing grim and dingy winter coats purchased at some Goodwill.

At a stoplight, I lean back. The lamps are jiggling beside me as my car sits at uneven idle. The woman's face will not leave me. I see her standing there, waving hopefully from behind the curtain. I see the mailman pulling up to my dented mailbox. The dead farmer's hand beckons to me from the snowbank.

I close my eyes and drift off. I see Don's blue Econoline churning up the twisting forested roads. Then I'm out over the Oregon coast, watching the thin line of breakers crash on the distant shoreline. I fly north, past Haystack Rock, past the broad mouth of the Columbia, around the Olympic Peninsula, over Puget Sound. In the distance the San Juans rise in the mist. Gossamer wisps of fog float among the coves and inlets. To the east, Mt. Baker and Mt. Rainier stand majestic above the clouds.

I wheel, veer south, pass over the spreading lights of Seattle.

Then I'm following the giants—Adams, St. Helens, Hood. Endless folds of forested hillsides stretch before me. The blue eye of Crater Lake stares up at me. The scent of fresh-cut cedar fills my nostrils.

Soon the redwoods loom, and I pass beneath their towering branches and refracted, cathedral light. Then down through Mendocino and Bolinas and memories of fresh crab and bottles of wine on the beach at Point Reyes. Into the great bowl of lights of the Bay Area and a million forgotten feelings.

Farther, to Monterey Bay and Big Sur, and bonfires and solstices and drumming all night, until the first warm kiss of a San Luis Obispo sunrise, and the missions, and the God-touched sparkle of the Santa Barbara channel. Over L.A. and its arteries of traffic and lavender sunsets that caress like velvet. Into San Diego—all sea breeze, white sail, with tuck-and-roll, sailor-drunk Tijuana thumping right outside the door.

A honk breaks me from my reverie. The light has changed. A man in a giant pickup truck behind me is flashing his brights angrily and revving his bulldog engine. I place my hands on the lamps and pull away slowly.

Louise stares incredulously at the man standing before her with snow dripping off his beard and eyebrows, fulminating about bulletin boards, pickup trucks, lonely old women, and winter. It's a torrent of non sequiturs held together by a thin thread of rage and frustration.

She says nothing. She has heard this all before.

I hear my own voice, as if disembodied. I'm pleading. "No, this time it's different," I'm saying. "It's bigger. We can't live our lives waiting for someone to deliver meaning to our door. I don't want to end up like some old woman staring from behind a curtain or some dead farmer waving from a snow bank."

She listens patiently. She's a wise and insightful woman. Our years together have given her a fine sense of when to indulge my elliptical forays and when to cut them short. But my erratic gestures and irrational metaphors convince her she's dealing with a man unhinged. She decides to cut to the chase.

"So what's this all about?" she asks.

My answer comes instantly. It surprises me with its adamance. "I want to go back to the West Coast."

She stops in mid-stroke over the vegetables she's chopping and fixes me with an icy stare. It's what I've come to call the North Dakota Wind—a bequest from her mother, who was raised in an isolated hamlet on the bleak windswept plains several hundred miles west of here. It involves responding to a suspect idea or statement with a frozen silence that blows across the speaker with all the chill of a winter gale blowing across the empty prairies. It's a masterpiece of timing, pacing, and psychic withdrawal. In its presence, everything withers.

"You want . . . to go back . . . to the West Coast," she says. The slow, measured repetition of my own fumbling words leaves them hanging out there, as alone and naked as the grey November trees.

"No, not for good," I say, grasping for a handhold. "At least, not yet. At least, I don't think so. Just a trip. Just to see."

Her silence is a frigid, empty space. I rush to fill it with words.

"We talk about moving out there all the time. You know you'd like to do it. Maybe it's time to consider it. We can't live our lives trapped in the middle."

She turns her attention to the half-chopped pile of carrots and scallions. The silence is excruciating.

"So," she says, meticulously gathering the scallions together into a neat pile. "You think we should trade our cow for some magic beans."

"Or a beanstalk maybe," I respond brightly. "A way to climb out of here."

She purses her lips and walks to the window. I can see the thoughts turning. She's considering various responses, trying them on like winter coats, then discarding them.

She has seen this coming. We both have. For the past several weeks, there have been seismic rumblings just below the surface. With each darkening day I've heard myself waxing lyrical about that old Volkswagen camper and how it was rigged to pump wine rather than water from its sink. I've caught myself recycling tired tales of college life in the Bay Area, my time living in a monastery in British Columbia, my roustings by police in Crescent City, Berkeley, and San Diego. She's heard me recount for the umpteenth time the stories of the basketball games in the prison at San Quentin and the nights falling asleep to the sounds of breakers on the beach at San Gregorio.

She has heard, and she has endured. She knows me well. The West Coast is my old lover. Until I put her out of my mind, once and for all, I'll never be at peace with this cold outpost that we now call home.

She turns from the window and faces me. The wind has passed; there's a wry smile on her face. "You might not like your traveling companion," she says. "He's a lot older than that twenty-five-year-old kid you went with last time."

That's as close to an approval as I am likely to get. But it emboldens me.

"Admit it," I say. "You think about it too."

She gestures out the window at the heavy darkness and the whorling snow. "Is it November?"

"We could go together," I offer. "Take Nick, over winter break. Check it all out. Seattle. Eugene. The Bay Area. Make a family vacation out of it."

"No," she answers. "These are your demons. We'd just get in the way."

I nod wistfully. But, secretly, I agree. I need to do this one alone, with my mind, emotions, and memories finely tuned. That way I can be fully present to whatever I encounter. If it comes out well, we can make a more leisurely visit together in the spring. But this time it has to be a solo enterprise.

She gestures at me with the end of the knife. "Just be sure," she says. "We've got one move left in us. I'd do it, you know that. I'd love to. But I don't want to go chasing some fool's paradise."

"I know," I say. "And I don't want to be the fool."

She focuses those wry and skeptical eyes on me. But somewhere, far below, a twinkle is trying to break through.

"One question, though," she says. "I've got to ask. Why now? Why this time? What pushed you over the edge?"

"Just a minute," I answer.

I run out to the car and bring in the lamps and place them on the table. She stares at them in disbelief.

"They have good bulbs," I say.

She doesn't even dare ask me what I'm talking about.

TWO

KEROUAC'S GHOST

So now, the branch has broken, and I'm falling, tumbling, sliding down the hillside and I can't stop myself and I don't want to stop myself.

I'm making plane reservations, cleaning the gutters, arranging to have the driveway plowed if we get hit by an early blizzard. Louise and Nick watch from a distance, curious and wary, like people observing the movements of a dangerous animal.

I keep feeling that I should stop and reconsider. But I can't—I'm giddy with possibility.

Where is this coming from? Do I really think there's a better life somewhere else, only waiting for me to turn over the proper rock to find it? I've lived long enough to know the tired truism that wherever you go, you bring yourself along. And, to the best of my knowledge, I'm not in the throes of some midlife crisis.

In fact, I'm really quite pleased with this point in life, and find it far preferable to being "eighteen with a bullet" or thirty and rudderless in the larger sea of life's meaning. I have a good wife whom I love dearly, a son who is the light of my life, several wonderful stepchildren whose first steps into adulthood I'm watching with fondness and joy, good friends, a meaningful intellectual and spiritual inner life, work that constantly challenges me, and a home on the edge of a pine-bordered lake. I would be an arrogant fool to think I deserve more or that I could find better. And I don't.

So what's driving me?

I am afraid it's this infernal sense of being suspended in the middle—the middle of the country, the middle of belief, the middle of my own time on the planet. It's not a crisis, but it is an urge for mid-course assessment. I've made a virtue of balance and objectivity, and when that doesn't feel like wisdom, it feels like inertia and stasis. I want to pull my elbows from my sides, blow the cautionary caveats out my tailpipe, and drive. Kerouac may be dead, but his ghost still whispers.

Then there's that other thing. That "over the next hill" thing. That thing I tried to capture in a paper I wrote while I was at Stanford and that my professor decried as turgid and overblown:

We measure our land from east to west—a subtle historical imperative following the footsteps of our forebears and the ceaseless transit of the sun.

But who were we that we could not give ourselves in simple pleasure to this land, and live upon it lightly like those whose homes we entered when we first set foot upon this shore? What was it made us hold our breath for the journey yet unmade, and made of our arrival a beginning?

Somehow east to west traced the trajectory of our dreams, and the deserts and the mountains fit the drama of our story. To persevere, and then be stopped, to rise above our greatest fears, and then slide down that magic slope to some Edenic conclusion seemed just right to the deeper movements of our souls.

To travel east to west was to put our childhood at the end—a teleology of hope to stand against the tomorrow and tomorrow and tomorrow of the lands from which our forebears had fled. It gave our journey an ecstasy, like some Arthurian quest, and made our path through history into the myth we did not have.

America. We live upon her not as land, but story. We are the travelers, the seekers, the children of El Dorado and the Rapture and the Holy Grail. To move, and move again, is our redemption, until we learn to hear the voices of the stones as clearly as the voices of our dreams.

Perhaps that's it. "To move and move again." "A teleology of hope." "Putting our childhood at the end." The West Coast is our Eden, our El Dorado, our prelapsarian paradise where people get younger instead of older and can live off the fruit they pick from trees and the gold nuggets they find on the ground.

We know it's not true. But myths don't have to be true; they just have to give us a story by which to understand ourselves and shape our dreams.

I guess I just can't face living without the myth. Or at least I can't give it up without a fight.

Grim-faced farmers plowing rocky fields don't inspire me. Barricaded *posse comitatus* types growing chickens and hothouses of dope don't ennoble me. I can't find meaning in strip malls and shopping expeditions and profit margins and portfolios. Even the great north-woods myth of the plaid-shirted outdoorsman with his loons and canoes—the myth that keeps infusing fresh human fodder into our bleak local landscape—is hollow to me.

Only the myth of the West and the road and the world over the next hill puts light in my eyes. I'm an American through and through, and my wheels are always rolling. And the direction they always want to roll is toward the sunset.

I think I first felt the tug when I was about twelve, while my family was on the only real vacation we ever took during my childhood. My father had borrowed a car from my uncle, and we had set off from our home in Minneapolis to visit the Black Hills in South Dakota. My father distrusted the newly built interstates, so for several days we drove in unair-conditioned agony on buckling asphalt two-lanes through the scorching heat of a South Dakota August.

One afternoon, while we were passing through another of the endless railroad-siding, grain-elevator, "population 300" towns, I heard a rumble outside the window. I looked up from my sweaty backseat lethargy to see a group of motorcycles with sidecars warming up on the dirt apron of a cafe. This was pre–Hells Angels and designer

Harley days. Touring cycles were almost unknown, and the people who owned them were eccentric *Popular Mechanics* types.

I watched from my car window, like a dog staring out a screen door, as men in porkpie hats and women in jackets with their names embroidered on the back climbed on bikes festooned with handlebar streamers and carnival midway light bars, and wheeled out of the dusty parking lot off down the razor-straight Dakota highway toward the setting sun.

I don't know what that did to my parents as they sat there in the sweltering heat trying to live out their postwar American Family Vacation Dream, but I know what it did to me. I can't remember a thing about our visit to Mt. Rushmore or the Badlands or the chairlift at Harney Peak. But I can see those motorcycles pulling out, one by one, in my mind's eye, and heading off toward the west as if it were yesterday.

And then there's another image, even further back in my past, that may touch even closer to the core. It's an old black radio, about the size and shape of a bread box, that had belonged to my grandmother. It had suffered some kind of electronic stroke during a particularly vicious lightning storm, so only one-half of the dial worked. Discarded by the adults as worthless, it had ended up on the table at my bedside, where it became the first grown-up object in my stuffed-animal and toy-soldier life.

The radio was of an ancient technology—full of vacuum tubes and resistors that glowed and hummed as it crackled its way to life. Each night, after my parents thought I had gone to sleep, I would cover myself and my radio with a blanket and turn the dial through its various screeches and whistles in search of distant signals that would carry me to faraway places and unimagined lands.

KOMA in Oklahoma, WLS in Chicago, stations from nameless outposts in Canada where people spoke in a rapid-fire French—these became the destinations of my imagination, and as surely as train whistles in the night, they fueled my yearnings and placed distance in my dreams.

As I got older, those disembodied voices still called to me. I would climb in my battered fifty-dollar car, fill it with gas, throw a box of wrenches in the trunk, and drive off into the night in search of those same lights and sounds and distances that the old black radio had fired in my imagination. With one hand on the car radio dial and one on the steering wheel, I would home in on a signal, then isolate its location on a map, and turn south or north or whatever direction it commanded.

When, years later, it came time for me to choose a graduate school, and I sat at my kitchen table staring numbly at brochures from the University of Chicago and Stanford, I blindly chose Stanford—not because of its academic programs or reputation, but because the memory of driving over the pass on I–80 and looking down on the lights of the Bay Area held greater magic in my imagination than the memory of rounding a curve on a rainy Illinois night and seeing the towering skyline of Chicago rising in the fog before me.

If I hadn't realized it before, I knew right then that the myth had claimed me. And when a senior professor in my graduate program told me that I would never become an academic because I was a "moving thinker" rather than a "sitting thinker," I knew that its claim ran far deeper than any simple fascination with travel and the road. It was the cornerstone of my epistemology and the metaphor for my life and dreams. I had, in my own small way, joined the Joads, the Donner party, Neal Cassady, Lewis and Clark, and everyone else who had ever been part of that great American pilgrimage. I had become one more child of El Dorado, and I remain its child to this day.

There is one last piece of business, and it's a hard one.

I go into Nick's room and sit down next to him. He is ten now and misses nothing. He's heard the late-night discussions and the dinner conversations and seen the maps open on the dining-room table. He knows something of consequence is going on.

"Do you know what this trip is all about, Nick?" I ask.

"Well, sort of." He's a circumspect boy, inclined to keep his counsel as much as possible.

"You know I'm going out to the West Coast for a couple of weeks."

"Yeah. You're going to drive down from Washington to California."

"Yes, but do you know why?"

He looks down. Pauses.

"Dad," he says, "I don't want to move."

I move closer to him and put my arm over his shoulder. "I know you don't. I'm not sure I do, either. This is just . . . well, you know I used to live out there. It's kind of like if you moved away from here, and sometimes you missed it and just wanted to remind yourself what it was like."

"But I'm not going to move away from here. Ever."

His lips are tense, his hands are clenched. He keeps his gaze fixed squarely on the floor.

How does it happen? When is that moment when the fantasies of faraway places so infect the spirit that they overcome that innate childhood conservatism and rootedness? Nick spends days in his room reading books about wizards and dragons and boys on adventures. He has a map on his wall with pins in Egypt (the home of the pyramids), Hawaii (a fond vacation memory), Alaska (the site of his and my most recent trip together), and Loch Ness (where he expects to set up a camera and be the first person to get a good photograph of the monster).

These are his fantasies as surely as the voices on the radio were mine. But, as was the case with me as a child, they are fires in the imagination, not destinations where one might live out a life. In his world home is here, and will remain here. Like the wizards in his books, he will be able to wave a wand and be somewhere else, then wave a wand and be back here with his friends and family and all the familiar pieces of his life. There will be no disruptions, no starting over—no deaths, physically or metaphorically. He will have it all.

Now I've cast this in doubt. I, the father, the protector, am shaking his faith and confidence to its foundations. This journey of mine is a betrayal of all that he holds dear.

I decide to push just a bit.

"Nick, you know, you're not always going to live here. Sometime you'll have to move."

He has no interest in pursuing this line of thinking. "But I don't want to move now."

He rolls off a litany of friends and small events he cherishes, unaware of the sad truth that within a year or two he and most of these friends will be living lives as separate as if they had moved a thousand miles away from each other. I toy with the possibility of mentioning this to him and naming close friends from his past who now have moved and about whom he has almost no recollection. But what good would that serve? He doesn't need lectures. He needs to be reassured with some kind of solid knowledge he can grasp.

"Nick, listen to me. When you go to another school for a chess match or something, do you ever wonder what it would be like to go to school there?"

"Well, yes."

"Does that mean you're going to go to school there?"

"No."

"But isn't it worthwhile just to imagine it? Give you something to compare your school to?"

"I guess."

"It's like that for me. Sometimes you have to go away from home to appreciate what you have. Like Dorothy in *The Wizard of Oz*."

"So we're not going to move?"

"Nick, we're a family. Anything we do, we decide together."

"You promise?" He picks away nervously at a pile of dirty clothes on his bed.

I reach out my hand. He looks at it tentatively, then takes it in his in a weak grip.

"What have I told you about my handshake?" I ask.

"It's better than any promise."

"It's a rock. You can build your house on it."

He cracks a tiny smile. "How can you build a house on a handshake?"

I cuff him on the shoulder. "Come on, let's go see Mom."

We go downstairs together, father and son. Abraham has kept the knife beneath his cloak. I can only pray that somehow, before this is all over, a ram will emerge from the bushes.

The final weeks before the trip are spent trying to keep the family mollified. Louise is no problem. I simply have to endure her references to her "Oz-intoxicated husband" and her strategically-timed whistlings of "We're off to see the wizard." But Nick is not so easy. His natural wariness and his child's unerring instinct for survival have kept him at a distance. But, eventually, his curiosity has gotten the best of him, as I knew it would.

I have shown him the maps of the general area where I intend to travel. I've pointed out the terminus of the Oregon Trail, Sutter's Mill, and the redwood forests. I've shown him the places where I used to live and told him stories about each.

"Here's where that man shot at me in Mt. Rainier National Forest. Here's where you get on the boat to go to Alcatraz. Here's where I picked up that crazy hitchhiker who was going to the desert to wait for the spaceship to land."

Gradually, he has gotten into the spirit. "Did you take that guy all the way to the desert?"

"No, here's the desert. See?"

He looks. "That's a long way from where you picked him up."

"Six hundred miles."

"So, how long did you have him with you?"

"Overnight. All the way to San Francisco. Here."

It's a strange history and geography lesson. But I'm pleased to offer it. When he's old and talking to his grandchildren, these are the stories he will cherish, the way I cherish the stories of my mother's childhood in Wisconsin or my late father's reminiscences about chasing ice wagons down the back alleys of Minneapolis.

More than that, these stories breathe life into this journey in a way that makes it seem justifiable on its own terms. Who wouldn't want to visit the place where the hitchhiker built a circle of stones to signal the Venusians that he was on his way to their landing site?

All I want is for Nick to look upon this journey as an adventure rather than a gallows walk being led by an autocratic and fantasy-addled father. And I think I've succeeded. He has reduced it in his mind to just one more crazy thing that Dad does. It will allow him to become the man of the house, and he and Mom will get to have time alone together. They'll make popcorn every night, read books to each other, and laugh about things that never seem as funny when Dad is around. All in all, it will be just fine.

So when I ask him to help me pack, he does so willingly. He happily runs to the closet and grabs my old aviator bag and throws it open on the floor.

We consider shoes, choosing work boots and sandals, belts ("Your belts sure are big, Dad." "I stole them from Santa."), T-shirts of various colors, a few sweatshirts, one semi-decent long-sleeved shirt, some Hawaiian shirts that Louise refuses to let me wear in public, and a collection of jeans. Each of these he duly deposits in the green bag, stuffing it until it looks like a bulging military sausage.

Over the years, this bag has almost reached the status of personal friend to me. It was made by my uncle during World War II while he worked as a parachute repairman in the navy. It's faded and torn and covered with oil stains. But it has that military utilitarianism and indomitability that allows me to trust it and forget about it. It was constructed to be dragged through the jungles of Saipan; it can surely sit in the rain in Seattle or fall from the trunk of a car in East Oakland.

What it can't do is absorb clothes that must retain a modicum of decorum. It welcomes jeans and T-shirts and sweatshirts and work boots. It abhors, and gleefully brutalizes, sport coats and pressed slacks, so I never use it when I'm asked to present myself in any public forum. But there will be no public forums on this trip. This is a guerrilla mission, a reconnaissance patrol of a thousand miles of coastline from Canada to San Francisco. No suits or sport coats or anything with a crease will be needed.

This is my kind of travel—a bag of clothes in the trunk of a car, no deadlines, no scheduled stops, no obligatory visits to old friends or relatives. I could be a salesman, a fugitive, or the illegitimate son of the pope. No one knows, no one cares. I am traveling below radar, surfacing whenever I see fit.

In my younger days, I traveled even further below radar—hitchhiking, hopping freights, staying with people I met on the road, occasionally sleeping under bridges or in thickets by the side of the freeway. But the bones creak too much now, and the streets are meaner. And a man of my age walking the side of the highway has the spore of a vagrant, not the sparkle of a young adventurer. I'm better served by the comfort and anonymity of a car, and better preserved by putting these old bones in a bed at night.

Still, I want the immediacy of the street-level experience—the ordinary people, the casual encounters, the *ad hoc* turns and serendipitous decisions. At heart, I'm no different from the kid with the jalopy, fifty bucks, and time on my hands: no itinerary, only intention, and an appreciation for the moment that reveals the universe in a grain of sand.

Nick is curious about this. He has had a few encounters with my travel habits on our journeys together. The most legendary moment came on our recent trip to Alaska when I decided to take nothing but left turns for ten minutes. We ended up against the back wall of some industrial park on the outskirts of Anchorage.

He sits on the side of the bed and watches me struggle with the zipper on the engorged aviator bag.

"You sure travel weird," he says.

"It has its virtues," I tell him. "I just follow my nose."

"Yeah. To the back walls of buildings."

"It's not always that bad. Remember the beached fishing trawler in Seward? Or the grave of that pioneer woman on the Oregon Trail?"

He nods. Those were good moments.

"It usually works out," I say. "How can I know where I want to go if I've never been there?"

"You could look in a book."

"And go to all the places everyone else wants to go, or all the places that sell Tastee Freezes or have theme parks? No, thanks."

In fact, I'm not really so jaundiced about guidebooks. They provide deep background and interesting context. But they just don't create the right kind of travel for me. I want travel to be about discovery, not about destination. Otherwise, everything becomes a process of waiting for the end points, a kind of "connect the dots," where the lines between the dots have less weight than the dots themselves. It makes travel into a series of nouns rather than a continuous verb.

I'd rather follow a shaft of light down a particular lane, or take the advice of someone I meet in a cafe, or pluck a note from a bulletin board and go off in search of an address where an old woman is selling lamps with good bulbs. These are the ways to get down to the streets, to smell the sweat of a place and sense its spirit.

I guess this all began in high school when my childhood friend, Steven, and I bought a Bondo-ed up '47 Chevy for nineteen dollars and forty-three cents. The owner had wanted twenty-five dollars, but when we couldn't come up with that, he sold us the car for what we had in our pockets. We had limped it home, changed its oil, and written the name "Fred" on the side, in honor of a friend who had wrapped himself around a telephone pole on a motorcycle at eighty miles an hour.

Every weekend Steve and I would pool our money, hop into "Fred," and head off into the wheatfields of western Minnesota or the woods of northern Wisconsin—anyplace where the roads weren't marked and the towns were small and scattered. We would each take turns giving directions for ten minutes.

"Go down this road." "Take this turn." "Back up and go into that field over there."

No maps were allowed, and the only purpose was to get as lost as we possibly could. To this day there are places in my memory I couldn't find again if you offered me a million dollars. And those weekend trips to nowhere rest as fondly in my memory as any visit to the museums of Manhattan or the monuments of Washington, D.C.

In fact, it was Steve's daughter, Christina, who, years later, put a name to the pleasure that this type of travel offers. At about the age of five she began accompanying us on our journeys. An only child being raised by a single father, she was an easy traveling partner because she had a rich inner life and occupied herself without difficulty.

"Want to hit the road?" we'd ask, and she'd run to her room and grab her little pink plastic suitcase she kept packed and at the ready. She'd climb in the backseat, spread out her books and crayons and tablets and puzzles, and sing softly to herself as her father and I set off down roads for no other reason than because we liked the view of the horizon they presented.

One of Christina's passions in life was snow angels. She drew them, she discussed them, she gave them names. She even determined that real angels would come down and live in them if they were made in just the right shape. Whenever she was out walking in the winter and saw a fresh and unsullied patch of snow, she would drop on her back and begin waving her arms and legs to make the magical form she believed would call an angel down to earth. It was a standard neighborhood joke that Christina could never get lost, because the parade of snow angels would always lead her home.

One summer day, when the three of us were on one of our road trips up near the south shore of Lake Superior, her father and I saw an abandoned homestead we wanted to explore. Christina was in the backseat sketching some imaginary animal. As we pulled to a stop in front of the collapsing barn, she turned to her father and said, with all seriousness, "I like going on trips with you and Kent, Daddy. It's like you're always stopping to make road angels."

I lever the recalcitrant zipper closed and slide the bag across the floor to Nick.

"That should do it, buddy," I say. "Let's take this out to the car."

He grabs the handles of the bag and drags it behind them.

I'm off to find some road angels.

I know it's quirky, but when I fly, I like to arrive places in the dark. I think it has to do with wanting to spend time alone with my thoughts before immersing myself in the activity of my destination. So I've chosen an evening departure. I should get into Seattle about midnight.

I had given some thought to driving the whole distance, but then the journey would have taken on a different shape. There would have been a sense of arrival and completion upon getting to the coast, and I would have had to retool my tired and image-laden psyche for what would have amounted to a second, almost separate journey.

Better in this case to do what I call a "Dorothy" trip: the house is lifted up, spun around, and deposited in a strange, unfamiliar place full of new and different sights, sounds, smells, and colors. That way, the senses arrive more alive and ready for action. It's a distant echo of the birth experience and allows me to see the world with a freshness that ground travel never quite achieves.

I drive to our small local airport alone, as is my practice. Honks and waves and backing out of the driveway seem far preferable to clumsy last-minute hugs and kisses in an antiseptic terminal on the edge of town. I like to have my family there when I return—that seems to be a legitimate celebratory event. But there's simply too much tension involved in check-in and boarding to allow for any meaningful sharing of intimacies prior to departure.

I'm sure it was different in days when travel was more leisurely. I have no doubt there was great drama and significance in standing at dockside and waving hankies at departing loved ones as the great ocean liners left the pier. But air travel has gotten too crowded and frantic. Better to say our good-byes in the kitchen than in a terminal full of plastic chairs and nervous strangers, even though our little airport has only a fraction of the tensions and hysteria of the large major metropolitan terminals.

So when I leave, it's without fanfare. We all hug, make promises, and I'm out the door.

The plane is late. Something about bad weather and the always comforting "maintenance problems." I pass my time reading every word in the local paper. There's a photo of a man and his son standing proudly next to a suspended deer carcass, a story about a family being burned out of their trailer and counting among their losses the husband's collection of thirty-seven guns. The want ads offer the usual pickups ("some rust") and snowblowers ("needs work"). The real estate ads present their usual bifurcated reality of run-down in-town houses ("fixer upper," "doll house") selling for slightly more than the price of a car, and high-priced "executive" lake homes aimed at the local automobile dealers and real estate speculators. I see an ad for a lot for sale around the shore of our lake. I know the spot. Its price is a desperate fantasy. The last page I look at is filled with recipes for casseroles made from canned mushroom soup.

The weather apparently has cleared, and the maintenance problem has been solved. The plane arrives and departs without incident. It takes me uneventfully over the miles of forests and lakes, past the blips of small towns, over the ever increasing suburban sprawl, and deposits me safely in Minneapolis, where I go through the herding and queuing and checking of boarding passes necessary to get me onto the leviathan that will carry me to the rainy runways of Sea-Tac International.

I've tried every crafty maneuver in my arsenal to avoid being jammed into a seat between two other unhappy passengers, and, thus far, it appears to be working. I'm in a row by myself.

I watch with gimlet eyes as each succeeding passenger enters, checks his or her boarding pass, and wanders down the aisle in search of the proper row and seat. Finally, the flight attendant pulls the bulkhead door closed. I have succeeded; my row is still unoccupied. I'm facing three hours of private thoughts without the elbows of strangers pressing uncomfortably against my sides.

The plane waddles out to the runway, lets out a roar, and thunders down the tarmac. That familiar giddiness clutches my stomach as we rise at an impossible angle in defiance of all human reason. Far below, the lights of Minneapolis recede into a great puddling of illumination on the flat Midwestern plain.

I have heard that ninety percent of all crashes occur in the first minute after takeoff or the last minute before landing. So, silently, I count to sixty as the plane noses upward in its metamorphosis from lumbering beast to flying bird.

. . . Fifty-eight, fifty-nine, sixty.

Now, at least until the first hint of turbulence, I'm safe. It's an absurd conceit, I know. But no more absurd than the fact that I'm hurtling through space in an aluminum projectile made by a thousand hands working a thousand hours in a giant hangar on the south end of Seattle.

I know the truth. I have had jobs. At least one of those workers came to work drunk or hung over, or smoked a joint on his break, or had a fight with her husband, or hates his boss. At least one was irritated at his pay, enraged at being passed over for a promotion, or just plain sick of his job. Was he the one responsible for that certain rivet, that single crucial winding in the wiring harness?

But this is not a line of thought to pursue. I have issues enough to ponder without allowing my mind to run to dire fantasies.

All around me people have settled in. You can tell the pros. They're already set up to go—computers out, headphones on, shoes off, collars loosened—only waiting for the "all-clear" signal from the cockpit so they can become reconnected to the world below.

The rookies and the dilettantes, on the other hand, are still staring out the tiny porthole windows at the receding sea of lights, or jabbering mindlessly and trying to get comfortable in a situation that defies all efforts at comfort. Some of them have adopted a casual air. But, like a parent awaiting a phone call from a teenager who is two hours late arriving home on a dark night, or the patient in the doctor's office waiting for test results, their casualness has an internal stiffness that cannot be disguised. It is obvious that thoughts of windshears and flaming engines are still close to the surface for them, and their nonchalance and busyness belie a taut-wire vigilance.

I fall somewhere in between. My fear is real, but it's not so much fear of mechanical failure as fear of cosmic destiny or spiritual retribution. I cannot shake the belief that time and space form our sacred boundaries, and that we risk some divine disapproval when we transgress them.

I know it's irrational. I scoff at the notion that God helps professional football players catch passes or basketball players make free throws. But I'm utterly convinced that God is keeping an eye on me at all times, mostly watching for unwarranted arrogances or tiny moral transgressions.

I think back to a time twenty-five years ago when I was in charge of a Saturday open gym at a high school in Eugene, Oregon. I was desperately poor—dumpster-diving poor—and this measly six hours of minimum wage work per week was all I could find in the depressed Eugene economy.

One Saturday, while putting away the basketballs after the gym had closed, I noticed one old scuffed ball that had been stored, half deflated, on a back shelf in the locker room. Despite the echoing lessons of my father, who had worshiped Abraham Lincoln and his "walk five miles to return a nickel" honesty, I took that ball. After all, I figured, it was a reject, I was working for next to nothing, and no one would get more pleasure out of owning that abandoned ball than I.

Two days later, while playing in a pickup game, I tore up my ankle so badly that the local hospital brought in a photographer to take pictures for use in training future doctors in the treatment of severe ligament and tendon damage.

Another person, less schooled in a Catholic sense of guilt and less willing to believe in the minute moral scrutiny of a nit-picking God, might have found no correlation between the two events. But my God is always numbering the hairs on my head and keeping track of each sparrow that falls. So, in my mind, there was no doubt. The theft had caused the injury, and that was that.

Now, if God were willing to smite me and tear up my ankle just because I stole an old abandoned basketball, how much more might he be willing to do if I became a thief of time?

Here, sitting in this seat, stealing what should be days or weeks of honest earth travel in order to arrive at my destination in a few short hours, I can't help but contemplate the possibility of divine retribution for our human hubris. Lot's wife stealing a glance at Sodom, Prometheus stealing fire from the gods, Kent and his fellow travelers stealing time from the natural order. Sinners all, held like a spider by a thread over a pit of flames. One snip, and we all fall down.

And then, of course, there's the alternate possibility, equally dire, that in a seat in some distant part of the fuselage there is someone whose number has just come up in the cosmic lottery. The leg bone's connected to the thigh bone, and if he goes down, so do I.

Add it all up, and I'm awash with uneasiness in that corner of my brain inclined to cosmic connections. Somewhere God is squashing ants for his own pleasure. I just have to hope he remains occupied for the next several hours. And then, of course, there is the possibility that one of the engines could simply inhale a duck.

Soon the plane has achieved its cruising altitude, and the surging sounds of the thrusting turbines have been replaced by the benign hum of a machine at peace. The soporific drone of the jets, the laconic cowboy confidence of the captain's lazy Southern drawl as he gives us our flight route, and the familiar scurrying of the flight attendants with their bags of peanuts and carts of soft drinks have mitigated our separate terrors and set us all at ease. We are once more a small gaggle of social animals, rather than a tense collection of solitary souls contemplating our own mortality and more or less imminent deaths.

I recline my seat and close my eyes. The time has come for me to make the shift from conscientious father and husband to willing pilgrim and lone traveler. It's a hard transformation, because the tendrils of responsibility and familial expectation are still wrapped tightly around me. There is this lurking sense—amplified by the skeptical looks on my neighbors' faces for the past several weeks—that this is a journey of selfishness, a personal *ubi sunt,* of value to no one other than me.

But I know better. I've watched the light go out of too many of my friends' eyes as their lives turned from a crazy garden of weeds and wildflowers to a well-manicured lawn. I'm not ready for that yet. I need "bears behind trees"—surprises in life that are bigger than a plugged sewer line or an unexpected finance charge on my credit card at the end of the month. If I don't have them, my life becomes just a long-term maintenance project. I become a custodian of my own tiny plot of earth, and something in my spirit dies.

My family deserves better than that. Louise needs a husband who still has a little stuffing in him. Nick needs a father who doesn't spend his life complaining about bills and bosses and the guy down the block. The only way I can assure that they will get the man they deserve is to blow out the pipes now and then. And the best way I know to do that is to set off on a journey into the unknown. It takes some of the spiritual shrimpiness out of my soul and makes me humbler, more appreciative, and less cynical. In some indefinable fashion, it keeps me young.

But, above all else, I've got to confront that infernal American myth one more time. I've got to go head to head with it, stare it in the eye, wrestle it to the ground like some dark angel. Until I vanquish it, or at least make my peace with it, I'll feel as if my life is a journey left half undone. My eyes will always be fixed on the distance, and my heart will always be looking over the horizon. This isn't fair to anybody, especially my family. For their sake, as much as for my own, I've got to descend, one more time, into that American Eden, to see if her fruits still seem as sweet.

If they do, fine. We'll find a way to pack up and leave the snow and the loons and the dark and the peace, and start over one last time. But if she's just one more fantasy lover grown beautiful in memory, I want to know, so we can leave her in peace, embrace the simple centeredness of life in the heartland, and get on with the business of listening for the voices in the stones.

THREE

PRAYING TO THE PLASTIC CLOWN

What they never tell you is that Dorothy must have been slightly insane when that house finally landed. Why else would she have so blithely accepted a Technicolor world of witches and munchkins right outside her door? But, then, it is exactly this kind of caution and skepticism that I've come out here to lose.

I decide to sit for a while in the terminal before setting forth into the wet Seattle night. There is something about the manufactured air of airplane interiors and the collective suppressed hysteria of a group of people hurtling through the sky thirty-seven thousand feet above the earth that causes the cautious traveler to take stock before surrendering to the thrill of being earthbound once again.

It is not unlike the caution necessary when you're first set free after six weeks in a leg or ankle cast: the temptation to run and jump is overwhelming, but wisdom dictates that you return to normal life by a series of baby steps.

I choose to go the route of baby steps—sit, collect my thoughts, let the turbines of my psyche slow, and take in what my senses offer me.

As always, it's the air that strikes me first. The earth has, literally, held its breath during the flight. We've been offered up some awful oxygenated gruel consisting of recycled human breath and filtered jet fumes. It has not been calculated to energize the brain cells. So the last real air my body remembers is the aching Midwestern winter cold that turns skin to scabrous parchment and lungs to wheezing refrigeration units. But with my first step out of that plastic tube into the Seattle dampness I was hit by the thick, wet Pacific atmosphere—a northern rain forest of smells and textures so bracing and rich it almost howled me over with its pungency.

The faces, too, fascinate me. Airport faces anywhere have a raw, frantic edge to them, but the baseline expressions of the culture are still there. Here there's a lightness in the eyes. It's not the mirthful, laughing look of people in warmer climates—this is, after all, still the North, and rain does not lift the spirits toward mirth any more than do arctic winds and swirling snow. But there's a fluidity and mobility in the faces—a willingness to change expressions quickly—that winter had frozen out of the faces of my Midwestern compatriots.

I don't want to make too much of these observations, but I find them heartening. Though I have, indeed, come along with myself, at least there is something new and fresh for that same old self to observe. Time will wreak its changes. My horizons will drop and my senses will acclimate. What is unique will become commonplace. But for now, everything is fresh and delicious. I'm as alive and sensorially febrile as I could ever hope to be.

Soon my mind begins to catch up with my body, and I'm ready to move. I make my way to the baggage carousels, processing everything in shorthand leaps: goretex, not goose down; a greater fundamental athleticism (less sense of gravity, both physical and emotional); more laughter, brighter colors—and so it goes.

Above all else, I'm struck by the casualness. America everywhere is casual now, much more so than in my youth. But here the casualness has a sense of style.

Despite the nonstop efforts of catalogue companies and trendy outfitters to place us all in ripstop nylon outer garments, Minnesota still has more than its share of people who are committed to green parkas and heavy woolen coats. There is a comforting kind of honesty in this. But it does have just the faintest whiff of Balkan refugee about it. There are moments trudging through the wind and blinding snow when you feel as though the score from *Alexander Nevsky* should be playing in the background. Still, I would be some kind of hypocrite to disparage my Soviet-looking countrymen as I stand here waiting for my tattered green canvas aviator bag to come down the baggage chute amidst all the shiny, black, ballistic nylon luggage cases and designer outfitters' packs.

At least I didn't travel east, where both my luggage and my personal appearance would have porters automatically pointing me to the nearest Greyhound stop. Here, I'm just a garden-variety frump, and there are enough frumpy people in the general Pacific Northwest populace so I blend into the crowd without seeming like a vagrant or a Bolshevik.

The elements of arrival—baggage claim, rental car, and so on—go rather smoothly. At the rental-car counter a woman in a gabardine power suit does slow me down by launching into a diatribe against the rental agency and viciously badgers a well-meaning but slow-witted janitor who has slopped her shoes with some cola slime he's been mopping from around a bank of chairs. The man simply cocks his head like a confused bird and mops with renewed vigor. The rental-car agent mollifies the woman with an upgrade, and she clicks off, hair swinging, toward an opalescent pearl Lincoln Town Car that has been brought up from the VIP row by a man in blue jeans and dreadlocks. She hops in and disappears into the night.

I consider my shoes and the vigorous mopping going on adjacent to them. I, too, would like a Lincoln Town Car. But my sweatshirt and jeans strike no administrative fear into an agent's heart, and he goes indifferently through the process of getting me the midget car to which I'm entitled. I look at him sheepishly. He looks at me, considers the car that has been allotted me, and understands perfectly.

"I don't give a shit," he says conspiratorially. "It's one o'clock in the morning. Pick what you want."

Confronted with absolute freedom, I choose with typical Midwestern caution. "A Bonneville would do nicely," I say.

The man grins. "Good choice," he says. I swell with a tiny pride.

This is a good start. Soon I'm settled into one of America's most commodious and steroidal vehicles, with maps and cassettes piled on the seat beside me, staring at a dashboard as exciting and complex as that of a 747, heading northward through the water-soaked freeways of south Seattle toward the great Canadian night.

As I had anticipated, the weather is cold and rainy. Anyone arriving in Seattle in the winter would be a fool to expect otherwise. What I failed to anticipate is the way the rain would put a damper on my spirits. I should have been ready for this; after all, I lived in Oregon for three years. But the intellect cannot anticipate the response of the heart. The rain drops over me like a curtain made of stone.

The windshield wipers slap hard rhythms against the pummeling of the downpour. Seattle floats, tearstained, before me, its towers and pinnacles of lights emerging as if from a dream. In the darkened sky I can see phantom clouds moving. The surrounding hills are indistinct dark masses.

The city draws me like a moth to a flame. It's an absolute, a fixed point of reference, representing something human and protected. But there's nothing for me there, not at this hour. A few people will be coming and going from bars and late-night cafes. A few of the fallen and unfortunate will be huddled in doorways and makeshift shelters. It will be essentially a ghost ship of a town, retaining its shape, but devoid of life. A visit there would only increase my sense of disconnectedness. I decide to pass her by.

I stare at the passing hillsides. The lights in the houses call to me like hearth fires. I imagine people gathered together in their living rooms sharing friendship and family. I am overcome by a forlorn sense of isolation.

I must be careful now. The giddiness of arrival has whipsawed into the melancholy of the lonely traveler. None of these emotions can be trusted. I need to ride this out, like a sailor in a storm-tossed boat. The sea will be calmer in the morning. But thoughts of family overwhelm me. What have I gotten myself into? If I could, I would click my heels and return home immediately. I could sneak quietly into the house, kiss Nick on the cheek, and crawl silently into bed next to Louise. When she awoke in the morning, I could say the flight was canceled and I decided to skip the whole thing altogether. We could all go out to breakfast, take in a movie, come home and make cookies, and sit in front of the fire. This mad junket would be only a dream.

But it is no dream. I'm here, two thousand miles from my family, on the dreariest of Seattle nights, with ebbing fantasies and escalating fears.

I drive on into the darkness. The radio and the sweeping wipers are my only companions. On the side of the highway blue lights flash eerily in the mist. A man is leaning spread-eagle against his car. Police are frisking him. Soon, he too, recedes into the mist. Everything is evanescent. Nothing seems real.

Five miles, ten, twenty. The lights become fewer. The rain settles into a steady drizzle. My headlights cut a foggy swath through the night. My mood is dark, my spirits low.

Far in the distance, over a hill, I see a spectral, vaporous glow. As I get nearer, I see it's a truck stop. Eighteen-wheelers and log trucks are rumbling in rows at the back of the parking area. Reflections ripple up from the puddles on the pavement.

I decide to stop. I'm fading fast, and the melancholic cast of my spirit needs to be countered with some bright lights and human energy.

The air is alive with the dull throb of idling diesels and whirring compressors. Truckers are leaning against their rigs smoking cigarettes. Their ashes glow like fireflies against the night.

I wander inside past the shelves of road atlases and diesel additives to the restaurant. In a far booth two stocky short-haired women in engineer boots and flannel shirts laugh harshly and poke cigarettes into ashtrays. Aside from them and the waitresses, there are no women here.

This is not a family place with senior discounts and kids' specials and baskets of crayons to use on connect-the-dot place mats. This is a truckers' place, and these are truck stop hours. Men with an overnight stubble of beard are staring at mugs of coffee while holding cigarettes in cupped hands and paging through girlie magazines with names like *Beavershot* and *Jugs*.

I take a seat at the counter next to a plate of congealed brown gravy and a half-eaten hot beef sandwich. Normally I'd find a seat as far from that plate as I could. But it's late, and I'm tired. The waitress will remove it soon enough.

Without thinking, I've lugged several books in from the car: Barry Lopez, Annie Dillard, Wallace Stegner, and a few lesser lights in the world of western and nature writing. Perhaps the reading and a cup of coffee will improve my outlook and keep me awake.

The waitress thunks a white ceramic mug in front of me and fills it with thin, greasy coffee. She leaves the plate of congealed food. I cast a quizzical glance at her, but she has already turned away.

I'm about to shove the plate farther down the counter when I hear the heavy thud of caulk boots behind me. The owner of the hot beef sandwich has returned. He was just off in the rest room.

I'm embarrassed. We are adjacent to each other when there are plenty of seats available along the counter, and this is clearly a restaurant where one does not violate another's personal space.

I look up sheepishly. "Didn't know anyone was sitting here," I say. "I'll move down."

"Nah, it's okay," he responds. "I can use the company." He slides onto the stool with a cowboy's grace and digs back into his sandwich.

He stares at the books. "You a perfessor?"

He has a worn face, a haggard beard, and long stringy hair that hangs down almost to his shoulders. On his head is a filthy baseball cap that carries the insignia of some trucking firm. His must be one of the semis parked outside, engine rumbling.

"No," I answer. "Just traveling."

He spears a triangle of bread and swishes it around the gravy on his plate, then stuffs it in his mouth. He looks at the books again. "I went to college for a while," he says. "Out in Yakima. Bunch of bullshit."

I say nothing.

"What're them books?" he asks.

"Oh, just some nature writers," I say. "Travel stuff." I would rather take the conversation in a different direction.

"Let me see," he says, grabbing one from the pile without asking. He riffles through it, then puts it down.

"Speed reader?" I ask, regretting my flip words even as they leave my mouth. But he has taken no offense.

"Nah. Print's too small." He grins at me with rotted teeth.

He grabs another book. The print is bigger. He begins reading intently, running his fingers along each line as if tracing the words. His face settles into a scowl.

I cringe, for I can guess what's coming. He has grabbed one of the more saccharine books, a wide-eyed paean to the western open spaces by an overly self-absorbed and self-congratulatory writer. I don't even know why I brought it along.

"'Today I helped to birth a calf,'" he reads. He flips the pages and picks out another passage. "'I have learned to love sleeping outside at ten below. The stars dance . . .'" He slams the book on the counter. "What a bunch of bullshit!" He stabs at his hot beef sandwich.

"So goddamn proud of themselves, these assholes. It's all a kid's game to them. Big fucking kid's game." He shoves a chunk of beef into his mouth. "Fucking assholes."

He leans over toward me, so close that I can smell the tobacco and Listerine on his breath. Gravy beads are hanging from his mustache. "You know what's wrong with assholes like that?"

I smile weakly.

"They never did a real fucking day's work in their lives. Let them hook chains on a rig in a snowstorm or sleep in a froze-up rig at ten below, then let's hear them talk about fucking dancing stars. You ought to wipe your ass with them books. Bunch of bullshit." He is looking at my pink writer's hands. I quickly pull them under the counter.

He ladles a mounded teaspoon of sugar into his coffee to emphasize his point, then drains the cup as if it's a shot of whiskey.

"Well, I got to get back to work," he says, hoisting himself up from his stool. I can't tell if it's a simple statement or an accusation.

He slaps a five on the counter and starts toward the door. Then, as if he has forgotten something, he pauses and turns back toward me. A slow grin crosses his toothless face, and he pulls the corner of his jacket back to reveal the butt end of a revolver sticking out of his pants.

He taps the gun twice with his thumb. "Now that," he says, "ain't bullshit." He cuffs me hard on the shoulder, "Have a good trip . . . perfessor. See you down the road," and walks out the door.

I hear the sigh of air brakes releasing, followed by the low drone of a semi pulling out into the wet Washington night.

It is late. The clock on the wall says two forty-five.

Soon I'm back on the highway. The stop has shocked me into the present, but it has only worsened my mood. Mr. "Bunch of Bullshit" has made me feel even more uncertain of myself and my purpose.

Is this what I've come out to find? Truckers on uppers with NRA stickers all over their rigs can be found anywhere. Guys who think guns are equalizers elect half the politicians in America. And what did he mean, "See you down the road"?

I look at my soft hands on the steering wheel. A Bonneville! A real man would have asked for a pickup. From now on I've got to park in the back when I go to a truck stop, or at least I've got to drive through some mud so I don't look like a suburbanite on his way back from the car wash.

My mind continues in this downward spiral, full of doubt and self-loathing.

The road curves like a serpent through the night. I'm out of my mind with exhaustion. I haven't slept in over twenty-three hours. I'm dizzy, lonely, depressed, confused—a jangle of emotions with no fixed point of reference. If I were even halfway in control, I'd pull into the first motel I see and take the first room they offer. But I'm not. I'm a wobbling gyroscope, spinning out of control, running on some kind of adrenaline spillover, and absolutely resistant to the logic of my circadian rhythms.

I grip the wheel with grim intensity. The 747 lights on the Bonneville dashboard dance and merge. My eyes begin to sag; sleep drifts across me. But nothing can make me stop. I'm intent upon making the Canadian border.

My head is starting to loll. I jerk upright, open the window, pull air in with a cupped hand, slap my face. But I can't fight the fade.

I mutter something out loud and stick my head out the window. The rain chills me, but can't make me alert.

"Sleep! Sleep!" my body says. But my mind won't listen. A legion of little gremlins are stoking its overheated blast furnaces and playing "The Anvil Chorus" on my brain.

"Drive! Drive!" they chant.

"Sleep! Sleep!" my body shouts.

"No! Drive!" the gremlins respond. Their laughter echoes up and down my cerebral cortex.

I know this battle: the gremlins always win. I slap my face and push the pedal harder. The gremlins send up a cheer.

My body knows it's in trouble. If it can't stop me I'll slip into unconsciousness and slide off the highway into some bridge abutment. I can see it now: "Minnesota Man Dies in One-car Accident North of Sedro Wooley." Nick and Louise, weeping at a casket.

My body refuses to let this happen. It fights back with the only trump card at its command.

"Hungry," it whispers. "Hungry."

I open my drooping eyes and squint. Yes, I am hungry. I've been hungry since the "a la carte" cold sandwich and cellophane-wrapped cookie on the airplane. I should have ordered something at that truck stop. But that man, that hot beef sandwich. Yes, hungry.

The body has won. It has fired its silver bullet. The little gremlins curse silently, put away their hammers, and crawl back into the darkness.

Yes, hungry.

Armed with this new focus, I turn off the freeway and plunge into the night. I have no idea where I am.

Through the dense foliage, I catch a glimpse of a distant rim of harbor lights. They're a string of pearls around a center of liquid darkness, a curve lying low against the night. Surely there will be something open there.

I take a quick left, head through a densely wooded neighborhood. Soon I'm completely lost. The road has doubled back on itself, reversed its course, gone over some hills. The harbor is nowhere to be seen.

Suddenly, I break forth onto a franchise strip. The garish assemblage of neon assaults my senses, but at least it blasts me awake. I pass through the jungle of emblems and insignias, scanning the horizon for a logo that speaks of food.

My brain is glowing bright orange. In its fevered state, each sign becomes a brassy carnival barker standing with his hands in the air. "Choose me! Choose me!" they each shout. It's a parade of arrogant, selfish men with no sense of dignity or decorum, no concern for their neighbors, no sense of responsibility to a larger community vision. Each is out only for himself, trying to make as much noise as possible, trying to get me to come into his tent so he can take my money.

Conoco, QuickStop, Jack in the Box. Screaming venal men, waving their neon hands in the night, bellowing out, demanding my attention. I hate them all. But I want to eat. One of them must be open. One of them will get my favor.

Finally, I see a likely candidate. I splash into the drive-through and come to a stop before a neon menu board. A muffled voice, like a prisoner with a sock in his mouth, speaks to me through a microphone embedded in the sign.

"Wudyubeinneresdednaspshlnstrfut?"

"No, that's fine. Just give me a couple of tacos and a cup of coffee."

The voice garbles out an unintelligible response and directs me forward.

I drive through the reflecting puddles to the prisoner's tiny window.

A hand emerges. I place some money in it. The hand withdraws, returns, and passes me a sack. I throw it on the seat beside me, grab my coffee, and drive off.

What a strange act of cultural faith. Here I am, two thousand miles from home, at a restaurant I've never been to, in a town I can't even name, and I don't even check the contents of the sack before I drive away. Then again, why should I? No one is going to hand me a bag containing an old shoe, a wad of counterfeit bills, or a kilo of contraband cocaine. This is America. I've done this a thousand times in a thousand places, and the results are always the same. The sign tells me where I am; the weight of the bag gives me an approximation of what's inside; the wrapped objects bespeak a uniformity of product that takes away all uncertainty and doubt. The only variable will be the amount of condiments and lettuce piled on my tacos by the invisible hand that constructed them, and these I will scrutinize and judge as if their measure really matters. I will eat as I drive, tasting little, caring less.

I aim back in what I think is the direction of the freeway. The string of harbor lights is no longer of interest to me. The town had what I wanted; it gave it to me expeditiously, and now I want to leave. I've left some money here, and a wealthy franchise owner is a few pennies closer to a new home while a disinterested high school student is a few pennies closer to a new alternator or a prom dress or a six-pack of beer. By daylight I'll forget I was ever here.

I'm not proud of this transaction. This is a town with a history and a character. A person could spend a day or a month or a lifetime here, just listening to stories and staring out at the sea. There's a past to be explored, the echoes of Native belief to be heard. But I have no time for these things. I'm on the fly. I got my food, they got my money, and my feet never touched the ground.

How did I let this happen? This could be the place. My family could have lived here. But the neon strip broke my spirit. It convinced me that this is the same place I'm trying to escape, not somewhere with a magical life force all its own.

I'm overcome with a deep sense of gloom. "This is America, now," I think. "One great drive-through." It's platted into our cities, built into our economies. The ghosts of former cultures are silenced. Downtowns are dead or gentrified. The vibrancy of our culture resides in these endless strips of neon hawkers who have as their sole purpose the extraction of money in exchange for real or perceived service. The elderly, the poverty-stricken, those who by choice or circumstance are reduced to the odd and suspect status of pedestrian no longer have access to the centrality of civic experience. Like the main streets that used to give them succor, they are vestigial, allowed to exist only because no one has yet figured out a benign way to get rid of them.

My mind drifts to a time, years ago, when I had first arrived in California to attend Stanford. It was a late hour, much as it is now, and I was hungry. I was on foot, for I had not yet completely lost the habit of walking. I wandered up to the door of a fast-food restaurant and found it locked, though there was activity inside. A paper-hatted employee gestured at me through the glass and directed me toward the drive-through, apparently believing I had merely stepped from my vehicle in a misguided attempt to get service across a counter.

I walked around the curve of asphalt and spoke my desires into a plastic clown. My order was duly acknowledged and I was directed forward. When I arrived at the window, properly spaced between a pickup and a sputtering Dodge, I was told I could not be served because I was not in an automobile.

At first I thought they were joking. But this was no joke. I was at a drive-through, not a walk-up, and without a car they were not going to serve me.

I protested and made clever banter about being a '56 Chevy doing undercover work, but to no avail. Tempers flared, horns honked, and I was ultimately offered the option of moving on or receiving a visit from California's Finest. They, I was assured, would find my demands neither humorous nor entertaining. I left, unsatisfied, unserved, and educated in the ways of an automotive culture.

Thirty years have wrought some changes in our drive-through culture. Hours are longer, and provision has generally been made to accommodate the occasional late-night pedestrian who happens by. But the basic premise of the automobile as the key to our civic experience has only taken deeper root in the design and daily activity of our American life. And it has permeated our economic bloodstream until it has infected the smallest burgs and hamlets in the most distant corners of our land.

The last vestiges of this costal town are passing before me now. A tire store. An auto parts store. Gas stations glaring into the night. Through the window of a convenience store I see a young turbaned Sikhman sitting behind a glass wall staring at a television. He seems as distant and alone as a statue.

My gloom is overwhelming. I'm living in a nation anchored by car lots and shopping malls. We've become good at transactions, but progressively weaker at meaningful human exchange. We sit in front of our televisions and computer screens thinking we're part of a community, but really we're part of nothing more than a set of commonly experienced electronic images. Like these neon signs I'm passing, we glorify our individual isolations. Like this small harbor town, we survive by that which electrifies our edges, while our centers are gradually going dark.

I plunge further into the night. I'm awash in that most dangerous isolation that comes from being alienated by that which we find most familiar. Things are not going well.

Don't ever let anyone tell you that a "motorhead" isn't real. In a world of social adaptation disorder, gambling addiction, and an almost endless set of behavioral quirks defined as infirmities, "motorhead" deserves to be near the very top of the list. It could be defined in the textbooks as "the imbalanced but obsessive need to keep driving an automobile when all reasonable indices stipulate that the body should stop. It tends to afflict males more than females and is especially prevalent during late-night hours. Synonym: white line fever."

There's no other explanation for why a reasonable man, twenty-four hours into wakefulness, would think that two tacos and a weak cup of coffee could provide sufficient fuel to keep him functional on rain-soaked roadways in an unfamiliar landscape.

But I did. And they couldn't.

I awake with a mouth like the inside of a vacuum cleaner bag. The car windows are covered with condensation.

If I remember correctly, I'm in a grove of trees somewhere north of the Canadian border and somewhere south of Nome. I have a hazy recollection of a customs crossing, an even hazier recollection of some side roads, a dead end, and getting a jacket from the trunk. I'm swaddled in various pieces of clothing, like a retreating soldier trying to make it home from the front. Shreds of lettuce and some empty taco wrappers are on the seat beside me. A bleak and heatless light pushes in against the steamed-up windows.

I start the engine and turn the heater up full blast. My teeth are actually chattering. I'm appalled at myself. Only a fool of the first magnitude would have allowed things to come to this. Arrive early, get a room, go to a restaurant, retire at a reasonable time, and let your mind cool—this is the way of the prudent traveler. But, no. Arrive late, drive until you pass out, wake up in some woods with no sense of where you are or what you're about. I've done it again, and it isn't a pretty sight.

I look at the dashboard clock: nine twenty-five. Pacific time? Central time? I do the quick computation: eleven twenty-five. Almost noon.

I wipe the condensation from the window. The day is no more hospitable than the night. Dark, heavy clouds stretch to the horizon. Everything is damp with mist.

I drive to a nearby gas station. Under the guise of needing to use the rest room, I take all my toilet articles, plus the coffee cup from last night's taco extravaganza, and prepare to put myself in order for the day.

I wonder: Is this my own dirty little secret, like men who keep porno magazines under their workbenches? Or are there hundreds out there like me, who change for speaking engagements in McDonald's rest rooms and wash their hair using paper cups at sinks in Amoco stations? Perhaps it's one of those underground societies, kept hidden from view by the shame of its members.

The irony is, this is the shadow side of something I view with pride. I take it as a badge of honor that in middle age I can still sleep anywhere under almost any circumstances. Though the man who wakes up is less agile than the young man who first started this practice, it still feels like a connection to the ways of youth. It's proof to myself that I'm not yet ready to be put out to pasture and carted around on Greyline tours. But the end product of such excursions is too often a morning like this, with furtive runs between my car and a public rest room while carrying armloads of clothes and toiletries. I try to look casual and relaxed, but I'm sure my manner has all the subtlety of a first-time shoplifter. I emerge with ribbons of wet toilet paper dragging from my shoes.

But there is no escaping the truth. I've made my own non-bed. Now I must lie in it. I navigate my way across the grimy tile floor of the rest room and set my toilet paraphernalia on the edge of the oily, stained sink. I wash up as best I can, keeping the slop and mess to a minimum. There's no reason for this; the rest room is already filthy. But my childhood lectures about zero-trace camping run deep. Somewhere high above, my father is watching. He'd be appalled at my circumstances, but proud of my conscientiousness. We take our self-respect where we can get it.

Washed, coiffed, and freshly T-shirted, I'm ready to go. This should be good enough. After all, the French only bathe once a week.

The Bonneville is quickly becoming "Spaceship Kent," with maps and tapes and piles of papers on the front seat, changes of clothes spread out in the back, and the contents of my friendly aviator bag strewn haphazardly inside the trunk. My biggest challenge is to keep "Spaceship Kent" from becoming "Tenement Kent," a rolling slum of newspapers, fast-food wrappers, and discarded soda bottles.

Never one for "desk management" or orderly folding of socks and underwear, I have, in the past several years, gotten even worse. I start with a clean slate, then become messier by degrees, until I'm living in an intolerable chaos that undermines all my efforts at emotional and mental balance. Eventually, when things get too bad, I peck around at the edges of my mess for a week or two, until a day comes when I'm unable to tolerate my life anymore, and I attack the chaos with a vengeance. I bring things back as far as I can. But somehow, I'm never able to restore my life to a complete state of order. One pile of papers, one set of notes—something of the chaos always remains. That's why I'm keeping such a close eye on the Bonneville. It was delivered to me in pristine condition. Like the child whose mother has cleaned his room and said, "There. Now keep it this way," I'm faced with the daunting task of changing all my behaviors at the drop of a hat. Already I can see the chaos creeping in: a hairbrush on the passenger's seat, a brochure that must have been handed to me at customs, a jumble of caseless cassettes that have slid out of the plastic bag in which I brought them, a notebook, a couple of cheap ballpoints, a micro-cassette recorder, and a scattering of receipts.

This is how it starts; I know that. Vietnam falls, and the whole world goes Communist. But I don't care. I might need all these things. I'm not going to move any of them.

I hang my wet towel over the back of the front seat and throw my muddy sandals on the floor.

I am, once again, my own worst enemy. I am, once again, traveling with myself.

As it turns out, I'm only a few miles from Mission, a small town in British Columbia a dozen miles north of the U.S. border. I once lived in a Benedictine monastery there for six months back in the early 1980s. I'm driving slowly through the rain, trying to decide whether I want to go up to the monastery for a visit.

Never have I had such mixed feelings about a place. It had a dark and potent spirituality that annihilated your sense of self and brought you within listening distance of the voice of God. But it was a harsh and heartless place as well, where human foibles and dreams were seen as nothing more than dust and ash. And I was there because of my human foibles and dreams.

I had gone there to sort through a terrible relationship that was complicated by the presence of my partner's young daughter, who had, over the period of our years together, become as dear to me as if she had been my own flesh and blood. I desperately wanted to end things with her mother, but I was the only father that young girl had ever known. To stay in that relationship, which I did not have the courage to ratify, much less consecrate, through marriage, was as great a betrayal of myself and my belief in love and commitment as would be my betrayal of the heart of that child if I chose to leave. I thought perhaps a stint in a situation of pure prayer would clarify this spiritual struggle. Maybe God would whisper some answer in my ear, either filling me with love for a woman from whom I felt increasingly distant or giving me the courage to leave.

Of course, God gave me no answers. Perhaps he was off assisting someone with a free throw. But I think he simply wanted me to work things out for myself.

In exchange for the hospitality of the Benedictines, I had offered to create a sculpture for the monastery. The result was a life-size figure of Joseph, the father of Jesus—a man asked to raise a child not his own, a man who lived a humble working-man's life in service of God's will. It was a perfect meditation for me, and I had invested it with every ounce of spiritual understanding I possessed and every dream I had for a worthy fatherhood. It was to be installed in the new chapel they were building as I left. I have never seen it in place.

Should I go? A visit there would bring me a few moments of warmth and friendship with men I grew to love and would allow me to see a work that contained the best of my spiritual and aesthetic understanding at a very difficult time in my life. But it would also resurrect a time that even today echoes with pain and darkness.

In the last analysis, I decide not to go. Perhaps I'm afraid to reconnect with that past; perhaps I simply don't want to stand in the warm glow of remembered friendships. But no matter; the decision has been made. Someday, I vow, I'll bring Nick to that monastery. It will help him in his long unraveling of his father's history, and he can look into the eyes of that figure of Joseph and decide how close I came to achieving the ideal fatherhood I had so long ago envisioned.

But, for now, my fatherhood has a different task, as does my husbandhood. The man who wrestled with dark angels in that monastery is long in the past. The question is not whether I will accept my fatherhood, but how I will carry it out. Joseph has to decide whether to pile his family on a donkey and ride across the desert or to set up camp and raise a tent upon the land.

I should turn and drive south. But I can't resist the urge to take one last side trip. My memory is hazy, but I think the road I'm on— Dewdney Trunk—dead-ends at the base of the mountain range a few miles above the monastery. North of that is nothing but hundreds of miles of jagged, mostly unexplored, mostly unnamed ten-thousand-foot peaks. I want to stand in the clearing at that turnaround and stare into the ultima Thule before I begin my trip into the hothouse reality of American culture.

Being back in Canada has begun to put me at peace. Even my short half day here has opened the shutters and let the winds blow through. It's strange how I've always felt at home in this country, sometimes more so than in my native land. There's no national betrayal in this: I'm an American through and through. But I've always felt a spiritual affinity for Canada that I can't deny.

I came to this affinity early. Minnesota abuts Ontario and Manitoba, so Canada was always on the north end of my consciousness. As a child, I would hear adults talk about fishing trips to places like Great Slave Lake and Sioux Narrows, and this would send me scurrying to my parents' road atlas to try to locate these exotic-sounding destinations. I would pore over the map, tracing the thin lines of roadways and railways and imagining what it must be like to live in such inconceivably remote locations.

One line, above all others, haunted me. It was a small, cross-hatched railroad line that angled north from Winnipeg, passing near towns with names like Flin Flon and The Pas and dead-ending at a place called Churchill, Manitoba, on the shores of Hudson Bay.

Dead end! Hudson Bay! It was Robert Service, Jack London, red-jacketed Mounties, and fur trappers with knee-high moccasins and great round, bushy beards. It was knifings in barrooms and big-bosomed women named "Lil." I found it inconceivable that anything more exotic could exist on this continent. Go to the end of the line, get on a dogsled, mush out onto the frozen wastes, and start a fire with a single match. How could it be otherwise?

I don't even want to brush against what I found when I finally did take that train up to Churchill. But reality did nothing to dampen my fascination with Canada. She had something that I longed for, something that seemed lacking in my "God shed His grace on thee" American existence.

We Statesiders—Canadians consider themselves "Americans," too—tend to presume for ourselves a political and moral centrality. We're the stake pounded in the center of the universe. If aliens were to land tomorrow and ask who it is they should talk to, we'd feel sorely put upon if any nation suggested it was anyone other than us.

I've always found this a little unseemly. I don't much like people at parties who monopolize the conversation or wear lampshades on their heads. So why should I find it attractive in a country?

Canada has always seemed more willing to take a seat at the foot of the table. She doesn't stand up and thunder her point of view to everyone else. She doesn't give lectures on proper behavior while eating all the food in sight. She questions; she struggles; she keeps quiet and tries to judge other countries on intrinsic merit rather than on the litmus test of her own ideology.

Yes, her Anglophones and Francophones are always in a fistfight. Yes, they play too much hockey and are always on the verge of coming apart at the seams. But they have a humility in the face of nature and an honesty in the face of their past. How can you not admire a nation that looks at its history, sees the wrong it did to the indigenous people, and gives them a province of their own?

Try to give a state to the Indians in the United States. We couldn't even leave them Oklahoma, or the western half of South Dakota. Every time we tried to leave them a little chunk of their own native soil, we took it right back as soon as we saw some economic value in reclaiming it. Now we've got them on little plots of land we've deemed worthless, and we're trying to bribe them into taking our garbage and our nuclear waste. Canada took a chunk of land as big as the whole Great Plains and put it under Native control.

No, in some fundamental sense I like Canada better, and it's in no small part because she's a country where praising another nation doesn't cause wild-eyed flag wavers to come up, blast beer breath in your face, and shout, "Then why the hell don't you move there?"

And, in fact, it's a good question. Why the hell don't I move here? I like the idea of living in a place where people are united not so much by a political philosophy as by the spiritual awareness that comes from waking up every day with a thousand miles of untracked wilderness right outside their back doors. I like the idea of living in a place where lights dance in the midnight sky and you can never quite forget that somewhere north of you icebergs as big as cities are floating silently through the night. It provides a sense of perspective about life that we Americans can never fully understand.

Ours is a culture of history, not nature. We do lip service to nature, but, at heart, we understand ourselves as a great drama—a national journey from east to west, full of pilgrims, powdered wigs, coonskin caps and muzzle loaders; of slaves and antebellum mansions and men in blue and grey; of men in covered wagons and women in bonnets and babies buried in shallow graves, until it all morphs into our current reality of highways and housing developments and limitless shopping experiences. The land, majestic as it is, remains only a backdrop, a stage set on which it's all played out.

Even when we choose to challenge the national plot line, or to demand that different players get leading roles, we never challenge the primacy of the drama itself. The play's the thing, and the show must go on.

Here in Canada, the set remains bigger than the actors. Sure, they can turn south and face the rock and roll juju of American culture. But, even so, it's hard to get too full of yourself when you're giving the play on a glacier or a thousand miles of unmapped mountains.

If I were younger and alone, I just might consider this place. I could find some hamlet in Nova Scotia or Newfoundland or Vancouver Island or inland B.C. I could even take the ultimate plunge and go off into the northland where men look like bears and bears walk like men.

But those days are past me. I don't have the stomach for expatriate reality, and neither does Louise. We have to be satisfied just knowing that a Canada exists, visiting her on occasion, and praying that the mountains and the winds and the icy fingers of the north can hold our American fast food hustle at bay. Our own task is to find a way to make our peace inside the room called America. We've got to accept the fact that our lives will be spent doing the Yankee Doodle dance.

I follow the road past the monastery. I'm right; this is the route. As with almost all Canadian north-south roads, the pavement soon begins to narrow as it moves toward its inevitable dead end. I continue chunking along, watching the vegetation creep ever closer to the side of the road. Soon the pavement turns to gravel and becomes little more than a path through the forest. In short order, I reach its terminus at a small earthen turnaround huddled in a grove of towering fir and cedar.

I step out into the moist, fecund air. Fog moves silently among the distant mountain peaks. Mists float dreamlike through the treetops. There are no sharp sounds, no clear edges. Everything is muffled by the presence of dampness.

The mist settles around me and collects on my skin. I feel clammy, vegetal, leaflike. A single droplet falls from far above, splashes on my hair, and runs down my cheek.

I walk along the trail until it reaches a gurgling stream. A rotted, moss-covered stump beckons. I remain there for almost an hour, smelling the pungent cedar and listening to the wind and the rushing of the waters. The icy emptiness of the mountains whispers to me. The tidal pull of the Pacific calls out to me. I can feel the cold breath of the distant north.

Eventually the wind builds and the rain begins. It sweeps across the land in sheets, closing down the day. I hurry back to the car and turn the heater up full blast. My mind is calm, my spirit is clarified. I have, for a moment, gotten my head screwed on straight.

I turn the Bonneville around and face south. It's time to rock and roll.

FOUR

CALL ME ELMER

Rock and roll doesn't play well in the rain.

The heavy weather continues, moving from dismal to dreary and back again. I should have known: a line on a map, an agreement between nations, doesn't change the music of the land.

I make my first contact with the actual coastline just north of Bellingham. This is not yet the great thundering sea; this is the gentle wash of the protected beaches of Puget Sound. But no matter. The vastness is there—the sense of infinity and a grey eternity, rolling.

Despite the rain, I run from the car to water's edge. I make a ritual touch, place my hand in the froth and bring it to my lips like Holy Water. The sense of release is palpable. I can only imagine what Lewis and Clark felt as they stood at the mouth of the Columbia, looking out for the first time on what they believed was the great Pacific, and penned those words that even today jump off the page with their potent and inarticulate sense of relief: "Ocian in view! O! the joy."

It was Columbus in reverse: men of land touching the sea. In some dark but joyful way, it was the completion of our American journey and the beginning of our American dream.

Yet what is surrounding me here, as I stand in the rain at water's edge, is not our American dream, but something far darker. I am on the Lummi Reservation, one of the many small reservations that dot the Pacific Northwest. For the Lummi, as for all Native Americans, the journey of Lewis and Clark is but the first chapter of the saga of a dream gone desperately wrong.

I don't know much about the Lummi. I seem to remember that they've done better than most of the tribes in America, keeping possession of their seacoast and, thus, access to the ocean's bounty. Still, they live like the Native people on almost all reservations, amid half efforts and incompletions and junk cars and shabby houses. In this, they're no different from the Ojibwe of my own northern Minnesota or the Lakota I have known in the Dakotas.

How did we as a nation come to this? Driving in, along the freeway, there was a standard-issue highway sign that read, "Lummi Reservation. Next Exit." It might as well have said, "Gas, Food, Lodging," or "Wendy's" or "Burger King." A people who once owned this land, built their philosophy around it, found the presence of God on it—reduced to a civic division and roadside pulloff.

I know this doesn't bother most people, at least not in the way it bothers me. For most, the real issues of American colonialismo—if, indeed, they see any such issues at all—are framed in terms of oppression of blacks and exploitation of workers in foreign countries. But I have lived too long among the trees and lakes. And my little town's placement between three major Indian reservations has had its effect on me. For me, the voices of the indigenous peoples are always present.

I can't escape the purported words of Chief Seattle: "And when the last red man shall have perished, and the memory of my tribe shall have become a myth among the white man, these shores will swarm with the invisible dead of my tribe; and when your children's children think themselves alone in the field, the store, the shop, upon the highway, or in the silence of the pathless woods, they will not be alone."

As much as this might sound like spiritual mumbo jumbo to most people, I believe it with all my heart. I feel the Native presence on the land, and it haunts me.

I don't quite know how to explain it. Maybe it was best revealed in a moment I experienced a few years ago on a Nootka reserve a few miles north of here on the west edge of Vancouver Island. I was with a group of my students from the RedLake Ojibwe reservation. We were guests at a feast being given for a young boy, no more than eleven, who had written a poem that had won some national contest. He and his family were soon to depart for Japan, where his poem would be read in an international celebration of the works of the world's youth. In the traditional manner of the Nootka people, a feast was being provided—fresh salmon smoked on open fires—and the young boy was being raised up before the community.

We all sat on folding chairs in a small gymnasium while the young boy stood, blushing, at the front of the hall. His parents were with him, as was the head man of the tribe. Too shy to read his poem aloud, the young boy chose to acknowledge the audience with a traditional dance. He donned a simple box-shaped helmet decorated with the designs of the raven, and, placing a blanket over his shoulders, he began to dip and weave in time with the singers who were chanting and drumming in the corner.

For fully ten minutes he danced. Part of him was no more than a little boy at play; part of him was swept up into a world of dreams and visions. Swooping and gliding, bobbing and soaring, he turned the music into wind and floated upon it. Though his eyes were closed, he would turn the mask toward us, and we would feel observed and acknowledged.

When he finished, he slumped clumsily into a chair in the corner. He was once again the embarrassed boy. The families in attendance applauded lightly. He had done well. He soon faded into the crowd and ran off to play with his friends.

The feast went off as planned. We all sat outside, near the pounding of the surf, sharing freshly-cooked salmon beneath fogbound, swaying cedars. There was much joking and friendly banter. Nothing more was mentioned about the poem or the dance or the small boy. But as the fog wove its wispy fingers among the branches of the trees, a raven winged its way out of the mist and floated silently to the ground. No one said a word, but we all watched. In the bird's lyrical descent to earth we saw the movements of the young dancer. And in the rhythm of the surf and the singing of the wind, we heard the beat of the drum and the chanting of the voices to which he had moved his wings.

This was not conceit; it was connection. And I mourn the loss of this connection. Nothing good can come of a deafness to the land.

I drive down a long, forested roadway toward the center of the reservation, a place called Lummi Village. Real-estate "For Sale" signs dot the sides of the road, and they're not promoting reservation shacks and trailers, but fine, expensive, glass-and-cedar suburban homes.

I don't know the story, but I can guess. These are probably white-owned houses, legacies of sales and barters and outright thievery performed years and generations ago.

The rough historical outlines are always the same. The encroachment of European settlers drove the Indians onto ever smaller and smaller plots of land, which they accepted with heavy heart, until they had only tiny areas left of their aboriginal homelands. The Dawes Act of 1873 further segmented those remaining lands by dividing them into individual pieces of property, so the Indians could be "civilized" by learning the ways of forty acres and a plow.

Having no tradition of personal ownership of the land and even less of capitalist values and ways, the Indian people soon found themselves trading away the rights to that land for goods or in payment of debts—real or fictitious—that white merchants claimed they owed. Soon even the reservations were mostly in white hands.

I don't know the specifics of the Lummi situation, but I'm sure I could find stories here equal to that of the Ojibwe family in northern Minnesota who had to give up their entire traditional family hunting grounds, including a half mile of pristine lakeshore, to a local dentist who claimed he had not received proper compensation for a filling.

Maybe with a little luck, the Lummi will be able to buy their reservation back, piece by piece. But they're going to have to sell a lot of fireworks and T-shirts and raven ashtrays.

As I approach Lummi Village I see that it is dominated by a casino. Through the drizzle I can hear the drone of the idling tour buses.

Here, in the cruelest irony of all, is the Indians' last best hope for getting their lands back: offer white folks a shot at the American dream at a quarter a chance. Unfortunately, the bags of money that this produces too often disappear into a void of graft and corruption protected from regulatory eyes by the tortured legal definition of tribal sovereignty. The ordinary folk are going to have to make it on the fireworks and ashtrays.

The casino is like so many others—a cheap, cavernous building meant to serve no other purpose than housing slot machines. Queues of elderly white people are disembarking from the buses and pushing their way through the doors.

I wait until the crush is over, then follow the crowd inside. Near the entrance, a young Indian woman sits disinterestedly behind a glass case containing god's-eyes, dreamcatchers, and bad miniature totem poles made in China. She doesn't even look up as I enter.

The light inside is garish. Like all casinos, this one is supposed to fill a person with an electric sense of possibility. Bells are ringing, lights are flashing. The slot machines gleam in the darkness like the rocket's red glare.

As my eyes focus, I see a uniformed Caucasian bus driver leaning against a one-armed bandit, passing the time with a teenage Indian boy dressed as a croupier. The Indian boy looks as odd and out of place in his white shirt and black bow tie as the Indian men in nineteenth-century photographs looked when they were dressed in starched-collared shirts and waistcoats for trips to Washington, D.C.

I don't like this place. It's like being in a bar during the daytime or watching television in the afternoon. Old white men and women sit hunched over the nickel slot machines. Plumes of cigarette smoke rise from their ashtrays. In some distant corner a bell starts clanging, and the hollow tinkle of coins hitting a metal trough fills the joyless cavern of a room. The hunched men and women look up for a moment, then go back to their machines with renewed intensity. The woman at the gift counter files her nails.

Eventually, the croupier boy leaves, so I strike up a conversation with the bus driver. He's from Spokane.

"Come down a couple times a week," he says. "Charter. Gives the old folks something to do."

"It just feels wrong to me," I say.

He scowls. "It's a free country."

"I mean, for the Indians. To be reduced to this."

"Reduced!" he says. "Shit, they're getting fucking rich. I wish I could get a bunch of bored old people to throw money down a hole for me. You want to be reduced to something, try driving a fucking bus."

This conversation is going nowhere, so I walk outside into the heavy morning mist. Seagulls are perched on weathered pilings out in the muck of the tidewater. In the distance I can feel the restless movement of the sea.

The croupier boy is standing on the dock. I want to approach him, but there's an air of impenetrable distance around him. I watch him carefully. He takes a cigarette out of his pocket, taps it on the back of his hand, and lights it. His gaze is empty and without focus. He stands there, before the open sea, smoking. Drag, hold, exhale. Drag, hold, exhale. At first I think he must be smoking marijuana. Then I realize he is simply breathing in cadence with the heavings of the sea.

Suddenly something catches his attention. He snuffs out the cigarette in a single gesture and flips it into the grey water, as if the act of smoking would divert his attention, or reveal him. His eye follows something in the sky. The intensity of his focus is almost frightening.

I squint to see what he's watching, but all I see is fog. Then, ever so slowly, a sea bird emerges from the mist, floats silently down, and lights on one of the pilings. The croupier boy relaxes. He takes out another cigarette from his pocket, tamps it on his hand, and lights it. His gaze empties. Behind him the door of the casino opens and the ringing of the whirring slots can be heard.

He turns, blank-faced, and walks back toward the door. Someone has just hit a jackpot. The jingling of coins hitting a metal tray fills the misty air.

I want something more of this day. The greyness in the sky has induced an unrelenting greyness in my spirit.

I drive on into Bellingham, a city I remember with deep fondness. In the back of my mind this is a place where I've always felt I would like to live. Louise, who visited here during a summer she spent as an intern at the *Seattle Times,* agrees. It's the perfect "baby bear" of cities for us—not too big, not too small, but just right. It has a university, a semblance of a cutting-edge civic vision, proximity to the sea and the mountains, a good bookstore and restaurants, decent coffee, and the nearby, but not too nearby, presence of Seattle and Vancouver, two of our favorite large cities on the North American continent.

But theory is worth nothing in the rain. This day defeats me. Its grim dreariness drains any sense of adventure from me. Forty below zero, where metal snaps and spit freezes on the way to the ground, I can understand. You just have to swaddle yourself in goose down and cover every square inch of your body. The cold hammers at you like the wind at the door, fighting in through every crack until it dulls you and numbs you and reduces you to a state of torpid lethargy. But if you're well enough packed, it can't defeat you.

This cold is different. It's more pernicious, more subtle. It begins at the surface as simple chill and wetness, seemingly able to be toweled off and forgotten. But then, without warning, it moves deeper. Your bones become soggy, and your life force becomes as grey as the skies. Like a dark river, the damp moves to the core of things. Your body and your spirit become entombed in boggy despair.

I learned this lesson well when I lived in my Oregon cabin. A young couple, crazed from living too long by the chill of the sea, wanted to trade me their home on the coastal dunes for my home deep in the folds of the coastal hills. Since I was crazed from the spiritual claustro-phobia of living in a dark valley, it seemed like an intriguing prospect.

On a cold and sunless day in March I went to check out their home. As it was only several hundred yards across some dunes from the ocean, I decided to walk to water's edge. But the wind was so wet and lashing that I couldn't even navigate that short distance. After a half hour of trying, I retreated to the house and sought to warm myself by the fire. But the house was cinder block, and the dampness was in the walls and the floors and the ceilings.

The fire dried me. The tea and cider nourished me. A blanket and a good book swathed me in warmth. But the cold had gotten in. Like a worm in my bones, it ate away at the very center of my hope and resolve. It made a sepulchre of my body. I didn't lose the chill until June.

Today that same chill is moving into me. Bellingham seems as inhospitable to me as New York City does to an Eskimo, or northern Minnesota does to a beachcomber from the Florida Keys. Still, I've promised Louise I would look closely at the place.

I go up to Western Washington State College, halfheartedly pick up a little material on the journalism program where she thought she might be able to teach. I make a few peremptory inquiries about their course offerings and educational philosophy. The woman at the desk has no interest in me, and I have none in her. I'm simply a dead man walking. I turn and shamble back out into the rain.

I'm profoundly depressed. This town is one of our secret fantasies, a trump card up our familial sleeve. Everything I see confirms my belief that it's the perfect balance of nature and culture, rawness and civility. But I'm as blind to it as I am to the charms of a swamp. It has turned in my mind into a place I merely want to escape.

I know this is purely the spillover from the relentless rain and travel fatigue, and I know that the other side of this all-pervasive greyness is a blue, luminous, sea-blessed brilliance. But my mind can't lift the heaviness from my heart.

I guess this is for the best. Major life decisions, such as those about spouses and places to live, are best made with clear-eyed knowledge of the extremes. I've seen far too many people make choices based on fantasies built on casual encounters under optimal circumstances. I need only look at my own native northern Minnesota, where we see a yearly hegira of backpack-wearing, hiking boot–clumping young people and RV-ensconced retirees who think the warm summer sun and the idyllic loon-call lakes make ours a perfect place to live. By January they're chewing the door lintels and banging pails on the floor. In short order, they bolt for the sun.

I lived long enough along this northern Pacific coast to know I could once again master the rain and lack of consistent sun. But the question I can't answer is whether I now have the will to do so. Just because there are people happily riding bikes through this drizzle doesn't mean I have the wherewithal to make that shift again in my life or, even, that making the shift is desirable. All I know for certain is that I can't fight this battle today.

This morning, at breakfast, I was reading the coastal entries in the journals of Lewis and Clark. Passage after passage began, "Rained all the last night & today without much intermition"; day after day was filled with observations like "Showery wet and disagreeable." I can't shake the image conjured up by the Christmas entry of 1805, in which Clark wrote, "We would have Spent this day of the nativity of Christ in feasting, had we any thing either to raise our Sperits or even to gratify our appetites, our Diner concisted of pore Elk, so much Spoiled that we eate it thro' mear necessity, Some Spoiled pounded fish and a fiew roots."

It wasn't until January 3, 1806, that he was able to write, "The Sun rose faire this morning for the first time for Six weeks past." Then he had to follow up in the next sentence with, "The clouds soon obscure it from our view, and a Shower of rain Suckseeded."

I haven't yet been reduced to eating spoiled elk and sleeping in wet, rotting blankets infested with "very troublesome flees," but the rain that fell on him for six weeks and defeated his spirits is no different from the rain that is falling on me and defeating mine. And it's no different from the rain that would fall on Nick and Louise as they set out each day for work or school.

Maybe, when all is said and done, Nick, Louise, and I are people of the snows and the North. Maybe we have been claimed by the land, and there's no further reason to resist. I do know that even if our Christmases had turkeys and dressing on the table rather than "Spoiled pounded fish and a fiew roots," spending the holidays under a freezing and relentless drizzle, rather than beneath snow-laden pines on the edge of a silent, frozen lake, would unhinge us all.

With heavy heart I drive south toward Seattle, one of my favorite American big cities. I could easily make it there by nightfall, but I decide to stop for the evening somewhere on her outskirts. I owe her better than to drag myself into her center under this pall of gloom and defeat.

I choose to overnight in Edmonds, a bedroom community a few miles north of the city. Edmonds is a ferry town, and the traffic making its way to the ferry is intolerable. I stop-and-go my way down one more rancid strip of car lots and squat franchise restaurants, wondering if there's any relief anywhere from this commercial dreariness.

After several stops at squalid dives that want a half a month's mortgage for a sagging bed and a TV with tinfoil wrapped around the antenna, I find a motel that's both reasonable and clean. It's run by an Arab family who will not let me leave until I take a room. Each time I pause in a sentence, they lower the price another dollar.

They're friendly folk, quite willing to talk. They took this job to get their children out of the city, they tell me. Too many gangs, they say, and too much racism. Their dark skin made them targets; their children were falling in with the wrong crowd.

"Edmonds is nice," the woman says. "There are many rich people here." Her voice is full of pride, as if by rubbing shoulders with wealth she has bettered herself. Through the curtain separating the office from the living quarters I can see a teenage boy playing Nintendo. He's eating a hamburger.

I nap for a bit and noodle around with the television, but I'm feeling restless. I decide to go down to the ferry terminal and watch the boats on the sound.

The sky has lifted, and the rain is falling in short, wind-driven bursts. Cars course by on the shiny, slick streets, spraying roostertails onto the sidewalks. Far out in the harbor I can see the ferries moving like floating temples on the darkening waters. Their horns blare muted and melancholy into the growing night.

I make my way to the pier and stare down into the inky waters. The lights of the ferry terminal wiggle and melt upon the surface. I imagine, for an instant, that I can see my own reflection staring back at me. It's a thing of beauty, but with a shudder of fear. I'm set against the darkness, liquid and primordial.

The rain starts up again, this time with a vengeance. It comes in sheets, driven on a heartless wind. It splashes on the ground, on the windows, on the cars. It pummels the pavement with perfect indifference and claws at any exposed flesh with the fury of an animal. I push my way back toward the car with shoulders hunched and eyes squinted. The torrent pelts me, cold and relentless, loud in my ears, sharp on my face.

I'm parked several blocks away. The wind is vicious; each step is torture. I'm so cold I want to weep. If someone offered me the choice between a warm bed and a personal audience with God right now, I'd take the bed.

A young couple runs past me, laughing. Their coats are pulled over their heads. They duck into a nearby restaurant. I follow, hoping to find some relief until the rain lets up.

There's a pay phone in the entrance. Against my better judgment, I decide to call home. If I can't feel any warmth in my body, at least I can feel some warmth in my heart.

Nick answers. "Hi, Dad. Where are you?" I begin to respond, but he's not really interested. He's working on some project in school—a report on the explorer Shackleton and his expedition to the Antarctic. He just wants to talk.

I listen to his breathless exposition of the travails of Shackleton and his ship, the *Endurance*. I don't even hear the words, just the music of his enthusiasm. His voice is the sweetest melody ever composed. Would I be crazy just to shout, "Nick, I love you"?

He continues to jabber, then drives the knife in. "Dad, are you going to be home pretty soon?"

"Another week or so," I say, with false brightness in my voice. Rain from my hair is dripping on the collar of my shirt and coursing icily down my spine. I hear the disappointed silence on the other end of the line.

"It won't be long," I promise. I'm trying to put some perk in my voice. "So, that Shackleton was a pretty brave man?"

"Really brave. Mr. Wade says he's a real hero."

The conversation continues in this vein—the sodden landlubber, two days out, listening to stories of the intrepid explorer who survived a winter locked in a floe of Antarctic ice.

Luckily, Nick is full of himself right now and doesn't push me any more about my situation. Finally, he reaches the end of his story.

"That's great, Nick," I say. "I can't wait to read that report."

"It's going to be good," he says, full of the naive confidence of a child on fire with a new enthusiasm.

"I'll bet it will," I respond. "I love you, Nick."

"Okay," he answers. He's at that age.

"Can I talk to Mom now?"

"Sure. Bye, Dad."

"Bye, Nick."

"Bye."

The rain runs off my eyebrows and drips onto the receiver. A happy group of diners, finished with their meal, stops in the entryway to open their umbrellas.

Louise gets on the phone. "So, you heard from young Shackleton. How are things going?"

"It's just awful," I blurt. "Right now it feels like the biggest mistake of my life."

Ever the realist, she tries to comfort me. "Things will get better."

"I know. I'm just having some adjustment problems."

"What's that sound?" she asks. The diners have just opened the door.

"Rain," I say.

"Oh." Her voice softens. Though her stay in Seattle took place in the summer, she saw enough dismal days to have a hint of the depression that's weighing me down at this moment.

She shifts her focus. "Did you stop in Bellingham?" There's a slight anticipation in her voice.

"I couldn't see it," I tell her. "The rain was in the way."

"Oh. That's too bad." I can hear the wind going out of her sails.

We move to small talk about concerns on the home front. But the dispatch has been sent, the communiqué has been issued. This planet will not support human life.

I feel like a failure. I've just slammed the door on one of our optimal relocation fantasies, and it's simply because I wasn't strong enough to stand up against a day and a half of heavy Pacific rain.

I wander back into the street, an absurd and sodden poodle. My son is working on a report about an intrepid and indomitable explorer. My wife is going to a job she dislikes and maintaining a household by herself while I gallivant around the country supposedly in search of a better life for all of us. And I'm standing in a doorway whimpering about the rain.

Forget Lewis and Clark. Forget Ernest Shackleton. Don't call me Ishmael; call me Elmer Fudd.

FIVE

DOUBLE SKINNY CAP AND A BULLET

What a difference a night makes.

I woke to a sun-blessed day, dressed frantically, and drove to a small downtown park on the edge of Puget Sound. Now I'm standing before a panorama of blue vaulting sky, lapping waters, and wind-washed hills. Across the sound, the white eminences of the Olympic Mountains stand in ancient majesty. The fog lingers, primeval, among their peaks, then retreats in wisps out toward the sea.

I can't find yesterday in my memory. It was a different world then, a different life. The sky was a grey, impenetrable bank of heavy-bellied clouds. There were no vistas, only an all-enveloping atmosphere that moved sullenly between mist and rain. The leaden sky pressed down upon my shoulders, and a cutting cold penetrated, without compassion, to the very spirit of all living things. There was no sense of joy or hope, only a longing for relief, a prayer that the sky would lift.

Now, this morning, I'm in an amphitheater of the gods. The rains are gone. The atmosphere is cleansed. The light is so pure as to be almost blinding. All things are alive, luminous, and fresh. All around me a cosmic drama is being played out. The mountains call out to the sea, and the sea calls back on the fragrance of the winds. The sun dances on the waters, and the clouds lilt like great white sails across the sky. All surges outward, outward, outward, toward the open sea.

I breathe deeply, unable to fill myself. The air is too rich with life, too pungent with smells from the ocean, too sweet with the nectars of a million flowers, too strong with the incense of cedars and pines. I want to scream, to raise a mighty shout to the sky.

We have weather shifts in the Midwest, but nothing like this. Winter can be cutting and cruel one day and, the next, become a vesper of golden sun on silent snows. A summer day can change, in a matter of hours, from murky and fetid and pregnant with danger to a placid tableau of mirrorlike waters and whispering trees. But these are changes in mood, not fundamental changes in character. This change is of a wholly different order. It's as if the very world in which I've awakened is different. It's total transformation, like a shy young boy turning into a raven.

Maybe there's some connection here. I remember years ago, when I first saw a film, made by Edward Curtis in 1914, in which the Kwakiutl people reenacted the story of the abduction of a woman by a neighboring tribe. The film was grainy and indistinct, like looking through memory itself. In one sequence a man was shown standing in the prow of a canoe, wearing an animal skin and dancing the dance of the bear. It made the hair on the back of my neck stand on end. What I saw before me was not a man wearing a costume, but a man who had taken on the very personality and presence of a bear. It was magic. Not card-trick magic or cheap illusion, but deep magic, shamanic magic, the kind of magic that lives on the edge of spiritual possession. I was witnessing a total transformation.

This day, in its own way, is such a moment of magic. The entire world has been transformed.

How am I to understand this? It's much more than some simple shift in personal psychology. I'm resonating with some deeper truth. All I can compare it to is falling in love, or the one day each year in my northern home when we awake from an earth of lifeless browns to a world of noiseless, trackless white. All yesterdays are forgotten. The world has new raiment, and the heart is on a different path.

As I pass a bush with delicate pink flowers and green succulent leaves, I begin to get a glimmer of an explanation. Yesterday, all of creation was colored as if with pigment. Today, it's alive with light. What had been a fresco has become stained glass.

Perhaps there's a scientific explanation for this. Perhaps it's simply the sun reflecting off the liquid molecules from last night's rain. But that doesn't touch the heart of the matter. It's a complete change in spiritual presence, like the difference between the eyes of the living and the eyes of the dead. The form may remain the same, but without the light, you know that life has fled.

Today the light is everywhere. It's in the clouds, in the mountains, in the sea, in the smallest blade of grass and the whole vaulting firmament. The very atmosphere itself has been infused with luminescence. We have been changed—raised incorruptible.

The entire world sings an anthem to the sun.

Part of me feels that I should go back toward Bellingham. I could spend the morning poking around La Conner and the San Juans, giving them the time I denied them yesterday. But the sun is driving me southward. I want to get to Seattle.

Ever since I first visited her almost thirty years ago, I felt Seattle had a freshness and humility that set her apart from other large cities. Part of this, I'm sure, comes from being washed clean by the constant comings and goings of the fog and the rain. But part of it is due to the city's setting between the mountains and the ocean, and their ongoing conversation with the low-hanging, roiling, ever-changing sky.

To live beneath this dialogue of the great forces tends to keep a place humble. The inhabitants can never quite lose themselves in the humdrum, street-level preoccupations of the human. Even if they become subsumed into the minutiae of daily affairs, there comes the moment when the clouds lift and the great goddess, Rainier, shows her face. At that instant, the entire world changes, and all human concerns and pretensions are put in their proper perspective. Truly, if there's a large city in America where I could live, Seattle is it.

I decide to eschew the rush of the freeway and enter the city by the side streets. I'm know they're a tangle; I know I'll get lost. But I'm in "boulevardier" mode: just riding along in my automobile, with no particular place to go. Something will happen soon enough that will put a shape on my day. And, sure enough, it does. On a street corner up ahead I see the outline of a solitary hitchhiker.

Hitchhikers bring out a great ambivalence in me. So much of my past is tied up in rides given and rides received. From the merchant marines who had jumped ship and made me take them from Bolinas to Seattle, to the Humboldt County hippie with his flatbed full of hay bales that turned out to be hiding hundreds of kilos of marijuana, to the kids in the stolen Chevy who were shoplifting their way across America and wanted me to be their getaway driver, to the paranoid schizophrenic soldier who hadn't eaten in three days and thought I was an agent of the devil sent to poison his food—my experiences with giving and receiving rides have been some of the most interesting and bizarre in my life.

But these are meaner times. People take to the road for darker reasons. I have no interest in being the next notch on the gun butt of someone who's receiving messages from a five-thousand-year-old dog or who's willing to cut out my heart to get a snootful of coke. So, despite the value I place on the serendipitous encounter, I now pass by many more hitchhikers than I ever pick up.

But as I get closer, I see that the likelihood of this figure being some Hillside Strangler is slim to none. It's a young woman, maybe eighteen, standing with her arm at full extension and her thumb facing straight up in the air. She has a slightly defiant look to her, as if she's trying to convince drivers that she can take care of herself.

I fancy myself a student of hitchhiking styles. In my younger days it was a simple matter of survival. When you were stuck at the end of University Avenue in Berkeley with twelve groups of hitchhikers in front of you and ten behind you, or at an on-ramp in a rough part of Oakland as the sun was going down, your success, and, sometimes, your very survival, depended on your ability to convince passing drivers that you were someone who was not only safe to pick up, but interesting enough to make it worth their while. A wise hitchhiker worked long and hard to craft a successful technique.

Over the years, I have seen, and tried, a number of them. I personally settled on a style best described as "intellectual casual": a well-lettered sign—understated but literate-looking—and a leisurely stance reinforced by a benign smile and a thumb extended nonchalantly at about hip level. Under no circumstance did I want to communicate tension, desperation, or ignorance. I admired the panache of people who stood on the curb with crudely crayoned signs reading "Mars" or "Paris," though I had neither the chutzpah nor the insanity to do so. But I had no respect for those hitchers who aggressively shook their thumbs at drivers, or who walked along with their backs turned, or who sat on the ground, indifferent to the passing cars, with a sign announcing their destination. For me, the issue was simple: let them see my eyes, don't have a sign that speaks of hundreds of miles of possible togetherness, seem relaxed and courteous, and look as if I might actually have something interesting to contribute to their life.

It generally worked. And, with a handful of notable exceptions, I've tried to follow the same set of guidelines when picking people up. This young girl, with her strident, defiant stance, has a very different approach. But the day is gracious and her manner piques my interest. How can I not pick her up on this sun-blessed Seattle morning?

Still, I hesitate. I recall the caveat of our dearly beloved Minnesota political hack Hubert Humphrey, who offered the counsel, "Never be alone in a car with a woman." But I'm not a politician, and this girl looks neither litigious nor dangerous. In fact, her naive self-confidence reminds me of my twenty-something stepdaughters, and in that, she brings out my instinctive parental protectiveness. Perhaps by giving her a ride, I can save her from some lecherous ghoul or some madman whose brain is churning like the agitator in a washing machine.

I assess her carefully as I clear the maps and tapes off the front seat and signal my intentions to stop. She's dressed in one of the uniforms of contemporary youth: baggy fatigue pants; big, heavy, military-style boots; and an Italian laborer's ribbed sleeveless undershirt. She is manifestly bra-less, does not shave her armpits, and has one single gold pin through her right nostril. Her hair is done in a chicken cut, with bristles sticking out everywhere. Beneath its blond fluff I can catch just the slightest echo of a long-faded dye job—something between orange and magenta. She carries a green canvas backpack covered with buttons and patches, mostly promoting environmental and radical political causes.

I'm acutely aware of my potential to be seen as some aging Humbert Humbert, so I'm prepared to offer my most benign and reassuring "Hello" as I brake to a stop beside her. But there's no need. She hops in fearlessly and blurts out a loud and perky "Hi."

"Hello," I respond. "Kind of cold to be out without a jacket."

She snaps her gum. "Nah. It's fine. Got one in my pack, anyhow. You going to U.W.?"

Surprisingly, this simple question stops me in my tracks. "Yes" would be a lie, because I don't know exactly what, much less where, U.W. is, though I assume it's the University of Washington. "No" would be equally as absurd, because I'm happy to take her wherever she needs to go. But "I'll take you where you want to go" sounds ominously solicitous and overly focused on her importance in my life. I'm trapped in some kind of Prufrockian dilemma. Do I dare to wear the bottoms of my trousers rolled?

"I'm in no hurry," I finally say. "I'll be happy to take you where you're going. But you'll have to direct me. I'm not from around here."

She snaps her gum and nods. There's no sense of concern in her manner, and even less interest in my reasons or motives. "That'd be cool," she responds. "I work down by the campus. At a cap shop. Give me a ride, I'll get you one."

My mind is processing rapidly, discarding options to arrive at a viable interpretation of her statement.

"Cappuccino?" I say, hoping she didn't mean baseball caps.

She looks at me as if I've just gotten off the boat. "Yeah," she answers in a tone that falls somewhere between incredulity and scorn.

"It's a deal," I say. "I could use another shot of coffee."

That issue disposed of, she moves on to other matters. She snaps her gum again and looks around the car. "You a salesman?" she asks.

I pull on the ragged collar of my sweatshirt. "Do I look like a salesman?"

But she's already moved past the question. She's reaching into the backseat to examine my tapes. "Bob Dylan. This is far out. Who's Leonard Cohen?"

"Another old guy. Excellent poet."

"Cool," she responds. Her interest is sated.

I'm driving blindly while she appraises my tape selection. I have absolutely no sense of where I'm supposed to go.

"You've got to tell me where to turn," I say.

She looks around. "Oh. Yeah." She points across the road. "There."

It's almost an impossibility. I hit the accelerator and try to sneak in front of another car that's driving beside me. The driver speeds up as soon as he sees me trying to get into his lane.

"Son of a bitch," I say.

The girl looks at me and wrinkles her nose. "You must be a meat eater."

I'm getting a little exasperated with her. She's a sweetheart, but her presumptuous manner and nonstop snooping have put me on edge. I'm almost ready to launch into a parental lecture. But the day is too beautiful, and I think back on the supercilious pronouncements my parents had to endure from me for so many years. What's good for the goose is good for the gander.

"I'll turn around at the next exit," I say. "I need that cappuccino."

She's already in the glove box. "There's nothing in here," she says. "This car isn't stolen, is it?" There's a hopeful look in her eyes.

"It's a rental car," I say. "They come pretty empty."

She wrinkles her nose again, like an overgrown twelve-year-old. "You mean you don't even have a cell phone?"

I want to stop her manic movement. I've got to engage her in conversation.

"Tell me about the . . . cap shop," I say. The phrase sticks in my mouth, but I've pushed the right button. She turns to me with an excited look. She removes her gum and wads it up, then sticks it against the side of the ashtray. "It's awesome," she says. "The people who run it—Bob and Marie—they're really amazing. They have this, like, special coffee, from, like, Indonesia or someplace. It's grown on the side of this secret mountain, and they're, like, the only people who can get it, because they've got, like, this special connection with the natives. Bob was in the Peace Corps or Vietnam or something."

I don't have a clue whether she's deluded, lying, or possibly even telling the truth. I've been fully prepared for the coming of coffee varietals and enological-like parsings of soils and vintages. "Indonesian, west slope, 1996 planting" is surely on the American coffee marketing radar screen. But this girl's blurtings are so breathtakingly naive that I just let them go.

"Sound's amazing," I say. "Pretty special coffee, huh?"

But she's off again. "Bob says they're maybe going to sell franchises. Like, if they can keep the supply coming. My boyfriend and I—we're, like, maybe going to get one. I can get my dad to loan us the money. He's a lawyer. We'd probably go to Alaska. My boyfriend, he's a really good musician. He can sound just like Hendrix. Kurt Cobain, too. He's had some really good gigs. We'd be, like, the only ones there with this coffee. Bob and Marie, they said we could have, like, the whole state."

She's almost tripping over her own thoughts. She reminds me of a puppy trying to stop on a slippery floor.

"A franchise, huh? Alaska? Sounds interesting."

"Yeah, but not, like, one of those corporate things. You know, that rip off the rain forest."

"I know what you mean."

Suddenly she blurts out, "Ohmygod, there's Teresa." I about jump out of my seat. She rolls down the window and starts shouting and waving.

"Do you want me to stop?" I say.

She wrinkles her nose again and looks confused. "Why?"

Despite her skittery foolishness, the more I get used to her, the more I like her. Her naive freshness is as invigorating as the day. In some ways it's far healthier than the sullen, hunch-shoulder existential angst I carried around at her age. And though she may not know anything, the direction of her thinking is good. She's planted the seeds of a social consciousness in herself, and she has ambitions and dreams. Given decent nurturing and a bit of editing, she'll grow into a fascinating person, though I doubt it will be as the operator of a string of Alaskan "cap shops." I'd like to meet her in ten years to see what she's become.

Eventually, we arrive at her place of employment. It's a little storefront hole-in-the-wall, done up with lace curtains and divided-light windowpanes. Inside I can see people hunched over mugs of coffee reading the *Seattle Times*.

"Wait here," she says. "I'll get you a double."

"Skim milk," I holler after her, "and not too much foam."

She grins. "Double skinny cap, dry. Got it."

Soon she returns carrying a paper cup. "Here. Taste it. This is, like, that secret coffee I was telling you about. It's their own roast, too."

I sip it. It's very good, but no better than a thousand other cappuccinos I've had, and probably no better than the one served at the next shop a few hundred yards down the street.

"I think you've got something here," I tell her. "Good luck in Alaska."

She bounces up the steps, her fading magenta chicken cut gleaming in the sun. She turns and gives me a thumbs-up, the same gesture she was making when I first saw her. I give her a thumbs-up and drive off into the morning.

I could live with this. The sky overhead is a luminous, depthless, cerulean blue.

Since I'm near the university, I decide to poke around. University neighborhoods are especially dear to my heart. However, they all share one common curse: they're anathema to automobiles. If you live near a university, the best thing you can do is burn your car. Or, at least, that's the decision that was come to by a friend of mine at the University of Minnesota.

He owned an evil Volkswagen bug that defied the efforts of every mechanic to solve a recurring electrical problem. Time after time it would stall for no reason at all, always with no warning and always in the most inconvenient circumstances.

He would have it towed to a mechanic, spend money he didn't have, be assured that the problem was finally fixed, and within a week find himself stranded on another freeway or busy city street with a car that once again refused to start.

He would dutifully call a friend, who would dutifully come over and pull the beast back to his house. Then he would dial up the mechanic, who would shrug his shoulders and offer to try again for more money. My friend would get angry and curse the mechanic, then drag the car to a different shop, and the same process would begin all over. The only thing that changed was the balance in his checkbook, which had been almost nonexistent in the first place.

One winter morning he awoke to find the curbside in front of his apartment peppered with signs announcing that all vehicles had to be removed by eight o'clock so the streets could be plowed. It was already seven forty-five.

The Volkswagen, of course, refused to start.

He cranked and cursed and enlisted the aid of neighbors to try to jump the battery, but nothing worked. After almost inducing coronaries in three out-of-shape passersby who he conscripted to try to push-start the car, he shoved the beast into neutral, pushed it into the middle of the street, and began yelling, "If anyone wants this car, they have fifteen minutes to come and take it." But no one emerged to take him up on his offer. Perhaps it was because he kept referring to the Volkswagen as "the piece of shit that has ruined my life."

At any rate, the fifteen-minute deadline came and went with no takers. So he did what any reasonable man would do. He set the car on fire.

By the time I stopped by later in the day, it was only a charred carcass resting by the side of the curb. The firemen had come and put it out, and he, like Peter, had denied any knowledge of its ownership. His wife, who was expecting a child, was ready to divorce him. The kids in the neighborhood were ready to canonize him. But in his own mind, only one thing mattered: he was free. He bought an old black bicycle, too wretched to be stolen, and proceeded to ride it all through one of the snowiest Minnesota winters on record. He was a happy man.

As I drive up and down street after street in the elephantine Bonneville looking for a parking place, I consider the elegant simplicity of my friend's solution. Yet this is not my car, and, besides, I'm not about to let the streets defeat me. I'm the son of a man who would spend ten dollars in gas looking for a place to park rather than five dollars to park in a lot. And I have inherited his stubbornness in this regard. The only real evolutionary step I've taken is to see the search as an exercise in self-mastery rather than as proof of a conspiracy directed against me by a cruel and sadistic God.

Today, however, I'm wondering if God, perhaps, has decided to get involved. I drive for fifteen minutes and never see a single open parking spot. Blessedly, the beneficent sky and the novelty of the neighborhoods is keeping me from psychosis. Even if I have to walk twenty blocks, every step will be new. And, if I'm truthful with myself, I have to ask, "Twenty blocks to where?" I really have no destination.

Finally, I see a space up ahead. It looks too small for the gargantuan Bonneville and may be only the leftover space between two careless or selfish parallel parkers. But I'm determined to try it.

I speed to the spot and slam on my brakes. I don't want to have to throttle some young coed who slips into it frontward before I'm able to wheelhouse my way back into its tiny confines.

My window is open and I'm talking out loud to myself. "This is mine, you bastards. This is mine."

Suddenly, I notice a young black man sitting on the front steps of a house across the street. He's watching me intently. I pretend not to see him and begin cranking the wheel. I'm willing to spend fifteen minutes juking and jerking a quarter of an inch at a time if that's what it takes to fit me into this slot. I've got something to prove.

The man sits there, watching. His presence flusters me. I feel like a fat man trying to wiggle into a tight pair of pants. Back and forth, back and forth. The power-steering pump moans; the CV joints judder. I don't care. Nothing is going to deter me. After what seems like half an hour, I succeed, though the car is on an odd angle and its right rear wheel is rumped up on the curb.

I step out triumphantly and give the Bonneville a chuck on the hood. We've only been together two days, but I've begun to feel a real fondness for her. I've even dubbed her the "Tuna."

I cast a sidelong look at the man on the stoop. He hasn't moved. I shrug sheepishly. "Parking spot's like gold around here," I say.

"Tell me about it," he answers. "Sold my car a year ago." He pours himself a glass of orange juice from a pitcher he has at his side. "You really worked that sucker."

I'm smitten with his relaxed manner. He's in "boulevardier" mode too; he just isn't changing boulevards. He gestures me over. This is university territory; the streets are your entertainment.

I walk across and exchange pleasantries with him. He compliments me again on my fortitude in wrestling the Tuna into that parking spot. "A guy's got to do what he's got to do," I say.

I tell him the story of my friend and the Volkswagen. He lets out a hearty laugh. "Your friend's smarter than you are," he says.

Just then, the door behind him opens and a boy of about ten comes running out of the house. He has a puppy with him. The man gets stern, but keeps the twinkle in his voice.

"Now, Tarique. You ain't done with that homework. I know it."

"Sure I is."

The man corrects him. "Sure I am."

"Yeah."

"Say it, now."

The boy exhales theatrically. "Sure I AM."

"That's better. Using the wrong word is like wearing socks that don't match. Sooner or later someone's going to notice, and they ain't going to take you seriously."

I like the man's fathering style, and the kid is about as cute as anything.

"What's your dog's name?" I ask.

"Lester," the boy says solemnly.

I burst out laughing. I have a great fondness for animal names that catch you off guard, and this one blindsides me.

"Lester?" I say.

The man chuckles. He understands. But the boy is not so quick to accept the humor. His dog is meant to be taken seriously.

I try to mollify him. "That's a great name," I say. "I've got a cat named Dennis."

The boy is not quite sure what to make of me.

I'd like to introduce myself, but I don't want to force any familiarity. Better to use the dog as a common point of intimacy.

"Can I see Lester?" I ask.

"Bring him over to the man," the father says. Tarique comes over to me slowly, carrying the puppy. He's still not sure if he trusts me.

Dogs are one of my favorite things in life. I'll work on a dog—any dog, good, bad, mean, or ugly, longer than I worked on that parking space just to get a wag or a lick out of it. I've even got puncture scars in my wrist from some friends' killer Akita that tried to take off my arm when I was alone with it in their house. I simply wrapped up the wound with a rag, put on a long-sleeve shirt, and continued my week-long visit. To this day, they have no idea that their dog bit halfway through my wrist and almost sent me into shock. And, to this day, I'd still be happy to see that dog if I were to meet it again.

Lester is no such threat. He's in love with the world. I take him in my arms and he starts licking my face.

"Now, this is a fine dog," I say. Tarique swells with pride.

"You better take him back in the house before he gets hashed in the street," the dad counsels. Tarique obliges. "And you get on that homework."

With the boy gone and some intimacy established, the father and I begin to talk a bit. I tell him about my son and my travels. "I wish I could do that," he says. "Seattle's not a bad place. But if I was you, I'd stay in that small town. It's tough raising kids these days."

We're on the same wavelength. I tell him of my concerns about raising a son in a place where hunting and hockey are the measures of manhood.

"Better to shoot deer than cops," he says. "You should hear the shit my boy's friends talk." He takes a long drink from his orange juice. "Black boy in America these days, somewhere there's a bullet with his name on it."

There's not a whole lot I can say. I know it's true.

The man continues. "I don't tell him I want him to grow up to be president. I tell him I just want him to grow up. You know why I got him that dog? I don't want no dog; the city ain't no place for it. But I want him to have something to live for. Something he wants to come home to, when he's thinking about doing something crazy."

It's a harsh lesson I'm getting. This man is not much more than twenty-eight or thirty, but he's seen all the way through. He loves his boy, and he knows his odds.

"You ever think of getting out?" I ask.

"I think about it. But where'd I go? I think about Alaska some. See, if you're a black man, you can't go to no small town. Even if you're clean and working for the Man, no white lady wants to see your boy at her doorstep on prom night. You got to look for a city with a military base. Lots of black folks there. I think about Anchorage some."

This is the second person in one morning who's mentioned Alaska. "Alaska's pretty raw," I say. "I've spent a little time there."

"'It ain't what it is, it's what it ain't.'"

I shake my head. "Is that what it comes down to these days?"

He looks straight in my eyes. "That's what it comes down to."

It is a hard lesson from a decent man.

It feels like the right time to go. "Well, I got to get going," I tell him. "Good talking to you."

He nods and raises his glass to me.

"To good sons," I say.

"To good sons," he responds.

Tarique is in the window, watching me walk away.

I enjoy my time down by the university. If I were young and interested in attending a big state school, I could do a lot worse than this place. But I'm not young, I'm not going to school, and the compaction of humanity is beginning to drive me crazy. Seattle is great, but I guess I've lived too long in the woods. I just want to get out.

What a change this is from my youth, when the lights of cities drew me and their sense of infinite variety filled me with excitement. Now, I'm happy in proportion to the expanse around me. Like the clouds in the sky above me, my mind and heart need room to move. And right now I'm feeling constrained and constricted, like a man who's crawled into a narrowing cave. The open spaces between my thoughts, where contemplation and reflection reside, are under assault from all manner of external stimuli.

I owe Seattle better. She's a gracious hostess, and it would be impertinent and unfair to bolt from her party just because I feel there are too many guests. If I ever lose my almost pathological distaste for crowds, this could be a wonderful place to call home. As an homage to her graciousness, I decide to do the one thing that always calms me when I'm here. I decide to ride the ferries.

The ferries are Seattle's act of grace. Other places throw steel and concrete spans across every natural barrier. The Spanish are even talking about building a bridge across the Mediterranean to Gibraltar. But Seattle has committed herself to the ferries and, by doing so, has given herself to the rhythm of the sea.

Life here can be no more frantic than the ferries allow. "Come to the edge of the sea and wait": this is the injunction they give to

Seattle's residents. It's Ishmael's dream made into public policy. And, in its own way, it's every bit as responsible for Seattle's civil character as the great conversation of natural forces taking place above her head.

I top a hill and look out over Puget Sound. The ferries are moving in the blue distance. Their horns call out, low and mournful, across the sparkling waters.

I turn down the hill and head to the wharf. I want that lullaby of movement, that heartbeat throb of the engines, that gentle rocking balm to the spirit.

Down by the dock the passengers are queuing. I park my car and buy a ticket for the crossing to Bainbridge Island. It's not a long ride, but it's ride enough. The man who returns will be a lot less fragmented than the man who's departing.

Soon the telltale moan of the horn announces the ferry's arrival, and it emerges like an apparition from a low-lying layer of mist. It glides gently into the docking berth and cars pour forth from its belly like salmon swimming off to spawn. We foot passengers begin our orderly procession onto the deck.

In the upper-level passenger lounge a string quartet is playing for hat change. Under almost any other circumstances I'd stop and listen, but even Bach can't stand up against the lure of the sea. I place a bill in the hat, then proceed outdoors to the frontmost promontory—a small fenced area that juts like a catwalk over the lower deck of the ship.

A number of passengers are milling about, involved in easy conversation. But when the ferry reverses itself and churns back out into the sound, the spray from the winter waters drenches the deck, and everyone else goes inside. But I'm intoxicated by the sea. I stand mesmerized before the undulating waters—a manqué Admiral Nelson with his jaw jutting into the wind.

I'm reveling in the chill and the salt spray when I'm interrupted by a voice behind me.

"Nice to stand out here," it says.

I turn. It's coming from a white man in his mid-thirties, dressed in khakis and a windbreaker.

"Got to love it," I respond.

He reaches out to shake my hand. It's an unexpected gesture, but a kind one. We introduce ourselves and take our places side by side looking out at the churning waters.

"I'm from Pasco," he says. "You know, the Tri-Cities. I bring the family down sometimes. I like to stand out here when I get the chance." He's affable and earnest, and I understand his sentiment. I'm pleased to share the deck with him.

He points to a woman and three kids standing behind the windows just inside the cabin area. "That's my family," he says. "The Lord has blessed us with three wonderful children."

I shrink involuntarily. His invocation of "Lord" in everyday conversation sets me on alert. I'm here to feel the sea breeze. I don't want to be harangued by a zealot, no matter how benign. But, then again, what sort of cynic would I be to turn from a man because he sees his children as a blessing? I decide to stay present to him.

"You're a lucky man," I say.

"I know," he answers.

Then abruptly he changes direction. "Do you get tired easily?"

I take my nose from the spray and survey him closely. Where is he going with this?

"You know, my wife in there?" he continues. "She used to suffer from terrible depression. Just awful. Wouldn't get out of bed for days. Then a friend of hers gave her this." Out of his pocket comes a pamphlet, a packet, a glossy testimonial for some vitamin-and-mineral cocktail.

He's thrown me a curveball. I was expecting a pitch for Jesus, but he's coming at me with a magic elixir. I eye him warily. Does he just want to banter a bit about something he believes in, or is he a New Age vacuum-cleaner salesman who has now got his foot in the door?

"That's good to hear," I say. "I'll bet that was a great relief to her."

He won't accept the dodge. He keeps coming forward. "It gave her energy like you wouldn't believe. Incredible. Changed her life." He stares at me earnestly. "Do you have all the energy you want?"

I'm in trouble. None of us has all the energy we want. This is a setup, a canned rap from a training course.

He continues. "What would you say if I told you there is a new scientifically proven product that could give you more energy than you ever dreamed possible?"

I groan inwardly. This guy is good. He started with an invocation of his family, then went to a testimonial from his sick wife before making the pitch. Now he has me. Like Little Lil in some silent movie, I'm standing on a promontory, backed against the sea.

I smile lamely and curse my Midwestern upbringing. If I were a hard-bitten New Yorker, schooled in the efficient dispatching of hawkers and hustlers, I could be out of here in a shot: "Look, fella. I'm glad you found truth. I'm glad you got a lovely family. I'm glad your wife has energy. We should all be so lucky. But I'm here to look at the sea. If you want to look with me, fine. But if you're just trying to sell joy juice, you'd better go talk to somebody else, because I'm not buying."

But I'm not from New York. I'm from the Midwest, where no crime is greater than hurting the feelings of others. I put on my best empty face and roll over.

Sexual power. The ability to run marathons. New positive feelings. Inside of a week of taking this potion he had found a new job at three times his previous salary.

The stories cascade from him, as unstoppable as the spume from nearby Mt. St. Helens. He punctuates his monologue with questions that demand my affirmation: Would I like to be in the same physical condition I was at eighteen? Are there things I would like to do that I never seem to find time to complete?

I want to hate this guy, but I can't. He's a natural. He was a blank slate of yearning just waiting for something to align the fragments of his psyche. Now, with his elixir, his life has focus. He's no cynical gumshoe moving toward a sale; he's a true believer. He sincerely wants to convert me.

I'm backed against the rail, feeling the surge of the engines and the frigid mist of the spray, looking for a chance to bolt. But he'll have none of it. Do I want to see pictures of his children? Do I feel blessed in my life? A fundamentalist patina is starting to reveal itself. There's faith enough in this man to move a mountain. I glance over my shoulder. Only the port at Bainbridge will save me.

Eventually the announcement comes. The ferry is preparing to dock.

He grabs my hand earnestly. "Got to get back to my family," he says. "Nice talking to you."

His wife, full of energy and freed from depression, is smiling at us from the inside of the cabin. His children, blond and pressed and perfectly coiffed, are beside her, smiling. He pushes the pamphlet into my hand. "Read this when you get a chance. It'll explain everything. My address is on the back. We're licensed dealers."

I glance at the pamphlet. It's full of testimonials from homemakers, computer programmers, and obscure professional football players. The full system, with toxin-cleansing pre treatments and high-energy supplements, is a hundred and ninety dollars for a thirty-day supply.

I don't think I'll try it, though I would like more energy. Still, I'm glad I've met the man. His faith, if not its content, was buoying. And he was gracious rather than oppressive in his insistence.

I must admit, too, that in some ways I'm jealous. I, too, would like to have such an easy, earnest faith. I, too, would like to think that life's solutions could be found in a bottle. But I don't, any more than I believe a car's bad engine can be fixed by a cure in a can. Tarique's dad can drink all the elixir he wants. Somewhere, there's still a bullet with his son's name on it.

The ferry moves slowly toward the heavy wooden piers of the docking platform. Behind us the sun breaks through the clouds and bathes the island in a halo of golden light. The man is standing inside with his arm around his wife. He waves at me. I wave back. Then I see it. Like the transfiguration itself, Rainier has appeared. She rises above the ferry in resplendent theophany—singular, confident, like the face of the once and forever God.

I stay on the ferry for the return trip, then get back in the Tuna. Rainier is still glowing on the southeastern horizon.

It's with a strange mixture of regret and relief that I head out of Seattle. She reminds me of a Cadillac I once owned: commodious and relaxed, but just a little too big for my tastes. Still, I've had a day of ocean breezes and interesting people. She'll rest fondly in my memory.

I'm all the way to Tacoma before the atherosclerotic sludge of strip malls and car lots begins to show any meaningful signs of thinning out. Rainier or no Rainier, this metastatic sprawl has become almost frightening.

I turn on the radio hoping to find something that will fit my mood, though I'm not sure what my mood is, or what it should be. Should I put on classical music to induce a sense of calm? Should I go for some hard-driving rock to match the urban drumbeat in my corpuscles? Or should I listen to news and talk to focus the welter of ideas spinning in my brain? How about country? Or techno? Or soul? Or new age? Any of them will do. Only neutered oldies, radio ministries, '40s swing, and excessively jabbering rap are absolutely off limits.

I scan twice through the dial. Nothing is clicking, so I decide to try a tape. I reach into the backseat, but the cap-shop girl has pushed them all out of reach. I'm left with the radio unless I want to pull over on the freeway shoulder and risk the wind shear of a hurtling semi. I skip the "scan" button and click through the frequencies one by one. I endure the snippets of evangelists and ads for mattress stores and gigantic used-car sales, until I catch a bit of a station that causes me to start with recognition. It's playing traditional powwow music.

This is something I didn't expect. I'm accustomed to hearing an occasional show of powwow music on public radio stations in northern Minnesota and some parts of the Dakotas, but seldom anywhere else. I wonder where it's coming from.

The music goes on and on, from one powwow song to another. This must be a college station.

I click through the dial again. Country laments, news teasers, oldies, an unlistenable oboe concerto. When I finally finish the circuit, the powwow music is still there. It seems so anachronistic and out of place. It brings back my thoughts about Chief Seattle and the ghosts of this land. This endless sprawl of urban dreck can't be making them happy.

I listen as the powwow drum echoes the beat of the human heart, and the ululating voices mimic the cry of the animals and the song of the birds. This isn't the music of civilization; this is the music of a people who were close to nature, people who just wanted to be left alone.

I think of Tarique's father, longing for a world where his son could take a white girl to a prom without seeing fear in the girl's mother's eyes. Then I think of the father of the young boy dancing the song of the raven, hopeful and proud because his son still practiced the old ways.

How different these two men were; how different their visions. One seeks nothing more than a seat at the table; one asks only for the right to stay out of the room. Yet we lump them both together under the name of minorities, and neither of them gets what he wants.

My eye rises up above the self-storage units and doughnut shops to the distant forests and the solemn silent presence of Rainier. The Lakota chief, Luther Standing Bear, once said that civilization had not added one whit to his sense of justice, his reverence for life, or his love for truth, honesty, and generosity. As I stare out at the passing strip malls and auto dealerships, I don't doubt that he was right.

Eventually, the powwow music ends and an announcer comes on. It's a shock to hear the flat, unmusical prose of our English tongue. But my instincts were sound. This is a college station. It's broadcasting from Evergreen State College, outside of Olympia.

I've long been fascinated with Evergreen, though I've never actually been there. It was the Holy Grail for every disaffected West Coast academic when I was in graduate school. To get a position at Evergreen was like winning the lottery. I even remember perusing their course catalog one time and seeing a faculty member's specialty listed as "blowing the horn"—a far cry from the alphabet soups of M.A., Ph.D., J.D., and so on, that we were trained to put on like chain mail as we prepared to enter the trenches of academic warfare.

Eventually, curiosity gets the best of me. I decide to make a visit.

Driving down the forested roadway that leads to the campus center, I realize that my graduate-school fantasies were probably right. Along with U.C. Santa Cruz, this campus represents the best of the new wave of academic environments. The old wave, like the Ivy League schools and my undergrad alma mater, the University of Minnesota, were the traditional "hallowed halls of learning," with courtyards and promenades framed by towering deciduous trees and imposing neoclassical buildings. In their organization and physical presentation they embodied faith in order and intellectual mastery of space—a fine metaphor for their educational missions.

This new wave represents a paradigm shift. In these schools nature dominates. You reach them on curving roads and woodland pathways. Buildings are tucked back from view and integrated into the landscape. You can never forget you're part of the natural world, and everything about the setting says that your task is to learn to integrate with it, not to master it. It's a change that, at least for the foreseeable future, seems to be a good one. I imagine Chief Seattle and his ghosts would approve.

I park and walk through the grottoes of towering firs until I find the student center. It's a hike, but worth it. You're able to leave the world of cars far behind, and you don't even have to incinerate your vehicle to do so.

The students are about what I'd expect—a heavy concentration of the Birkenstock and granola brigade, some hip-hoppers sporting cornrows and oversized jackets, sad-eyed kids with pins in their faces, a few button-down student-leader types, earnest young Janes and Joes in jeans and sweatshirts and totem caps, and a smattering of second-career retreads. They're all mixing easily and milling around a series of food stands that reflect their various ideological and culinary predilections.

The easy mingling impresses me, as does the ethnic diversity. I have this fleeting notion that the whole issue of racial integration may have begun to solve itself in the bedrooms of these students' parents. In so many cases, I can't tell where one race leaves off and another begins. If I were Tarique's dad, I'd be aiming him someplace like this.

I get in line at a falafel stand. The conversations of the students swirl around me. There are a lot of "he said, she said's" and discussions of guys and parties and what's going on this weekend. But there are also serious discussions about ideas. And they're worldly ideas—global warming, genetic manipulation, Keynesian economic theory. Behind most of them is a burning social consciousness. These are kids who want to engage with the world.

I'm reminded of how much I really like this younger generation. It took me a while to get past their presumptuous assertion of parity and equality with every other human being; I would prefer to see a sense of honor accorded those who have lived longer or accomplished more. But it would be the ultimate in hypocrisy for me to hold this against these kids, considering the behavior of my own generation when we were in our twenties.

In fact, I'm afraid my generation is reaping its own whirlwind in this regard. We're the ones who fought for a leveling of false status distinctions and the dismantling of a cultural pecking order based on economic achievement. We're the ones who said that youth must be served.

Well, this generation may have finished the job. Fourteen-year-olds now feel comfortable addressing me as "Dude." My wife now has students who challenge her class assignments because, "I'm not into that. You're supposed to teach me what I want, not what you think is important." But these are the extremes—the worst manifestations.

At their best, these young people have about them an honest egalitarianism. So what if the young fellow who just took my order for a falafel sandwich greeted me with, "What can I get for you, man?" I should be happy he acknowledged me with an honest smile and be honored that he saw me as someone worthy of a human connection.

Besides, such innocent familiarity is a small price to pay to raise up a generation that may, finally, be able to see past superficial boundaries and arbitrary distinctions. Sure, right now they're balkanized into gangsters and skinheads and straight-edgers and ravers and a whole grab bag of manifestations in between. But these are the prerogatives of youth, and they seem as much like style statements and youthful explorations as legitimate deep-rooted cultural values. And if we stop to realize that they're coming of age in a society that provides them with no health care, a job market that sees everyone as fungible, and a political system that seems cynically indifferent to the real issues affecting this planet, it's amazing they try at all.

If they can just get to adulthood without killing themselves or each other or descending into a miasma of self-absorption or cynicism, they may become something special. They may be able to see past divides that my generation could only dream of bridging. They may, truly, become citizens of the world, citizens of a common human race.

I return from my internal ruminations and listen to the conversations going on around me.

A girl behind me is telling a friend about an upcoming symposium on urban planning and sustainable communities. They're discussing the necessity of a vegan lifestyle for societal transformation. Another boy is going on about Vedantic philosophy; he's arguing with a Korean student about the Hindu influence on Jesus' thought.

I'd like to get up on a soapbox and cheer. I'd like to stand up and shout, "Keep it up. Explore the edges. Stretch it as far as you can before you get snapped back.

"Don't listen to all these people who tell you to focus on MBAs and IRAs and 401Ks. Cover your ears when they say you have to get on the bus immediately or you'll be dragged behind it until dead.

"This is your season, this is your youth. This is the time when dreams can be dreamed and values can be questioned. Prod us older ones from behind. Make us uncomfortable. Rub our noses in the compromises we've made.

"Rail against the destruction of the rain forests, the depletion of the ozone layer, our overuse of pesticides, our unwillingness to redistribute the world's wealth. Be upset at our unbridled population growth and our wanton waste of finite resources, our continued racism and our never ending quest for self-gratification. Tear up the ground around us while we're paying our mortgages and trying to mow our lawns.

"Have the courage of your dreams. Don't let your youth be just a training session for a spot on the treadmill."

But old greybeards on soapboxes belong in Washington Square or the tweedy confines of a classroom. I'm just a guy in a raggedy sweatshirt driving down the coast in a Bonneville called the Tuna. I'd best get my falafel and move on.

I turn my attention back to the young man who's constructing my sandwich. He's as earnest as a rabbi, which he very closely resembles, with his long untrimmed beard and his yarmulke-like rasta hat.

"Everything's organic," he tells me.

I nod in acknowledgment.

He solemnly lays on layers of condiments and vegetables. There's a conscientiousness in his actions that was decidedly absent in the construction of the tacos I purchased on the night of my arrival. But when I think of it, how could it be otherwise? His actions are driven by belief. The taco builders were indentured servants.

He hands me my perfectly constructed falafel. "Enjoy, man," he says in his soft, almost feminine voice. "It's all natural."

I give him a five. "You've already paid," he says.

"This is for you. For doing what you do with a little bit of love."

He gives me a quizzical look, then takes the bill.

"Thanks, man," he says. "I appreciate it."

"No problem," I answer.

I move aside and the girl behind me steps up. She's talking excitedly into a cell phone. "I'll call you back after I order," she says, and slips her phone into a pocket on her backpack.

My rabbinic falafel maker smiles at her. "What's your pleasure?" he asks. I hear them conversing as I walk away.

The sun is going down as I walk back toward my car. A young couple is making out in a forested meditation grove. It seems only right. This is a meditation all of us can understand.

I stop before a bulletin board to finish my falafel. Tucked in among the ads for futons and mountain bikes and spring-break trips to Florida is a rambling single-spaced rant full of exclamation points and words written in capital letters. I pull it off and read it as I walk.

We still need 1 camera person and an audio person to document us as we sell our asses the only way we know how: by being idiots. We drink, smoke, eat junk food, cuss, we hate each other with a passion but we are going to BANK ACROSS AMERICA, we are sexist pigs and all we care about is getting our dough. Do you want to film us? Do you motherfucker? We can't write or read. We just want to do ART and get MONEY. THIS IS NOT A JOKE! So are you fuckin' jumpin on our bandwagon to the pit of deppression and failure with us? DO YOU WANT TO FILM US AS OUR GREAT HOPES OF MAKING LOTS OF MONEY ARE CRUSHED AS THE VAN (OR THE POSSIBLE RV DEAL IN THE WORKS ...) BREAKS DOWN IN THE SMALLEST SHITHOLE TOWN IN THE MIDDLE OF THIS PIECE OF SHIT CALLED AMERICA? But maybe that won't happen maybe we will do really well and have a swell time and maybe, just maybe the media will pay heed to our "RIDICULOUS" idea, maybe we will get MONEY, maybe we will get laid, maybe people will like us a lot, maybe we will actually have a sense of accomplishment when we end up on CNN and NBC and LATE NIGHT WITH CONAN

O'BRIEN. Nah. Nope, never not in a million fucking years. Can't see it can you? Well you maybe right but then again you maybe wrong. You wouldn't want to be on television anyway, would you?

At the bottom are the names, Shawn and Thom, and a telephone number.

On a whim, I try to call them. I'd like to hear their story—buy them a cup of coffee, maybe contribute ten dollars to their cause. But their phone has been disconnected. They're probably already selling their asses across America, or have already broken down in the smallest shithole town in the country—maybe in the woods of Oregon, or in a little burg in northwestern Minnesota, where they'll wake up one day, and then the next, until, suddenly, they realize it must be their home.

All I know is that they're gone. I wish them well. We're not so different, Shawn and Thom and me. Or any of the others I've met today. We're all looking for a magic bean or a miraculous elixir or the big score—our own personal Alaska, where dogs run free and we can go to the prom with whomever we want.

"Hello?"

"Hello?"

I can hardly hear. There are some horrifying squawks in the background. Nick is practicing his saxophone. It's one of the ever mounting proofs of his increasing strangeness—that, and an obsession with the career of Richard Nixon. Small wonder I'm thrilled to find him so enamored of a man like Ernest Shackleton.

"Well, so where's the intrepid traveler tonight?" Louise asks.

"Another fantasy school. Evergreen."

She perks up. She, too, is familiar with its reputation. "What's it like?"

"Grottoes, granola, and a five-mile drive through a forest."

"Sign me up," she says.

We talk for a while about the realities of Seattle and the whole Puget Sound area.

"So, how does it feel being back?" she asks.

"At its best," I tell her, "it's like listening to Miles Davis. All muted and distant and implied. Baptized with fresh light every day."

"But at its worst?" A true Midwestern question.

"Remember why Ken Kesey entitled his Pacific Northwest novel *Sometimes a Great Notion?*"

"No. Tell me."

"The line from the old song 'Good Night Irene': 'Sometimes I take a great notion, to jump into the river and drown.' On bad days, you take that great notion."

"So, what do you think?" she asks. "Would you like to live there again?"

"I'm already missing snow," I say. "I can't imagine Robert Frost writing 'stopping by the woods on a rainy evening.'"

"But he could have written 'sliding off a driveway on a snowy evening.' I just spent the last two hours rounding up neighbors to help pull me out."

The reminder of the realities of winter living brings me crashing back to earth.

"Are you doing okay?" I ask. "I mean, overall?" A loud saxophonic honk blats in from the background.

She gets a bit more serious. "No, really. It's beautiful right now. You know how that first real snow can be."

I do indeed. When I left, the ground was frozen and brown. Short fits of snow slop had frozen the fallen leaves into lumpen masses, and our gravel road was filled with half-frozen mud sinkholes. That first true snowy benediction had been only a dream. Now, it appears, it has become real. I'm filled with a sense of longing.

"I've got to say," I tell her, "in some ways I wish I were home."

"I wish you were home too, in a lot of ways."

It's a human touch, and a warm one, cut short by a surging version of "When the Saints Go Marching In."

"You'd better let me talk to Stanley Turrentine. I preferred Ernest Shackleton, but I'll take whoever I can get."

She calls Nick over. I hear a few more bleats and honks as he rolls to a stop. Then the clumps of his footsteps. Then the voice.

"Hi, Dad."

"Hey, Nick. Doing a little toodling?" I say. It's a diminution he hates. I hear the pause in his voice.

"Hey. Sorry," I say. "'Saints' sounded great."

He's mollified, and moves forward. "I've been practicing."

"I can tell. So how's Shackleton?"

"Did you know he took sixty-nine dogs on his voyage?"

"No. Was that for pulling sleds?"

"I guess. But none of them survived. I think they had to eat them."

"Better than eating each other."

"Shackleton wouldn't have allowed that," he answers, always the serious little man. "Did you know they were gone two years and Shackleton didn't lose one member of his crew? Not even to sickness?"

"You really like this Shackleton, don't you?" I say.

"I think he's great," Nick responds. It's amazing how simple his life is. Tarique's dad is worrying about his boy dodging bullets; I'm worried my boy is spending too much time in his room reading about Ernest Shackleton.

"You're really doing a good job on this, Nick," I tell him. "I'm really proud of you."

"All I know is it's the funnest project I've done this year," he says.

"Sure sounds like it," I say. I don't even bother to correct his bad grammar.

SIX

DEEP VOICES

Four thirty-seven. Red digital numerals on a tiny clock face.

I roll over on the bed and put my feet on the floor. Sit up, lean forward. Where are my glasses? Hands feeling around like a blind man. There. On the nightstand.

This floor is hard. Where am I? Where's Louise?

That's right, now I remember. Seattle. The cap-shop girl. Evergreen.

I rub my feet back and forth on the carpet. Feels like boar bristles. Strange. Some of these motels are so hard. Mattress like plywood, sheets as stiff as cardboard.

Four thirty-eight. What am I doing? It's too early to get up, too late to go back to sleep.

Shower? Coffee? Yes, okay. Why not?

I stumble into the bathroom and switch on the light. Where did they get that bulb? They could interrogate someone under it. Maybe Norman Bates's mother. Lock the door. Damn Alfred Hitchcock.

The shower helps. In fact, it brings me alive.

Ah, yes, another day.

The motel has a chill to it. I should have turned the heater on before I got in the shower. I've got to remember: cheap motels are cheap for a reason. This one has no central heat. The entire room is at

the mercy of a single wall heating unit. You turn the switch, some fil-
ament glows volcano orange, and a rattly fan blasts reedy, hot air into
the room. It'll take twenty minutes to warm the place up.

Towel dry, slip on my clothes. At least the place has a coffee pot.
Today I'll pick up a hot pot and some cone filters. I should have gotten some of those magic beans from the cap-shop girl.

Little by little, coming north to consciousness.

Ah, that's better. Bad coffee, that horrid shredded nylon in a package in lieu of cream. But at least it has heat. Maybe that will trick my
body until I can find some real caffeine.

Now I can sit down, begin to think.

I plop down on the edge of the bed next to the heater. The warm
blast is comforting. I think I'll aim for Eugene today, unless something intervenes.

Boy, yesterday was a roller coaster. But that's what cities do to me,
even beautiful cities like Seattle. There's just too much compression.
But I had better get used to it. There's a lot more ahead of me.

It's a real conundrum. I have no quarrel with civilization. I can't
imagine life without libraries, or Bach's *Mass in B Minor,* or the sculptures of Michelangelo and the paintings of Van Gogh. When I need
surgery I'm very thankful I've got a physician with anesthesia and
sterile instruments rather than someone dancing around me shaking
a gourd. But I can't abide the compaction of urban life and the shat-
tered mess it makes of my senses. Give me three hours in a big city,
even a beautiful big city, and I want to get out.

I keep thinking this must be a character weakness. I can't stand the
heat, so I bolt from the kitchen. I'm haunted by a conversation I had
with an old high-school acquaintance several years ago at a gas station
in Minneapolis. We talked a bit while the gas was pumping, catching
up on people we had known in common. One was the head of an
international corporation, one was on *Wall Street Week,* a third was
chair of the school of dentistry at some university. As we parted, he
said, "I'm glad I ran into you. A couple of us were having a few beers
together a while ago and your name came up. All anybody knew was

that your address was some post-office box in northern Minnesota. It seemed like such a waste."

Maybe I've done it wrong. Maybe I should have bored through life with a vengeance and become a professor of theology at some prestigious university. Or listened to that man I met at a conference years ago and taken him up on his offer of a position with Chase Manhattan Bank. Or perhaps I should have stood on my father's shoulders and gone to work for the Red Cross, organizing relief efforts to alleviate the suffering of humanity. These were the prerogatives of a good, middle-class upbringing in mid-century America, and they were all available to me.

But I went a different route. I followed passions, not career paths. I've treated life as a garden to be tended rather than an architecture to be built. In fact, when I think about it, I've traveled through life much like I'm traveling down this coast—following my nose and chasing shafts of light. I've never had any set plan, never any timetable. Sure, I got my degrees. Sure, I studied and worked hard at whatever I did. And I've tried to make a meaningful contribution in every way I can. But I never aimed for the stars in terms of worldly achievement. Whenever I had the choice between sitting with a man like Tarique's dad or meeting with a guy in a suit, I chose Tarique's dad every time. I've never even worn a watch.

Has it been a waste? Have I squandered my talents and hid my light under a bushel? Who's to know?

It's strange to be my age and to watch the connective tissue of humanity reveal itself—to know someone who went to school with the president, to see the names of friends on the credits of movies and the mastheads of periodicals, to see old classmates being quoted in articles on medical advances and world political issues. They became players, or, at least, so it seems from a distance. Then I meet them and they're twice divorced, or spiritually dead, or alcoholics, or cynical, or so arrogant and full of themselves that I want to run out the door. A couple of beers or a few stiff drinks and they lean close and whisper, "I really envy you, living out in the woods in a house on a lake. When I retire . . ."

When I retire! I've never even been hired. These are my friends, my comrades, my fellow travelers in time. These are the people who are running our country. They've moved the pieces on the chessboard. I'm sitting in a corner playing solitaire.

Yet somehow it doesn't seem wrong, what I've done. I've helped the elders on an isolated Indian reservation collect and save their fading memories. I've created some meaningful sculptures that will stand for a thousand years. I've written books that have touched people's hearts. I've raised a good family. I shouldn't have to apologize for these choices. I shouldn't have to justify spending my time in nursing homes and elementary classrooms rather than standing at a lectern in some university.

At least, I don't think I should.

Confucius said that our task in life is to "bring peace to the old, have trust in your friends, and cherish the young." That's what I've tried to do. And who's to say which touches have meaning? Who's to say if one of those children with whom I've shared my time may not grow up to change the world?

Still, there's the cruel cut of a friend who called these "housewife virtues . . . domestic sops for having done nothing of significance in life."

Should I have fought harder? Should I have grown up to be president?

I walk to the mirror and examine the bags under my eyes, the whitening beard. I was once like those young faces at Evergreen, struggling to shape my dreams into a meaningful way to walk life's unpredictable road.

But I've chosen my path, and it is what it is.

Now I've got to help Nick choose his. I'll be happy if he wants to be a surgeon or a diplomat, but I'll be just as happy if he simply becomes a good father and lives with a sense of the presence of God. I've tried to raise him by the precepts of the prophet Micah: "What does the Lord require of you, but to do justice, to love kindness, and to walk humbly with your God?"

If that's all the Lord requires of you, who am I to expect that he do more?

But I'm afraid for him, just as I'm afraid for the cap-shop girl and Tarique and those kids at Evergreen. We've become such a mean-spirited society, willing to grind our collective heel into the face of anyone who stumbles along the way.

It makes so little sense. Individually we're such a good and caring people. Yet collectively we're arrogant and selfish. What if Nick happens to be one of those who stumbles? And, in so many ways, he seems like a child who may well stumble. He's so sensitive, so willing to withdraw rather than persevere. He's always just off the "A" list for birthday parties, just beyond the fringe of the center when the other kids are picking friends and comrades. I remember when he was barely three, and we were driving to town. A dead raccoon was lying on the side of the road. He saw it and became disconsolate. He withdrew into himself for days.

Now I see him withdrawing into himself in a larger sense. Each hit, each slight, each party where he's not invited, and each phone call to a friend that's not returned, sends him back to his room, more inside himself, more private, less present to the common society of the other boys his age.

Maybe that's why I turn and run from cities—because they feel like places where will and ambition matter more than sensitivity and compassion. They laugh at someone who takes time to craft a falafel with care and love. They'll eat up someone who cries at dead raccoons rather than skinning them and starting a business selling their pelts.

Yet it's more than escape that keeps me in the woods. I truly believe that nature is as wise a teacher as culture. The Buddha didn't go to town when he sought enlightenment. Moses didn't come down from the mountain to find the tablets. Even Jesus, the ultimate man of the people, withdrew to the desert when he wanted to contemplate the meaning of things.

If Nick wants to come down from the mountain later, to try his hand at the game, so be it. For now, I've got to protect him, to help him. I want to assist him in shaping his spirit. I want him to learn that the day is a god; there's plenty of time for him to learn how to deal with life as a bullet.

I walk out into the misting dark to warm up the car and wipe the condensation off the windshield. I can feel a cold day coming; the wind carries rain on its breath. Better toss the sandals in the trunk and slip on the work boots.

I do a final reconnoiter of the motel room. No overlooked shampoo bottles, no jackets hanging unnoticed behind the door.

I zip up my aviator bag and grab it by its ragged handles. It now has a companion: a large green plastic garbage sack half filled with dirty clothes. I'll need to visit a laundromat soon. But not today. My heart is open, my mind is moving freely. I must take advantage of this. I've got to make this more than a day of encounters and conversations. I've got to go after the deep voices of the land.

It feels good to get an early start. The road is still empty. Truckers trying to beat the scales or make time against their log books are roaring by at bone-rattling speeds. Other than that, it's just me, the lights on the dashboard, and the hint of dawn in the eastern sky. It's a good time to drive.

The pavement glistens from an overnight rain. The fog floats above the trees and moves in phantom whispers across the hilltops. Spectral mists rise from the churning winter streams. It's no wonder I find myself thinking constantly on the ghosts of former cultures.

Nick weighs heavily on my mind, and I miss Louise. I'd like to call again, but I think I'd better wait until this evening. They're just getting up and it would seem strange for me to be calling again so soon. Besides, I'm in a pensive mood, on that quiet edge between meditation and thought. No matter how much I want to touch home, I can't afford to have my heart tugged away from here.

I lean back and listen to the hum of the Tuna's motor. My mind moves and probes like the fog and mists, dipping and weaving like the dance of the raven. I'm full of blue distances and quiet, melancholic evanescences.

This is what I've been waiting for—a resonance between my spirit and the landscape. I knew it would happen if I just gave it a little time. This land is too big, its voice too powerful, to be silenced by the chatter of my own thoughts and the nervous twitter of the shops and city streets. I just needed to slow down and listen.

I'm finally getting what I'm really after on this trip—the voice of this western land. All my concerns about being trapped in the middle and feeling closed in by the culture are really just superficial issues. The deep question is whether my own spirit responds more readily to this coastal landscape than to my northern woodland home.

But beneath even that is the fundamental question of whether it's the land that shapes our spirits, or if each of us has a special landscape that resonates within us and our task in life is to find that special place. If it's the land that shapes us, then my task on this journey is clear. I have to decide if someplace here in the West enhances the spirit in a way that I believe would be good for our family, then bring us out here together to see if we all share that belief and are all willing to make the move.

If it turns out that each of us has a spiritual landscape that lies undiscovered within us, it would be an act of profound arrogance for me to think I know best and an act of unjustifiable selfishness to force my wishes on my family.

It gets so complicated when your life develops context. When I was twenty-five and in a lather, moving from woman to woman and place to place, decisions were easy. Life was about self-discovery and wasn't tied to the dreams of others.

Now I'm carrying the burden of others' dreams. The only honorable decision is a decision that lifts us all.

Louise is easy. She thrives on the temporal. She loves to analyze the world and its goings-on. Give her a journal on politics, a chance to get involved in social issues, and opportunity to study, teach, or write about human institutions and their interaction, and she's in her glory.

Life for her is a dog's breakfast—you just scarf it up as fast as you can. If she can have a garden, a college, and enough space around her that she sees more trees than houses and doesn't hear the neighbor's television set, she'll do fine.

But Nick? He's still inchoate. He dreams of explorers and mummies and Loch Ness monsters. He laughs at stupid cartoons and cries at dead animals on the side of the road. There's no telling, yet, where he'll end up, and no way to know, either by watching or by asking, exactly what his spirit needs.

I so much want to nurture him. I so much want him to grow up to be happy and a man of good heart. I need to find the setting where he can best seek that happiness and develop that good heart. Putting him in the wrong place—whether it's where we live now or some other place I've not yet discovered—would be like spiritually binding his feet. Your childhood home stays with you for your entire life. I've got to listen carefully, choose carefully, act wisely.

So today I'm going to keep my eye on the sparrow. I'm going to listen to the big voices of the landscape rather than the small conversations of its inhabitants. I'm after the deep resonances that call out to the heart and shape the spirit. And I think I know where I need to go to find them.

The sign says, "Mt. St. Helens."

I take the exit and pass through a knot of roadside restaurants and gas stations. I crane my neck to look for the mountain, but the fog is still too low; the mountain is hidden in the drizzle and the mist.

At first I'm a bit put out. For reasons I can't fathom, I've always assumed that Mt. St. Helens would be right at a freeway turnoff. I pictured an exit that put me at the base of a great blasted stony mountain. I would drive up through rocky crags on tiny winding roads and look down into some smoldering caldera.

It was a cartoon understanding, a flatlander's embarrassingly naive fantasy, born of looking at too many *National Geographic* specials on Mauna Loa and Kilauea. Now that I'm actually here, what I confront is a trunk highway going off into a forest, framed on each side by towering Douglas fir that obscure the sky and close in around me. There's no sense of mountain, no sense of volcanic upheaval. This is just one more mist-laden roadway through a canyon of trees.

A sign announces a place called the Lower Visitor Center. I turn into its forested parking area and survey the dank fern- and moss-covered earth around me. Maybe I can get some answers here.

The place is silent with the dripping heaviness of a fogbound morning. There are no other cars. If this is a visitors center, where's the mountain? This glass and timber building sits under a canopy of great fir trees. It might as well be the entrance to some national forest.

The place feels cold and deserted, as if it's closed for the season. I go up and press my nose against the glass. The inside is still and dark—not even a custodian or a night guard.

I walk around the back. The wet branches of the trees overhead brush against each other, sending a spray of droplets down upon me. As I get to a corner, I smell the acrid scent of fresh cigarette smoke.

A bit further, and I see its source. A man is standing near the building, facing out into the misty woods, smoking. He's in his early thirties and is wearing a grey forest-service outfit. His long hair hangs down over his shoulders.

Strangely, he doesn't turn around as I approach. Maybe he, too, likes to be alone, and I'll be intruding upon his morning reverie. Still, I need to know where I'm at in relation to this mountain and if the road will be open and passable.

He smokes his cigarette methodically, like a man deep in thought. I approach hesitantly.

"Excuse me," I say. "Will I be able to see if I go up?"

He whirls and faces me. A shadow of panic or confusion—much deeper than a look of surprise—crosses his face. He holds up his hands like a man trying to stop the words coming toward him. Instantly I realize: he is deaf.

I ask again, speaking slowly and shaping my words deliberately, hoping he can read lips: "How do I get to the mountain?"

He brightens. He raises his hands like a man about to conduct a symphony or give a benediction and begins forming soundless words with his mouth. His hands make grand and sweeping gestures.

"Stop." "Come." "Follow." He touches my sleeve and pulls a map out of his pocket. "Here," he mouths, pointing, then weaves his hands to mimic the movements of the road.

"How long?" I ask him.

He cuts against his wrist. "Half hour, half hour," he mouths silently.

Then he does it. "Hoff owuh," he says out loud, having decided to trust me. It's an odd sound, flat and without nuance, as if mechanically generated. I can see he's a bit embarrassed, but relieved. I thank him with exaggerated gestures. They feel full and natural. I like our common language.

I run back to the car, full of anticipation. I can hardly stifle a smile. That was a man who would know what I mean when I talk about the big voices. He's set me on my way.

At first the road is but another forested pathway shrouded in fog. Shanty houses huddle in the early morning damp. It's a sodden world of muted hues, punctuated here and there by forest green spires poking through the shifting mists. There's a knot of anticipation in my stomach. Though I'm still in deep forest, I know I'm heading toward something big.

I remember the eruption well. May 18, 1980. I was living in the monastery in British Columbia only several hundred miles away on the day it occurred.

Though news of the outside world was sparse in the monastery, this was a significant event. Word passed that a gigantic volcanic eruption had occurred near Portland. I was transfixed—a mountain had exploded. But there was no deep curiosity among the monks. They were involved in a life of prayer; God's meanings would reveal themselves in due time.

Lacking access to television or newspapers, I had a difficult time finding out about the cataclysm. But there was an old radio in the basement of a guest cottage, and I could occasionally sneak in and listen to a few minutes of the CBC. From those broadcasts I learned that the mountain that had erupted was named St. Helens—the Native peoples had called her "The Sleeping Beauty"—and that she had been making ominous rumblings for some time now. I learned that the explosion had literally ripped off one entire side of the mountain, that a billow of fire and ash had risen miles into the sky, and that a sea of mud had coursed down the Toutle River, burying everything in its wake.

The reports beggared my imagination: millions of giant trees, as tall as buildings, incinerated in an instant and snapped like toothpicks, left lying in grisly formation up and down the mountainsides like bodies awaiting burial. Entire towns and houses buried. A rain of ash over Portland that blanketed cars and houses and blotted out the noonday sun.

In the evenings I would go out onto the monastery grounds and look to the south to see if I could still catch a glimpse of a glow in the sky. The blood red sunsets to the west told me that the floating haze of volcanic particles in the atmosphere was beginning to circle the globe.

Maybe it was being in a setting where thoughts of God's omnipotence were foremost in everyone's mind. Maybe it was finally being in proximity to an event that dwarfed human concerns and civilization. But, whatever it was, the cosmic significance of this eruption took root in my psyche, where it has remained ever since.

Now, years later, I'm finally going to stand in the presence of that eruption, hoping to catch a glimpse of its cosmic significance in the empty, smoldering remains.

The road continues through the forest. There's still no sign of the volcano. Through the breaks in the trees I can see a sky heavy with dark, moiling clouds. It gives me pause. Even a flatlander knows that darkness hovering over the peak of a mountain is cause for concern.

Soon the road opens and the ground fog lifts. I find myself in expansive, forested valleys stretching for miles in all directions. It's a world of a wholly other scale.

A sign says, "No Services Ahead." A twinge of concern comes across me. Such signs strike a note of dread into all but the most hardy travelers. Unless you know the road and its safe havens, or have made preparations for every eventuality, a warning like this is a stark reminder of the darker side of travel. The unexpected is your problem. Flat tires, broken fan belts, heart attacks will receive no special treatment. The land is in control.

I drive with increased vigilance. Secretly, I'm pleased. I'm ascending a volcano, and it seems only right that all illusion of security and human control should be stripped away. The road twists and climbs. It's new and fresh, a marvel of modern highway convenience. Upward we wind, rising and falling on long, loping hills. Interpretive centers have been built, stopping points have been established. I can walk to overlooks, take tours. There are analyses of geology, lessons in natural history. This is a laboratory for the study of the world made anew, a journey backward toward the moment of creation.

Mile after mile I ascend, up through the trees and into the mists, from interpretive sign to interpretive sign, informational walk to informational walk. At each stop I learn something new. It astounds me how much the full force of human enterprise has been brought to bear on this geologic event. Here, in the blast zone, where those millions of trees were snapped off by the concussion of the eruption and left lying, charred and muddied, in their corpselike formation, seedlings have been planted and grow now in uniform measure across the mountainsides. Banks have been graded, fences built. The road, smooth and glossy, winds inevitably toward the crater.

Eventually, after thirty miles, I reach the end of the pavement. A grand interpretive center reminiscent of a James J. Hill railroad hotel has been constructed at this point. It's complete with dioramas, time lines, gift shops, and telescopes.

Year by year, the road will push further toward the crater itself. But for now the casual traveler must be satisfied with the opportunity to peer through a telescope lens at the cleft in the earth where a sword of fire spewed forth into the heavens from the belly of the planet.

I buy myself a cup of coffee at the snack bar and wander into a darkened theater where an earnest but uninspired film on the eruption is playing. "The volcanic laboratory is both lesson and school," drones the narrator. I can't abide the monotone, so I wander back into the hall.

A ranger is giving a talk while standing in front of a wall of glass that looks out toward the crater. The shroud of diaphanous mist that hides the mountain has not yet lifted, and this has put him a bit off his game. I hear other visitors grousing about the lack of a clear view, when suddenly the building is jolted by a monstrous, violent, rumble. There's a collective gasp, then titters of nervous laughter. It was just a thunderclap, but we all know what we were thinking.

In that instant, it all becomes clear to me what I've been sensing and what I've been seeking.

I'm standing on the back of a great, unpredictable giant, able, on a whim, to turn stone to liquid and toss boulders miles into the sky. That the giant now slumbers makes it no less alive. Like everyone else, I've gotten caught up in the science of the whole affair. In my mind, the eruption was an event, now in the past. All the descriptions, all the interpretations, have focused my attention on that event and the earth's magical efforts at renewal.

Yet this mountain is a presence, an active, breathing life force, not merely a laboratory for the study of a single, time-bound event. We should be genuflecting before this force, not simply analyzing it. Next to the observation posts there should be kneeling benches, psalters, prayer rugs. Alongside the explanatory plaques there should be signs saying, "Look upon My Works, ye Mighty, and Despair!" and "Regard this Mountain and Know Who You Are."

But we have lost touch with that deeper knowledge. We don't see life in this mountain, only activity. We can no longer find truth in stories about the Old Woman Mountain, who was made beautiful by the Great Spirit because she kept her lodge fire going. Our stories are about strata and borings and ash flow and sediments. We've reduced this great, breathing presence to classroom lesson and geological narrative. It takes a thunderclap to shock us from our analytic stupor.

I walk outside and wander down a trail where the sediment piles have been left untouched. There's an eerie sense of newness to the shapes, as if they've been tossed there by a colossal and uncaring hand. The rudimentary life forms that scuttle in the standing water seem prehistoric. The wind blows with a freshness from the dawn of time.

A hard rain is beginning to fall, and it's turning to snow. The mountain is making weather. I had best retreat.

I look toward the mountain whose face is disappearing behind the sinuous misting shroud. The snow is cloaking her shoulders with a mantle of white. Soon she'll be completely invisible.

Once back inside the interpretive center I warm myself with another cup of coffee and begin reading a wall of writings done by schoolchildren who have visited the center. A poem written by a young boy named Nick Collins catches my eye. It's scratched on a piece of paper in a labored, youthful script:

> *In the winter the mountain is white with snow.*
> *But there are things you do not know.*

I take my coffee and walk toward the car through the pelting snow. Nick Collins's simple poem echoes in my mind. Maybe this is the way it should be. Let the geologists and seismologists and aquatic biologists take their samples and their measurements. Let them collate and analyze their findings to increase the store of human knowledge and our understanding of the earth. Yet when all is said and done, the nursery-rhyme wisdom of young children is not to be disregarded. There are things we do not know.

I make my way back down the road into the broad valleys, leaving the snow far behind. I feel like a confused Moses. I've gone up the mountain, and God's voice has spoken. Now I've come down with the tablets, but I don't know what to do.

But the day down here is blue and full of promise. No need for answers yet. As the monks said, God's meanings will reveal themselves in due time.

Soon the road meets up with the Columbia River as it bends north before turning westward out to the sea. I follow it backward, down toward Portland.

I love this stretch of southern Washington. It's such a musical landscape. The hills roll in long, sinuous bass curves covered with pines that punch staccato toward the sky. Beneath the pines, lower and more sensuous, the deciduous trees clump and mass in rich, melodic clusters. What a change this is from the austere, titanic mountaintop, with its cold winds and ethereal, vaporous mists. There the land spoke in the hollow voices of monks. Here it sings the "Ode to Joy."

A curve in the road brings me upon Kalama, a low, one-story town spread out in a broad, forested valley. The sweet intoxication of freshly cut cedar hovers in the air. The sky is full of low swirling clouds that touch the surrounding hilltops and tumble like puppies against each other. Behind its frothy movement lies a brilliant cobalt sky. The sun paints the hills with patches of golden light.

Kalama is like any valley town on a sunlit day; she feels cradled and embraced. At moments like this, it's easy to believe in the earth as mother.

But there's the presence of another mother here as well. Standing cinch-waisted, bulky, and towering over all, is a grey concrete cylinder as tall as a skyscraper. It looms without emotion in the center of this valley, like a sepulchre of the gods. It is the cooling tower of the Trojan nuclear power plant.

The plant has been decommissioned for years now, but the spent fuel rods still glow in its bowels, and the silent concrete structure casts a pall over this gentle bowl of land.

I pull off the highway and come to a stop on the crest of a low hill. Stretching out below me is a teeming log yard, with men milling like insects and great snap-jawed machines moving like toys with thirty-foot tree trunks in their mouths.

If I raise my eyes, directly behind the log yard lies a chemical plant with its tangle of tubes and piping and holding tanks. Behind that, in its singular deathly silence, the grey cylinder of the nuclear power plant stands mute and lifeless against the hillsides and the sky. In its sheer austere geometry it violates the senses; even a person who had no idea what it was would sense a malevolence in its presence.

From where I'm standing, the escalation of technologies is frightening. And it seems all the more ominous because of the progressive decrease in activity. The log yard is a beehive of motion. Front-end loaders snatch six, ten, twelve massive tree trunks in their twenty-foot claws and do pirouettes in the mud as they roll off to place them in piles. Men scurry and shout. The metallic screeches of saws cut the air. Trucks rumble in and out. The hollow thwok of logs being unchained and bouncing like tenpins off flatbed trucks mingles with the groans of machinery lifting, dragging, and hoisting.

Behind, the chemical plant emits belches of steam. But the activity is less. Vehicles come and go, stopping at a checkpoint, then proceeding back into the labyrinth of tanks and tubing. But there is no sound of labor. The work is being done silently, in hisses and bubblings inside of steel shells. The human factor is one of containment and control, not active interaction.

Still, for all its abstract lethal power, the chemical plant seems benign and within our intellectual grasp. Its tangle of tubes and pipes echoes tree roots and arteries. It is a chemistry set writ large, a world of beakers and Bunsen burners and corkscrew pathways dripping and mixing and catalyzing into something new. If it seems dangerous, it seems so in the mold of the mad scientist.

Not so the nuclear reactor. It is of a wholly different order. Nothing moves. There is no life anywhere. The mind runs to analogies and metaphors: tombs, monoliths, ancient temples to forgotten gods. It is something so great that upon the death of its usefulness it can only be abandoned; it is too large, too permanent, to be destroyed.

In that way, it takes the measure of the surrounding hills. Earthquakes, floods, the mudflow of Mt. St. Helens could pour down this valley and reduce the log yard and the chemical plant to memory. Yet the monolith would remain, half buried, undisturbed, like the fossil of some ancient monster, in the layers of the earth.

It's as if this silent presence resonates at a level that only the earth can hear. It carries on its dark activity so far below the human that it seems indifferent to our very existence. This, too, is a conversation among the gods, but one of our own design. If these gods ever clash, we will become witnesses to our own destruction at the hands of our own creation.

I try to focus my attention on the petty despoliations of the log yard. I can appraise, to my own satisfaction, the rutting of the earth and the ripping of trees, the piles of sawdust and puddles of leaking oil. The moral indignation they induce is on a scale I understand.

Such is not the case with the concrete monolith. It fascinates me and fills me with fear. I want to approach it, to move up close to it, like a man might approach a slumbering rhino or a wounded elephant. If it rises up against me, my destruction will not be susceptible to negotiation or argument. It will be simple, awful, and absolute. But this is not a rhino or an elephant. It's a creation of our own human hands. At least, in theory, it's a shackled presence, bound and gagged and rendered permanently immobile by the same technology that created it. Nonetheless, the sheer scale obsesses me, and its nearness titillates me. I decide to approach.

I head back up the freeway, take the next exit, and turn left on the overpass crossing the highway. A swath has been cut through the forest to make way for the road. Directly ahead, framed by the avenue of aspen, the cooling tower looms just across the river, less than half a mile away. It's way out of scale and frighteningly out of context. Grey, efficient, neutral, it seems almost beautiful in its awesome singularity.

In an unintentional act of cheap irony, a sign reading "Dead End" stands to the right of the road, just across the overpass.

I follow the roadway as it wanders down toward the river. A small sign announces a group of trailers and cabinlike structures huddled behind a fence. "Kalama Hunting Club," it reads.

Just past this, the road ends in a wide spot at river's edge. From here you have a full view of the cooling tower standing just across the water on a rock outcropping, surrounded by pine trees. A strange, copper-green cast, the color of a rotting fish belly, covers a spot in the concrete halfway up. Ladders run up the side.

I've never been this near to a reactor before. I want to see it as clearly as possible, so I get out to look. As I'm standing there, an orange truck—unmarked, but with a government-issue paint job—drives up and circles around me. It unnerves me and irritates me. To whom is my presence here a problem? The county? The highway department? The U.S. government? It's hard to know.

The driver pulls up behind my car and takes out a clipboard. I'm amazed. Why does a solitary man standing on a riverbank staring across into the morning need to be circled, inspected, and have his license plate taken down? If I were collecting insects or taking photos of lichen, perhaps I would be seen as harmless. But I'm just standing with my hands in my pockets, staring at a concrete monolith, doing nothing. This is the mentality of the military base: it's better to be seen doing something, no matter how absurd and irrelevant, than to be seen staring, thinking, dreaming. A man doing nothing is a suspect upon the earth.

The driver finishes copying down the pertinent information about my car and keys a handheld microphone. I hear squawking and feedback and unintelligible voices.

What's the fear? Will we guard this monolith for a hundred thousand years? Is our final legacy to have doomed this gentle valley to a thousand centuries of suspicion and paranoia?

The cooling tower stands as still as Mt. St. Helens, and as unapproachable. Yet there no one accosted me. Surely I posed as great a danger to that mountain as I do to this concrete crypt? Perhaps there I had the secret incantations, the magical formula, to bring the volcano alive again. It's no less likely than the possibility that I can somehow release the forces entombed in this dormant monolith.

The truck circles slowly, making sure I'm aware that I'm being watched. I'm tempted to begin some odd ritual, to wave my hands and chant strange foreign syllables in the direction of the reactor. But that wouldn't bother the driver; he'd merely think I was mad. If only I could reach in my trunk and pull out some black box with meters and dials. But I have no such box. I have only my wonder and terror and curiosity.

Eventually, prompted by the driver's ominous scrutiny, I climb in my car and skulk away. He follows behind me to make sure I intend to leave. I take one last glance over my shoulder at the great cement cylinder. The driver stops while I look, then pulls to within a foot of my bumper, as if to herd me along.

I want to get out and talk to him. I'd like to know if he finds it as strange as I that a structure built to withstand the power of a volcano needs to be protected from the presence of a solitary man. I wonder if he ever asks himself why we have so great a fear of the power in this dormant concrete cylinder and so little fear of that dormant mountain that slumbers restlessly only thirty miles away?

Instead, I drive away obediently. He's only doing his job. Like me, he's just one more simple man in a complex world, doing what's necessary to feed and clothe his family.

I continue toward Portland on a back road. The day is clear and bracing. I can't decide what to do. I had enough of big cities yesterday, but Portland is special. She's like the child who doesn't belong. The other large West Coast cities face out to the sea. Portland sits ninety miles inland, a river town, enclosed, devoid of the gracious Pacific vistas possessed by Seattle, San Francisco, L.A., and San Diego.

Like most "different" children, Portland has developed a life of her own, and is, in her own way, a secret treasure. A friend of mine once described her as an apple-cider kind of town, where people curl up with good books in front of warm fires and care about things that matter.

That may be true, but she's changeable in a way that is disconcerting. On a day such as this, under this lapis sky, she's a private Eden, nestled between the deep, wooded folds of the Pacific coastal range and the towering presence of the Cascades, and watched over by the gracious eminence of Mt. Hood. She feels intimate, contained, forward looking; offering up a humane and civil life to her inhabitants while remaining blessedly free of many of the tawdry encroachments that have placed a stranglehold on most urban environments.

Beneath this depthless blue sky she is truly the City of Roses, with Japanese gardens, rose arbors, and people picking blackberries from bushes that grow along the sides of roads. She seems a metropolis in miniature, an urban center on a scale human, manageable, and benign.

But on bad days, when the clouds close in and the rain hangs dark and heavy in the winter sky, she shows a different face. She becomes a small and brooding landlocked dungeon of a city. The rivers and the bridges and the confluence of the railroads cease to seem like elements of a children's play set placed amid a valley of green, and instead rise up and claim her with an overwhelming sense of industrial dinge and drear. The erector-set bridges that crisscross her two rivers, the Willamette and the Columbia, begin to look less like graceful parapets and spans and more like viable places from which to take that great notion. On such days, she becomes the only West Coast city that causes a person to scream out, "Give me space! Give me space!"

But there's something deeper in Portland that sets her apart; something that rumbles on a subterranean geopsychic level. She pivots on a different axis. Alone of all the West Coast cities, she opens to the east. Here the great north-south flyway of coastal energy is abruptly intersected by the Columbia Gorge, the great rift that cuts through the Sierra-Cascade range and provides the only level passage through the mountainous spine that runs down the coast from Canada to the southern California deserts.

This gorge—a purple, misty canyon of grand promontories and hanging ribbons of waterfalls—is like a crack that opens onto another world and carries on its winds the whispers of the high desert, the plains, the Rockies, and the rest of the American landmass. It is a floodgate, a fissure in space and time, a fracture in the geological consciousness of the continent.

It's hard to sense this in our contemporary world. We have breached the mountainous barrier and now flow in any direction we choose. But before the railroad, before the airplane, when people made their way on foot through the folds and creases of the land, this gorge was the only level pathway into the great garden of the coast. Those peoples, both ancient and modern, who made the journey, first felt the true pull of the Pacific at the site where Portland now stands.

More than Portland, it's this gorge that interests me. It has a power equal in scale to Mt. St. Helens, and it offers an antidote to the unease I've felt since standing before the reactor at Kalama.

Maybe tonight I'll come back into the city, grab a sandwich, and prowl the shelves at Powell's until the employees chase me out. But today I want to go into this great geological cleft. I want to hear the winds sing above me as they move from the desert to the sea, and feel the great silence of the cliffs as they stand watch over the Columbia's rolling passage. So I bypass Portland, with all her beauty and civic grace, and turn eastward to the passageway where the waterfalls plunge from cliffs as high as the sky, and mists the color of memory rise from rocks that sit like shoulders on the land.

I stay on the old winding roadway that parallels the freeway. I could as easily take the main highway. It really doesn't matter; all human creations are dwarfed here. But I want the quiet. I want to hear the leaves and mosses speak. I want to experience the gorge not as thoroughfare, but as a passageway between consciousnesses, a door between worlds.

The Columbia rolls along beside me, wide, flat, and powerful. I try to imagine her before she was neutered and dammed—a river flood-raging over cataracts of boulders as large as houses. It's an image that beggars the imagination, as surely as the imagination founders while trying to envision the millions of trees, snapped and charred and lying in eerie formation, surrounding Mt. St. Helens. But I try. I envision a river equal in power and majesty to these misted cliffs and massifs, a roaring, thundering deluge whose rumbling could be heard for miles, cutting eternally through the silence of the Cascade mountain nights.

Now, though imposing, she's a tame presence, a majestic procession of water controlled by a series of locks, dams, and hydroelectric modifications beginning at the great concrete barrier of the Grand Coulee near Spokane and ending with the Bonneville lock and dam near where I'm passing. In between, she's choked, throttled, and relentlessly pacified by dam and reservoir after dam and reservoir, until she's given up all wildness and fight and accepted her fate as a servant to the great god of hydroelectric generation.

This pacification of the river has rendered the gorge less terrifying, but no less imposing. It's still a wondrous fracture in the continent, and one cannot behold it without awe. All that has changed is that her voice now speaks more quietly.

In a rudimentary sense, I'm well attuned to this voice right now. Aside from my conversation with the deaf man and a few words with a girl in the Mt. St. Helens snack shop, I haven't spoken to anyone today. I've been inside myself, present only to my thoughts and the sensations born of contact with the land. It's the perfect preparation for the visit I'm about to make—a visit to the site of the Bridge of the Gods.

This site is a private obsession of mine. The current bridge that carries that name lurks in my traveler's memory as another erector-set span that crosses over the Columbia near the Bonneville locks. As it has been neither imposing nor essential to my prior travels, I've never paid it any mind. But since I've started listening more closely to the voices of America's original Native inhabitants, I've developed a different feeling for this bridge, or, at least, for the bridge that once carried this name.

According to the tribes of this land, there was a bridge that far predated this steel span. It was a natural stone arch stretching from one side of the gorge to the other and wide enough for many people and many horses to pass across at the same time. They called it the "Great

Crossover." Upon it the tribes from the north and south passed over the river to carry on commerce with each other.

Though roundly dismissed by contemporary historians and geologists, this land bridge is well documented in the tales and stories of many tribes. Some say it was formed by the gods to help the people share with each other and that the gods destroyed it when there was too much quarreling among the tribes. Others present it as a deeper myth in which the mountains, when they were people, quarreled over the love of the Sleeping Beauty and destroyed the bridge by shaking the earth and throwing fire at each other. Still other stories have the terrified waters of a great inland lake ripping a hole in a rock wall that existed on the Columbia and forming the great land bridge between the feuding, fire-breathing mountains.

Though these stories differ, they all share the singular truth of a great land crossover on the Columbia and a great inland sea that stretched back into the deserts of Idaho and beyond.

I want to look for the truth that lies behind these tales. I'm no scientist, but I am a great believer in the factual origins of myth. I want to seek out the geologic remnants of this bridge and to place it in my own knowledge, to reclaim it in my understanding.

In the history I was taught, this gorge was significant only as the most treacherous final stage in the journey of white settlers coming over the Oregon Trail or as a New Deal triumph of river management and civil engineering. I was asked to be satisfied with a historical consciousness that went back only to the time of European culture's arrival in this land. Nothing was said of any geological events or formations that may have shaped the development of culture on this continent before the arrival of European immigrants. Yet here is a story of such great significance that the entire course of precontact settlement on this continent may have been guided by the truth that it contains, and it's denigrated as legend and relegated to the status of "fascinating old Indian tale."

But what if there is something deeper? I want to find out.

I decide to begin on the Washington side of the gorge. I cross the erector-set bridge and head up the road that winds to the top of the cliffs. At a site above the existing bridge there's a pulloff where a road-side marker announces, "The Bridge of the Gods." There's a descriptive roadside plaque by the side of the parking area, erected by the Skamania County Historical Society in cooperation with the Washington State Parks and Recreation Commission and the Washington State Department of Transportation.

I begin to read: "Here the Bridge of the Gods spans the Columbia River." It's referring to the new steel bridge. It goes on to explain something of the geological history of the area and ends with the observation that "This was the site of cascade rapids. . . . Indian legend attributes the rapids to a collapsed stone arch that once spanned the river, a myth that still persists."

I proceed to the Bonneville locks where I find a bright-eyed young geologist manning an interpretive center. I ask him about the land bridge. He drags me over to scale models of the lock and dam and begins a long and complex explanation about the course of the river. He gestures out the window at layers of strata and begins an impassioned explanation of magma and flow patterns. He's proud of his knowledge and excited to share.

"But what about the land bridge?" I ask.

He sniffs and shakes his head. "We do not have the geology to support it," he says. "It's only a myth."

I cross back over to the Oregon side and go down to the Cascade locks where there's a little maritime park that offers paddleboat rides and camping facilities. "What can you tell me about the original Bridge of the Gods—the land bridge?" I ask the woman at the information counter. The question takes her aback. She's involved in a conversation with some cowboys who are showing a great deal of interest in her, and she does not wish to bother with me. She points me to a wall of the building where a long screed is written out on a plaque. It describes the work of a man named Jimmie James, who came to Portland in 1927 and became obsessed with the Native accounts of the Bridge of the Gods. He drew a sketch of how it may have looked, using charcoal he had found in the earth near here, and tried to get the U.S. Postal Service to create a stamp using the sketch to honor the Native belief.

There's a copy of his drawing. It shows a great rushing cataract coursing beneath a long archway of land that spans the river. It's very realistic and atmospheric, and quite believable. It takes me into the reality of the story. It deserves to be a stamp.

"Do you know any more?" I say to the woman.

She waves me off. "Go talk to the people at the museum," she says.

The museum is an old two-story frame house some distance down the way from the visitors center. Like so many local historical museums, it's an old settler's home now converted into a creaky-floored, dust-mote-filled series of rooms with display cases containing old ax heads and bits of domestic detritus. It's presided over by two older women who love their museum and are thrilled to talk to anyone who wanders into its confines.

I ask them about Jimmie James. "Oh," they say, "he really loved those Indians." They tell me again about the stamp and the drawing, and give me a copy of James's plea that was reproduced on the wall in the visitors center. I scan it quickly:

The Bridge of the Gods was a gift of great magnitude used by most of the tribes of the northwest and many of South America as well as those of the north. This bridge was made, undoubtedly, during the Cenozoic period, the age of man and mammals.

It goes on to describe a geological history that has a dam being formed by an earthquake that spilled rocks across the Columbia twenty thousand years ago, and a gradual erosion through this dam to create the bridge. He then recounts that "among the Indians of the plains I heard many of the old, old storytellers telling of the past. They told of the great crossover way out there where grandfather sun slept when it was dark." He ends by asking for support for his project to turn his charcoal sketch into a stamp. "The picture is now in

Washington, D.C., at the postal department awaiting a decision." The drawing was done in 1963. There still is no stamp.

"Do you know why it was never made into a stamp?" I ask the women.

"Probably no one cared, or no one believed him," one replies.

"Do you know where the bridge itself was?" I ask.

They're not sure. "It was somewhere back there," they say, pointing generally toward the west. "Would you like to see the rest of the museum?"

I decline as delicately as I can and head out to look for places where the cliffs appear to have calved off. There, I surmise, far above the rocks that formed the cascades in the river, I might see the echoes of the great bridge that stretched like a stone rainbow over this gorge. After all, I was trained as a sculptor, and I can sometimes see shapes in absences where other people see nothing.

The crowns and bluffs protrude and thrust, making it hard to get a panoramic view of the gorge walls. Each place I stand reveals a different vista. The young geologist at the locks had pointed out the place where the bridge was supposed to have been. I bounce the Tuna back over logging roads in hopes of finding a clear vantage point. It's impossible. I'm left with a half glimpse of towering cliffs that have piles of geologic rubble at their base. These could have been the remains, but I surely can't tell.

I try to imagine what that bridge must have looked like. Jimmie James must have done much the same. The cliffs rise majestically above me in the mist. Far below me the river churns on its roiling course. I look across to where the bridge would have touched the other wall of the gorge. A chill runs through me; I can almost see it.

I imagine a great stone archway looming above me, ragged and monumental, of a scale that leaves me breathless. The wind down the gorge howls and moans as it shapes itself to pass beneath this roadway in the sky. The sheer imposing presence of rock suspended above air is terrifying and fascinating. It's an inversion of nature that holds the heart in a suspended gasp.

I am transported. I feel the ghosts of all the peoples of the Americas moving north to south. I sense the gathering of tribes, the meetings, the sharings and tradings and suspensions of hostilities in order to allow common passage for all peoples across this bridge. It may be fanciful; it may be apocryphal. But what if it's not? Is it too much to think that the stories of the bridge reflect some underlying geological truth, just as the stories of the quarreling mountains and the Sleeping Beauty reflect the underlying truth of ancient volcanic activity?

The pamphlets and geological materials acknowledge active volcanoes and a collapsed wall of stone that existed seven or eight hundred years ago and forced the Columbia to back up and form an inland sea almost to Idaho. Could there not have been a prior cataclysm?

Were there not volcanic eruptions prior to that time? Why can there not be a truth more ancient? The only answer I get is, "We do not have the geology to support it." I know it's unlikely, and that geology should be able to speak clearly and definitively on the matter. But sometimes we're blinded by our own paradigms. It was not too many years ago that notions of a great earthly cataclysm caused by collision with an asteroid were laughed out of the academy. Now we accept them as doctrine. Was not geology first in line to mock those notions as well?

I work my way back to the main road. There's a fetid moistness in the air, and steam is rising from fissures in the highway. A sign informs me that I'm near Carson Hot Springs.

Hot springs are to me like bars are to alcoholics. I can't pass one without entering. I find the springs at the dead end of a small, winding, down-sloping road. They're contained in an old sanatorium kind of place, a turn-of-the-century "take the cure" bathhouse with a tin roof and an adjacent ramshackle hotel that's on the down side of quaint. I watch a cat climb in and out of a dumpster full of garbage bags that sits on the back of an old Dodge power wagon. This is truly my kind of place.

I pay for a soak and go inside. Two rows of chipped porcelain claw-foot bathtubs sit in an old institutional white tile bathing room. The plumbing is exposed. Pipes clank, and the smell of the minerals fills the air. I climb in my tub and soak blissfully for about a half hour, then go into an adjacent room where metal-framed beds with tick mattresses covered by white sheets are lined up as if in a World War I Balkan hospital. An attendant directs me to lie down, then wraps me in hot sheets and covers me with towels.

He's a jovial sort—surprisingly congenial for a man who does such a repetitive task in such tubercular surroundings. While he's wrapping me, I ask him about the land bridge.

"Don't know much about it," he says.

It would have been about twelve miles from here, if all accounts are accurate.

"Well," I ask, "what about these springs?"

"Oh, they were discovered by some old Indian in 1876."

I settle back into my swaddling of towels and drift off into a vaporous stupor. The image of Jimmie James's drawing floats high above me. The molten earth burbles and boils far beneath me.

Old Indian myths. Fire-breathing mountains. Ancient springs that were "discovered" a hundred years ago. Bridges that never were. The vapors from the steam seeping from deep in the earth's crust fill my nostrils.

I wish my Nick could meet Nick Collins. There are things we do not know.

SEVEN

GOD'S SANDAL

I drive along the broad, flat, expanse of the Willamette Valley, full of the righteousness of my own belief. Spent fuel rods entombed in concrete bunkers, volcanoes reduced to scientific lessons, oral traditions dismissed as myth. How can we be so deaf to the voice of this land?

I keep hearing the words of Luther Standing Bear, the Lakota chief: "The white man does not understand America. He is too far removed from its formative processes. The roots of the tree of his life have not yet grasped the rock and the soil." If a volcano doesn't make us humble, what's it going to take?

Sometimes I wish I didn't have this strange bifurcation in my character. It's an absolutely irreducible combination of moral arrogance and spiritual humility. I may not be worthy to loose the straps of God's sandals, but if he'll take one off and loan it to me, I'll gladly beat the hell out of everyone else with it. It's the hollow thunder of the self-proclaimed prophet, and it doesn't play well in most settings. But it's an occupational hazard of the solitary soul, and it's one I'm willing to risk. You just have to keep a sense of humor, and temper your convictions with enough perspective that you don't start handing out tracts on corners or threatening to bomb people if your manifestos aren't published in the *New York Times*.

With rare exceptions, I toe the line. And I don't think yesterday was one of those exceptions. I truly believe in what I was sensing. And I've filed it away, deep in my heart. But today I need to get a dose of perspective and humility. Two tablets and a sermon won't buy you a cup of coffee, and everyone from Savanarola to the Son of Sam had a set of tablets, too.

When I started this journey I made a decision not to visit old friends along the way. They can tug at the heart in strange ways, and muddy the waters of clear intention. But I think I'm going to visit George. He's not so much a friend as a force of nature, a human Mt. St. Helens who rumbles in my past from the days when I lived in Eugene. He'll blow me off my mountaintop.

I'm not sure exactly where he lives. But he won't be hard to find. Eugene is only a city of a hundred thousand people. And George is George.

I stop at a 7-Eleven near the University of Oregon campus and make a futile attempt to look him up in a phone book. Of course, he's not listed. The likelihood of George owning a phone is no greater than the likelihood of George owning a Lear jet or a tuxedo. I need to go to plan B.

A few ragged kids are lurking around outside the store. They're wearing neo-hippie garb and have the lost look of people who are for-lornly out of place and time. A smile and a nod are all it takes: a nervous kid in a Grateful Dead T-shirt sidles up to me and asks if I have any spare change for a Slurpee.

"Nobody slurps for free," I tell him. "I'll get you your Slurpee if you can tell me where George lives."

He looks confused. "George?" he asks.

I can see it's the confusion of impairment, not ignorance. He's been hitting his stash early. I hold my hand above my head to indicate scale. That jogs his synapses. "Oh, yeah. That George. I think he lives on one of those streets up towards Thirtieth."

I give him a couple of bucks. "You'd better be right," I say, "or I'll be coming back to get your Slurpee."

"Aw, man," he groans. He can't tell whether I'm serious or not.

He doesn't have to worry. A few passes up and down the streets near Thirtieth, and I find what I'm after. In the midst of row after row of neatly kept houses that could have come straight from the set of *Ozzie and Harriet,* one small postwar bungalow stands almost obscured by a jungle of shoulder-high plants and weeds. For some unknown reason most of the paint has been scraped off the house, though clearly this was not done in preparation for repainting. The driveway is filled with a carnival of multicolored figures made from tennis rackets, old bicycle seats, fire-hose nozzles, and just about every assorted piece of industrial flotsam and jetsam known to humankind. George is standing among them.

He hasn't changed much. He's still about six foot seven. His face is still beefy and florid, and he's still wearing the same type, and maybe the same pair, of bib overalls I remember him in the last time I saw him.

"Nerburn!" he bellows as I step out of the car.

"Hey, George, how're you doing?"

"Come here!" he says, as if our conversation had just stopped yesterday rather than fifteen years ago. "I want you to see this. Here, look at this. Is this great, or what?" He points to one of the little figures. It has a head made from a chrome piece of a car bumper or something similar. I start to respond. He grabs my shoulder and pulls me over to another piece before I can get a word out. "What do you think?"

I'm taken aback. The last time I saw George he was carving whales from pieces of redwood and seemed to have committed his life to them. "They're big, no one understands them, and people are always out to destroy them," he had told me shortly after he'd been released from jail, where he had attempted to eat a lightbulb. They seemed a perfect subject.

But these new pieces have an authentic aesthetic presence and, in their own way, are just as perfect. They're figures, garish and cartoon-like, with reflectors for eyes, bicycle seats for heads, hubcaps for hats.

But despite their childlike simplicity, there's a poignancy and loneliness about them. For all their caricatured gesture, they reflect real understanding and communicate deep emotion. They seem all too real.

"These are great, George," I tell him. "I think you've found your artistic voice."

"I know!" he screams. "That's why I can't stand what's going on. These are probably going to be on Oprah next week." Then in a perfect non sequitur he says, "How could I be stalking her? I can't even leave my house." He sweeps his hand across the yard area. "There's literally thousands, millions of dollars worth of art here."

"Wait a minute," I say. "What's going on?"

"Don't you know?" he shouts. "It's all over the news."

I admit ignorance.

"Here," he says, pulling a sheaf of folded papers out of his overalls. They include some disconnected pages explaining a series of works he's done called the "Amy Series," a search warrant for his house from the Lane County courts that specifies such objects as his work boots and overalls as well as his artworks and personal records, and a newspaper column in which a local writer berates him for harassing and stalking a woman named Amy through both his personal activities and his art.

George is shouting and gesticulating as I read, but I finally begin to piece the story together. He has created a series of sculptures called the "Amy Series." They are neither pornographic nor sexually explicit, but have all been named or titled something to do with "Amy." There are hundreds of them. The Amy to whom they make reference was once a friend and neighbor of George's. She has determined that George is obsessed with her and that he has been stalking her both in person and in his artwork. At an exhibition of his work at a local gallery, some of his pieces were defaced, clearly in response to the brouhaha about his "Amy" theme.

First Amendment and artistic-freedom types have come rushing to George's defense. Feminists and others concerned with issues of harassment have come to Amy's defense and have gone on the attack against George. Amy has moved, the police have been called, George's house has been searched, and the battle has been joined.

"You understand it, Nerburn," he roars. "You should write something about it. I'm just trying to make art. She's my muse. Every artist has a muse. Dante had a muse. Now they're saying I'm stalking her."

I wander among his works. Though their subject matter is nonsexual, they are all named "Amy." It is more than a little odd.

"George," I say. "These works are good. Why the hell don't you just give them another name?"

He erupts. "Don't you see? That's just what they want. No one had any problems until those people from CAT grabbed onto it. They just wanted an excuse. They're using her."

"CAT?"

"Center for Appropriate Transportation!" he shouts.

We talk a bit more. The story becomes both murkier and clearer. CAT, neighborhood coalitions, art galleries, political-correctness police, ACLU types, special interest groups. It's all in a whirl.

I continue among the army of figures. George stands, MacArthur-like, among them. Here's a bull made from a bicycle seat and handlebars. Here's a little man with a head made from the clutch plate of a car. I find a delightful piece with a toy cannon barrel for one arm and a sword upraised in the other. Something about it absolutely captures me.

"George," I say, "I'd really like to buy this one."

I believe in supporting artists, and I'd be thrilled and honored to own this poignant little figure created by the hand of a friend. "Would five hundred dollars be fair?" It's more than I have, but it's a statement, within my capabilities, of how much I value him and his work.

He shakes his head and gesticulates wildly. "Oh, no. Oh, no," he says. "That's 'St. George Looking for Amy.' It's worth thousands. Maybe hundreds of thousands. Look at it."

I back off. I hope I haven't insulted him. "You're right, George," I say. "It really is special."

We move away from the subject. He continues his tour, surveying his troops. After we finish our walk through the driveway and the jungle of a yard, he suddenly becomes very serious. He lowers his voice and beckons me closer to him.

"Hey, Nerburn," he says. "Do you suppose you could give me twenty bucks? Things are a little slow right now."

I look longingly at the little St. George figure staring at me from across the driveway. "Sure, George," I answer.

I give him the twenty. He quickly stuffs it into the bib pocket of his overalls. He's once again his old blustery self.

I begin walking back to the car. I'd offer to take him out to lunch, but never once in two years did I ever see him eat, and he probably wouldn't be willing to leave his yard anyway. It's best to leave things as they are.

"Well, I should be going, George," I tell him.

"You're really looking happy," he says. "I can't believe how happy you look."

"Thanks, George. A good wife and kids will do that to a guy."

I regret the comment the moment I make it. But if it bothers him, he doesn't show it.

"You write something, Nerburn," he bellows. He waves his arms over his troops, his children. "This is going all the way to the Supreme Court."

"I'll be watching the news," I say, and give him and the hundreds of "Amys" a good-bye salute.

I return to the 7-Eleven. I want to use the pay phone. I feel like calling home. Teenage girls in long tie-dyed skirts and their boyfriends in rasta hats are now dancing in circles in the parking lot, waving their hands and chanting. The boy with the Grateful Dead T-shirt is there among them. He sees me and cowers.

"I've already finished it, man," he says.

I clap him on the shoulder. "It's okay," I say. "I found him."

The boy is relieved. I give him another couple of dollars. "Treat your friends. Dancing can work up a thirst."

He flashes me a crooked grin and scuttles away.

I pick up the phone and dial our number. It's been a day and a half since I've called, and a lot has happened. I hope to catch Louise before she leaves for class, just to assure her I'm alive and well and to tell her I'll call tonight when we can have a more leisurely talk. But there's no answer. Instead, I get the machine. It's Nick's voice.

"Hi. You have reached Kent, Louise, and Nick. We can't come to the phone right now. But if you'll please leave your name and number, we'll call you right back."

I remember when he was preparing to make the recording. He spent a long time up in his room, probably scripting and practicing what he was going to say. If I know him well, he had probably been listening to answering machine messages for months in preparation for the moment when he would be allowed to record ours. Yet he would never ask. That would reveal too much. But, if the time came, he would be ready.

And he was. The message is "little man" serious, in both tone and delivery. It tears me apart. There's nothing harder than hearing your child's voice at a distance.

I leave a short message telling them I had a wonderful day at Mt. St. Helens and the gorge and am now in Eugene, where the town is up in arms about people being stalked by Pinocchio sculptures. That should whet their interest.

As I get in my car I see that the dancers are now sitting on the curb sharing a pack of doughnuts. I wave to the Slurpee boy. He waves back and points at the doughnuts to assure me that my dollars were well spent. He was a nice kid, just a little scared and confused. I wonder if Nick would end up beside him in a few years if we were to move here.

Actually, the idea of relocating to Eugene has percolated in my mind for years. It may even have been the subconscious impetus for this entire trip. Of all the cities where I've ever lived, this was probably my favorite. If I pick and choose my way through my memory, I can make a strong case for trying to build a life here.

It was such a different time. I was in a stormy and progressively deteriorating relationship with an American woman I had met years before in Italy. Expatriate reality doesn't always translate well to home soil, and ours had not made the journey successfully. We were now trapped in a relationship we could neither save nor figure out how to end. In addition, we were so poor that every day was an exercise in simple economic survival.

I knew where all the good dumpsters were, and which were likely to yield edible produce. I rode my bike no matter how heavy the rain, because we needed to conserve as much gas as we could, and we couldn't afford to have our precious but well-worn car break down. I remember vividly having a case of athlete's foot so bad I had to wear one oversized tennis shoe at all times, and not daring to spend the three dollars necessary to get some ointment to ease my suffering.

It was a frustrating time, because I was more than willing to work, but there was no work to be had. One day the local paper showed a photo of a line of people stretching the length of a city block waiting to put in an application at a convenience store. After twenty or thirty such applications, with no return calls, you tended to give up.

It wasn't just the economy that made life difficult; it was an entire conjunction of circumstances. The counterculture had discovered Eugene, and the city fathers and mothers, who were insular and conservative and used to complete control, hated the influx. Anyone with long hair or a beard or a long skirt and a whiff of patchouli was deemed an undesirable and had almost no chance of being hired, even if a job opened up. The civic policy, though unspoken, was to starve them out.

At the same time, the university supplied an abundance of cheap labor that could be tapped at work-study wages, so the few jobs that did exist were easily filled through sweetheart arrangements that allowed the work-study funds to be used to subsidize a portion of the employer's costs.

Add to that the poor overall state of the lumber economy, the proud Oregon tradition of self-reliance and the concomitant tendency to establish draconian social service policies to minimize the influx of ne'er-do-wells from California, and the willingness of a great many hippies to live in the most squalid collective realities imaginable in order to remain in the area, and the result was that those of us who wanted to work, but were not from local families and did not fit the accepted profile of a desirable Eugene resident, were left standing with our hands out.

One friend of mine—a gentle, literate, ponytailed intellectual—had been the teacher of the year at Oakland College in Michigan, but had lost his job in a tenure squabble and had migrated to Eugene to allow his wife to pursue her dancer's dream. He was the success story among us, because, after a year, he had managed to find a job scooping ice cream at a local sweet shop. He went to his job with the pride of a Depression era immigrant, which, in a way, he was.

The rest of us muddled along as best we could, making crafts and selling them at the Saturday market, or picking up day jobs here and there doing some backbreaking labor like bailing out a nursing-home basement after a flood. My own tally, in two years, included my ill-fated stint as the Saturday gym supervisor, a time doing temporary labor on an assembly line that packaged colored pencils and fuzzy bunny posters, and a short-lived tenure as a freelance editor for a crazed old man who was self-publishing incomprehensible religious ramblings. That particular job had been my great hope, because I had thought it would actually allow me to use some of my skills. But it had fallen apart when my employer announced that without his approval I could not change a single word, mark of punctuation, or the spelling of anything he had written. After a week of tolerating the minimal red penciling I was doing in an effort to make his writings intelligible, he informed me that I was incapable of understanding the nuances of his thought and sent me packing. I took my Ph.D. in theology and fifteen years of editing experience, and went skulking back to the want ads and the dumpsters.

In retrospect, it's a wonder I didn't hate this town. But I didn't. It had a character about it that I loved. Though the counterculture was economically brutalized, it was vibrant and diverse. The absence of work for well-educated transplants produced a cafe culture, where intelligent and interesting people from myriad backgrounds and far-flung locales spent time discussing ideas and producing visionary schemes. I remember one man who actually made some headway on a project to run a series of canals through the city, utilizing the abundant waters from the Willamette and Mill Creek.

And then there were the civic amenities like bike paths and jogging trails for which Eugene is justly famous. And the manageable size of the city. And the delicious sense of "island reality," which, when it doesn't turn on itself, makes a place feel friendly and enclosed.

No, I didn't hate this city. It was a great place to live, just a bad place to make a living. It set a stamp on me that I've carried ever since. It made me realize that what I've wanted in a home was a balance between amenity and civility, intellectual vibrancy and the presence of nature. Eugene may have come as close to achieving that balance as any place I've ever hung my hat, and that's why it has remained, tucked in my memory, as a fantasy and a possibility when I contemplate different places our family might live.

As I drive through the streets, all of this comes back to me. The city has gotten bigger, but it still has the same look, the same feel. There's the hospital where they put the cast on my ankle. There's the bike path I used to take to cross the river to sneak into University of Oregon football games at halftime.

The smell of fresh cedar from the mills is everywhere. The day is alive with crisp, sparkling winter light. I want to grab somebody and say, "I know this place. I used to live here." But nobody would care. I'm a stranger in a familiar land.

I drive by the civic center that was just in the planning stages when I lived here. It's a thing of beauty, utilizing indigenous materials and a humane, Pacific Northwest aesthetic. This is what I loved about the town—it had an appropriate sense of place, and the confidence to assert it. Even in those days, it was wary of the tyranny of the automobile and instinctively leery of the soul-deadening effects of suburban sprawl. The core of the town has remained true to its original vision and character, and the malevolent strip mall spawn has been relegated to the perimeter, where it seems unable to suck the life out of the central city on which it feeds.

I wonder about this place. I wonder hard. Would it work? Would we be able to make a go of things here, or would it just be an updated reprise of the squalid hand-to-mouth existence I experienced last time I tried to make this home? I know Louise would love it here. We traveled through here once years ago and she was completely taken with its sense of amenity.

But what was it that really drove me out? Think carefully, Kent. Think carefully.

The golden day has been overtaken by cloud. A light rain is starting to fall. I drive up the street that leads to the house where I used to live. If there was such a thing as happy domestic times here, that house is where they occurred. It was a humble, though warm, side-by-side duplex right off the commercial main drag between Eugene and Springfield. My girlfriend and I had moved into it after shivering for most of the winter in a drafty, falling-down '50s clapboard rambler twenty miles out of town. That house, like most university-town rental housing, had been owned by absentee landlords who didn't care at all. It was what in real-estate parlance is known as a "cash cow," and these absentee owners were milking it for all it was worth. Despite the drafty windows and ill-fitting doors, we had tried to make it homey. But it was heated only by an inefficient Franklin stove, and we had been snookered by a traveling wood salesman into spending our last seventy dollars on two cords of what turned out to be green, freshly cut maple that did nothing more than hiss and spit and fill the entire house with smoke. When we finally tired of chipping ice out of the toilet bowl in the morning and huddling around the oven for warmth, we had given up our dreams of rural bliss and moved into this duplex near town.

As I come upon it now in the dim, bitter drizzle, it looks anything but warm and inviting. It's crowded in among trailers and deteriorating shacks on a dead-end street full of potholes and garbage. The yards are filled with automobile carcasses. It's an urban Appalachia, a dirty and unhealthy environment that's far grimier and more brutal than I remember. Obviously, all semblance of landlord and tenant pride is gone.

It makes me sad. My memories had a much gentler timbre. What troubles me as much as anything is that I can't be sure this isn't exactly the way things were even when I lived here. It's so hard to pierce the veil of time.

This disconnect frightens me. In some distant sense, it must be analogous to the experience of a stroke victim: relearning things you already know and finding in their familiarity an infinite strangeness. I'm filled with an ineffable sense of sadness, betrayal, and something irretrievably lost. Are all my memories about Eugene equally suspect and untrustworthy?

The drizzle is turning to hard rain. The chill of winter's breath is on the wind. I'm near the freeway; I think I'll take it. I had intended to follow the back roads south, winding among the small forested hills and valleys. But the sky has closed. As was the case with Bellingham, the atmosphere would be a curtain of tears, obscuring the countryside and driving me inside myself. I would learn nothing more except about my own sense of isolation and disconnection. Better to make some time until the sky opens again.

I need to fuel up before heading out, so I stop at a gas station just over the bridge into Springfield. The now vicious rain cuts and blows in violent gusts as I step out of the car. The wind rips me, the water streams down my face. I grab the nozzle and flip the reset plate, but the pump won't reset. I flip it again. Nothing happens.

I look toward the station, hoping to catch someone's attention. Inside, a man moves leisurely toward the door. He makes an indecipherable gesture and slips on a raincoat. I'm cursing like a sailor and madly flipping the reset plate as he slowly proceeds toward me through the rain.

"Just a minute," he shouts. "I'll pump it." Oregon is still not a self-serve state.

He ambles up and takes the nozzle from me. My hair is hanging in soggy strings over my face, and my teeth are chattering. He makes a fist and thumps the pump hard. "You're treating it like a girlfriend instead of a wife," he says. "You got to beat on it a little." He bangs it again at about buttock height. The gauge responds and resets to zero.

"See," he grins, "it's all in the touch."

He fills my tank, I pay my bill, and climb, shivering, back into the car. I drive off into the rain and drear, thinking about Louise and Nick, and how much I'm beginning to miss my home.

Damn this rain and its accursed moods. I was moving toward something in Eugene, some kind of resolution between the sense of alienation and distant familiarity. I wanted to pursue it, to get closer to what it was that had kept me there, and what had driven me out. But the rain has dropped a wall between me and any capacity for meaningful reflection.

> *I try to recall the man I was when I lived there. I had gotten so cynical. I remember sitting at a bar with George, swilling beer and reciting doggerel I had crafted on the back of a napkin:*
> *I've got a big tall truck with a four-wheel drive.*
> *Talking about chain saws and jogging more than five.*
> *Thinking about becoming a real-estate dealer.*
> *With a well-trimmed beard while praying for whales.*
> *I called it my "Eugene Anthem," and it went on from there, getting progressively more bitter and assaultive.*

It was the worst kind of cynicism—an impulse toward violence, sublimated and turned in upon itself and made impotent by a kind of despair. George understood it perfectly. He just chose, instead, to eat lightbulbs.

What had driven me to this? Was it really the town? Predictably, I blamed my bitterness on external circumstances. I was still young, and I thought my Ph.D. guaranteed me something in life beyond the right to dig in dumpsters. In my mind, Eugene had betrayed me. It was denying me my rightful due.

I was also wracked by the spiritual torment of being in a relationship with a woman I no longer loved, but did not wish to hurt. Was that sense of spiritual entrapment what really made me cynical and drove me out? Or was it perhaps something deeper—an incongruence of the spirit of this land with my own spiritual yearnings? Or maybe it was something as simple as the oppression of the rain and the lack of four discreet seasons. Maybe I was just one more Oregon wannabe, driven to the edge of despair by being too wet and too poor and too hungry for too long. Maybe I was just taking that great notion.

There's no way to know at this distance, and no longer any way to find out. All I know for sure is that my long-suffering partner and I, like Shawn and Thom, and the cap-shop girl, were more than ready to embrace the time-honored fantasy of a better life somewhere down the road. After my desperate attempt to find spiritual clarity in the monastery proved a failure, we sold what we could, dumped what we had, packed the car, and headed eastward. It was five more hard years before we finally faced the fact that we were able to make each other miserable wherever we chose to live.

These are the kinds of thoughts that swirl around me as I splash through the dreary hillsides and head south on I–5. Cars have their lights on. The fog is descending from the tops of the hills. I watch the vestiges of Eugene disappear off to the right of me. I wonder if George is standing out in his yard. I wonder if he's covering his "millions of dollars worth of art" with a tarp. I wonder if the tarp is named "Amy." I wonder what he's going to do with my twenty dollars.

It helps me to think about George, even as it saddens me. He provides me with some perspective on my confusion about Eugene. It was always such a moralizing city, always involved in some clash of high-minded principles. Everyone had their own set of tablets. Self-satisfied joggers, crusading vegetarians ready to free all the minks and rabbits, strident political-correctness police of various persuasions, chain saw–wielding logger libertarians, thundering fundamentalists, Greenpeacers itching to rappel up the sides of boats or take a torpedo for the whales—something was always at stake, even in a yard full of Pinocchio statues.

But I, too, carried a heavy set of tablets, and that's what attracted me to the place. A belief in the spiritual dimension of the land does not find favor everywhere in America, but it did in Eugene. Living there, I felt, for a short moment, as if maybe I was a part of something visionary, and that maybe we could change things in a way we had failed so miserably to do in the 1960s.

But there was so little sense of humor, so little sense of moral compromise or human fallibility. Maybe I'm just too Catholic. I believe in salvation by works, but I also believe we humans see through a glass darkly. We can't always go around beating each other to death with God's sandal. Sometimes, we need to step back and take a deep breath. Sometimes a Pinocchio statue is just a Pinocchio statue.

That, I think, may be what ultimately drove me out. In almost every case, ideology trumped humanity. There was less concern with being your brother's keeper than with seeing that your brother got it right. People were concerned about George because he made ill-mannered Pinocchios, not because he ate lightbulbs and was half mad. If he'd been found dead one day, the first concern would have been to clear the landscape of his offending figures, not to wonder how he had come to such a tragic fate.

Social responsibility—at least when I lived there—simply didn't carry much weight in Eugene, except in the most high-minded sense, and somehow, somewhere, that began to wear thin for me. Though I was, relatively, on the bottom of the food chain when I lived there, I still believed we needed to carry the less fortunate on our backs. Sometimes a Pinocchio statue is a cry for help.

The sky is beginning to lift. The hills are appearing, and on their peaks and ridges I see a light dusting of snow.

I motor along down I–5 savoring the last sips of a cappuccino I picked up as I was leaving Eugene. All the emotional *Sturm und Drang* of my visit to my old hometown are receding.

Once again, the road is freeing me. A warm car, a warm cup of coffee, the open road, and the purr of a well-tuned engine—it's our American mantra, our true national anthem. "Oh beautiful, for spacious skies, for roads that never end."

That old prof was right—I am a moving thinker, not a sitting thinker. I think most of us are. It's in our national character. Progress and perfectibility are just the lure of the road translated into a philosophical point of view.

The signs for Roseburg are beginning to appear above the freeway. I–5 has done her job; she's allowed me to eat up some miles during the rain. I'd like to push on ahead before dark, but this exit coming up is one I don't think I can deny. Forty-five miles to the west, on twisting, curving, rain-slicked Highway 42, lies the little town of Bridge and the road to my old forest cabin.

Since I've opened the Pandora's box of my past in Eugene and the ghosts have now escaped, I had best let them fly free. I think I should see this other world that I've held suspended in my imagination for almost three decades.

This visit, too, frightens me. It's like meeting an old lover. You don't know whether you're more afraid that she's changed, or that she hasn't. There's no timeless George to temper the blow, no changeless absolute around which to pivot the experience. Don, the mailman will be old. The cabin may well be gone. Perhaps the valley will now be an upscale cyberhaven for urban refugees. Or, maybe, like the little town that existed at the end of the road only on plat maps, the entire valley will have been swallowed up by the forest. I cross myself and take the off-ramp into the coastal range.

The slippery pavement and the growing hills soon grab my full attention. I don't remember this road well. I didn't drive it enough to embed it in my memory.

Deeper and deeper into the blue-black hills. The roadway twists and curves; the pavement is slick. Walls of trees rise on harsh angles from the hillsides. This is no fairy-tale woods of the Brothers Grimm, with paths and witches and thatched-roof cottages. This is a dark, indifferent forest of hollow, dripping silences. Nothing is anthropomorphized; nothing is reduced to the human.

I wonder if I ever really understood this land. My own sense of spiritual scale has always been based on prairie distances and horizons, and intimations of great weather just out of the range of hearing. Here, everything is enclosure. The hills close in and brood and threaten. You don't think winsomely about the unseen; you take a fighter's stance and dare it to try to take you.

This is what made the people around here who they were and what so fascinated me about them. If someone messed with them, they didn't call for help. They stood in their front yard revving up their chain saw, saying, "Come and get me."

I remember a man whose son was being pursued by the sheriff. He got the boy in the house, blocked his driveway with a line of sawhorses, leaned his arsenal of rifles and shotguns against them, and then sat back in an old wooden chair to wait for the sheriff's arrival. He would deal with his son's misbehavior. But first he was going to deal with the sheriff.

And then there was the man who lured a deputy up a dead-end road, felled a Douglas fir behind the patrol car, and went home for the night. All up and down the valley people sat by their scanners listening to the deputy's desperate radio calls for help. But not one of them got up and grabbed a chain saw to go out and assist him.

This is why I decided to leave when the dead rats began showing up in my holding tank. Accidents happen, and the hills are deep.

But despite their rough edges and suspicion of all authority and the fact that most of them saw me as an enemy, I loved these people. They were full of a noble but self-defeating heroism. They would risk their lives to help another, but they would lose their own lives rather than accept that same help themselves. They hated the government, yet they were first in line to sign up for World War II. The women were abused and subjugated, but they didn't miss a beat when the men died or fell ill or left for the service. They just started up the log truck, threw a grease gun and a bucket of wrenches into the back, and headed out into the woods.

It was American self-reliance at its most elevated. But it was also self-reliance at its most stubborn and bullheaded. People routinely lived alone in their houses until they were ninety, killing chickens and heating their homes with firewood. A neighbor might stop in now and then, but no little couples in Oldsmobiles came by with Meals on Wheels. If they had, they probably would have been politely sent away. A person don't need charity. There's plenty of chickens, and I can manage just fine, thank you.

That's why the mailman was in such a dilemma. People weren't looking at his personal struggles and saying, "Maybe we can help him out by taking his route for a while." They were sitting back, with arms folded and guns on the sawhorses, watching. They would have defended him to the death in a fight, and they never would have sabotaged his efforts to keep his job. But let him slip; let him fall, just once . . .

Compassion, for themselves or others, simply was not in their character. What they knew was work, the harder the better. If you couldn't do your job, you were weak. And if you were weak, you fell. If you fell, you were culled. The mailman knew it. He was one of them.

I recall my astonishment at seeing one-armed men going off into the woods, carrying their chain saws in slings over their armless shoulders, and seventy-five-year-old mill workers who could barely walk struggling to tie their caulk boots so they could go out in the mill ponds and scale the timber. Half the men in town bore long gruesome scars or were missing the ends of fingers. But that's just how it was. The woods raised them, the woods fed and clothed them, and the woods would claim them. There was nothing to discuss, nothing to consider.

Small wonder, then, that they looked at me with something between contempt and hatred. There I was, able-bodied, long-haired, and sad-eyed, living alone in a cabin, appearing to do nothing, while they stitched up their chain-saw wounds with their wives' sewing needles and dress thread and went back to work.

Small wonder, too, that I could never make my peace with the high-minded moralisms of the Eugene counterculture as they disparaged the loggers and waxed philosophical about the plight of the spotted owl. I knew the people who were cutting down the trees where the spotted owl lived. I knew what these woods did to them, as well as what they did to these woods. And I wasn't about to reduce the complexity of their lives to an ideological argument, any more than I was about to make an ideological argument out of George's Pinocchio statues.

As I look back now, I realize I was just struggling with my lifelong ambivalence about ideological purity in the face of fallible humanity. I knew that clear-cutting was an affront to the earth's spirit, as well as bad forest management. I knew that a genetically supercharged, fast-growth MacFir didn't compensate for the spiritual presence and moral dignity of an ancient redwood or a grove of old-growth cedar. I hated the sound of chain saws and blanched at the sight of a scarred, denuded hillside.

But you don't pound spikes into trees to maim men who are simply trying to feed their families. You don't make widows and amputees to prove a point. I couldn't walk away from the humanity of the situation to make a stance for the ideology.

I wanted to see the issue as one of economic exploitation, not ecological morality. I dreamed of some Joe Hill, some Eugene Debs, some forest Cesar Chavez who would bring these two sides together in a common fight to save the forests they both loved. To me, it was a war of brothers. They should have been partners. The environmentalists had the long view; the loggers had up-close knowledge. After all, it was the loggers who trudged, day after day, into the woods, losing hands and limbs and friends and fathers to choker chains and chain saws. It was they who placed their muscles against these giants and felt them give way before their efforts, they who ate their lunches beneath the canopied magnificence, went home exhausted, and dreamt of trees.

The environmentalists should have seen the nobility in these people and found a way to join hands with them. If only both sides understood that the silk-suit, bottom-line corporate guys eating expense-account lunches in distant skyscrapers were the only ones who really didn't care. If only they could have worked together to save the forests they both loved.

But such groups never work together. It is the socialist's pipe dream—a union of the intellectuals and the workers. But here in the woods there was no time for socialism. Both sides had already pitched their tents. The accursed individualism and high-minded morality had taken away any possibility of meaningful collective action. One saw the forests, the other saw the trees, and neither was willing to see through the other's eyes.

Someone like me, who tried to see both the vision of the environmentalists and the struggles of the loggers, was simply a man without the courage of any strong convictions. I was lukewarm, worthy only of being spit out of the mouth.

Now, as I see the log trucks flying by me on the roadway, loaded with massive Douglas fir tree trunks, I wonder if, really, my broad-minded humanity wasn't really just one more spineless compromise. Maybe these Oregonians are right: you have to choose, then stand and fight.

I'm getting nervous about the weather. The sky has lowered again, and snow is falling. Highway 42 has become a pair of icy tracks through wet, snowy slop. Once again, my flatlander's uncertainty is overtaking me.

It only takes me an instant to figure out the realities of snow in the northern Minnesota woods. I can read its texture and its moisture and can predict how it will affect my car and my chances for successful passage. But add in hills and curves and make that snow into something akin to icy slush, and I'm without bearings. I don't know what my car can and can't do, and I'm not even sure how to find out.

I take the curves cautiously. A skid here, a slide there, accelerate into the curves, lay off the brakes. I think I'm getting the hang of it; the Tuna seems to be holding.

Then, several curves ahead, I see a gathering of red taillights and emergency blinkers. I ease on the brakes, gently downshift. There's a moment of panic; I'm going too fast. I push the brakes harder. A shudder, a mild fishtail, and I slide to a stop.

Whatever has happened is about two curves in front of me. Cars and trucks are sitting patiently, their windshield wipers flapping and their engines running.

I step out into the slush. My feet make puddled footprints in the slop. There's a thin glaze on the roadway, causing me to walk gingerly.

I move forward hesitantly. I'm not sure I want to see. Accidents on these winding highways always had an absolute dimension. The drops were too precipitous, the speeds too great. It was an all-too-common occurrence for a log truck to miss a curve or have a load shift and crash through a barrier, tumbling down one of these steep embankments, rolling over and over, until it came to rest upside down, disjointed, with its wheels spinning and its logs scattered like matchsticks, a flip of the coin whether its driver was alive or dead. Or for a car full of people, on their way to some church function in a nearby town, to meet a hurtling log truck head on and be reduced to a bloody box of metal that had to be sawn apart by rescue crews before the number, much less the identities, of the victims could even be ascertained.

So I approach with trepidation. But people are still in their cars. If it had been something gruesome, the dark human fascination with death would have drawn them all to the edge of the scene. Perhaps it's nothing more than a truck that has spilled its load.

Step by step I proceed through the mush. Water creeps in through the eyelets on my boots, soaking my feet. I pull the hood of my sweatshirt over my head and shove my hands into its kangaroo pouch. This is the Oregon cold I remember.

A few more steps, and the situation reveals itself. It's nothing as dire as I had feared. A portion of the rocky hillside has dislodged and slid down, creating a finger of boulders and scree about three feet high across the full width of the road.

Toward the front of the line of vehicles, a log-truck driver is sitting on the step of his cab, eating a sandwich. I figure he'll know what's happening.

He nods as I walk up. "Nice weather," I say, grabbing for my standard Minnesota conversational opening.

He shakes his head. "Fucking road . . . "

He's young, maybe in his late twenties or early thirties. He has a clean-cut country-western kind of handsomeness, with a well-trimmed mustache and long hair that's pulled behind his ears and hangs long down the back of his neck, Wild Bill Hickok style. His T-shirt is stretched taut over an athlete's body, and his forearms are like bundles of ropes. I can imagine him line-dancing, drunk as a lord, at two in the morning in some roadhouse with some woman he's picked up, or coldcocking an abusive boss on an assembly line somewhere in Tennessee. Instead, he's sitting here, leaning comfortably against the cab of his idling diesel, eating a sandwich in the Oregon winter mist.

"Been here long?" I ask.

"Twenty minutes. Cat's coming." He tosses his head to the side, a shorthand gesture to indicate he's called in for assistance on the CB in his truck.

There's really nothing more to do. I can turn around or I can wait. I figure I might as well pass a little time with him as long as he's willing.

I look at his sandwich. I can't suppress a smile. It's one of the true abominations of American cuisine: fried egg on white bread, dripping with ketchup. It's exactly what the mailman used to eat every day for lunch. When I'd go with him on his route, we'd stop at his house about noon and he'd whip up a platter of greasy, inedible fried eggs, throw a loaf of Taystee bread and a bottle of ketchup on the table, and tell me to "fill 'er up." After weeks of making excuses, I finally managed to find a way to doctor the eggs sufficiently to get one sandwich down. Just the thought of that lunchtime routine and its inevitable cuisine was almost enough to keep me from accompanying him on his route. Now, I'm staring at the same accursed creation that used to cause me so much gastric consternation just a few miles down the road. I begin to wonder if it's a local specialty.

I tell the logger the story. He smiles and takes another bite. "Better with beer," he says.

The snow is still falling. I wonder if I really want to continue on this road, even if the slide is cleared. I figure I'll give it a few more minutes.

"This your truck?" I ask. I might as well keep the conversation going, and there's not a hauler alive who isn't happy to talk about his rig.

"Yeah. Bought it a year ago. I'd been living in Fresno. Horseshit. Didn't want my kids raised in that shit. Christ, gangs, you wouldn't believe it. No trees, either."

He begins a long rant on spics, niggers, and the deficiencies of the Central Valley. "Rather be poor here than rich there. What I make is mine. I got damn sick of paying for some prick's home in the Sierras. Now I just got to pay for the pricks in Washington."

I'm listening, but not attentively. My thoughts are on the weather. I'm scanning the forested hillsides, watching the line of the heavy snow descend, and trying to gauge the likelihood of this turning into a full-scale blizzard. He notices me looking around at the woods as he talks. I feel obligated to justify my inattention.

"That's a hell of a clear-cut," I say, pointing to a naked gash in the hillside. It's an innocent comment, more an observation than a judgment. But the very fact that I've noticed alerts him to a potential bias in me.

He stops eating his sandwich in mid-bite and fixes me with a hard look. I rush to clarify myself. "I could never understand the logic of clear-cutting. Seems to violate the natural processes of the forest." It's a calculated risk on my part, meeting the issue straight on. But the man seems intelligent enough, and I'm curious as to how he sees things.

He gives me a funny stare. I can't tell what it means. But when he responds, it's with an odd, aggressive sincerity, like a candidate answering an unfriendly question in a political forum.

"I'll tell you the logic," he says. "I'll tell you the logic. The logic is, if you were two hundred feet tall you wouldn't be talking like that."

It's an exceedingly strange response. At first I think he's joking. But there's no humor in his voice. He's not pulling my leg.

I let out a nervous laugh. "Well, I'm about a hundred and ninety-four feet short," I say, not knowing where else to go with this.

"Yeah, well, think about it." He's shifted to the edge of the step. This is an important issue to him. "Farmers grow wheat, corn, all that shit. They plant it, they cut it down, they plant it again. But nobody says a damn thing. 'Poor farmers. Just trying to make a living.' Loggers cut down trees, plant new ones, let them grow, cut them down again. Everyone's up our ass. What the hell's the difference?"

I give a simple shrug. It's not a question I want to touch. But he does.

"I'll tell you what the difference is. Tree takes longer to grow, and you're standing underneath them. If you was just an inch tall, standing under a stalk of corn, it'd look like a tree, and you'd be out hugging that fucking ear of corn. 'Save the corn.' But you don't give a shit about the corn. You're looking at it from the top. It's a crop. Tree's a crop, too. You're two hundred feet tall, you'd be looking out over these fucking trees, saying, 'Harvest them.' 'Poor loggers.' Instead you're saying, 'Stop it. You're clear-cutting.'"

I'm on very fragile footing, and I'm not pleased that he's turned my innocent comment into grounds for full-blown ideological warfare. But this man has really thought this through. Despite some gaping holes in his logic, I just want him to keep rolling. And I don't want to make him mad; I don't have forearms like bundles of ropes.

"I never thought of it that way," I say.

"That's the trouble," he says. "People don't think. Their heads are up their asses. All this shit about bio-fucking-diversity. You don't hear them saying that stuff to farmers. You think them fields would produce all wheat or corn on their own? Hell, no. But they talk about crop rotation, not bio-bullshit. Good forester, he understands crop rotation. It's all about time. A tree takes a long time to grow, longer than we live. A head of lettuce, or corn, that only takes a short time. They cut it down before any fucking tree hugger can fall in love with it. You don't see us fertilizing the shit out of the hillsides to get stuff to grow where it shouldn't. We're the ecologists. Why the fuck ain't you on the farmers?"

He's getting worked up. How did he get to seeing farmers as the enemy? But, more importantly, how did I end up in his crosshairs? I want to get out.

"Hey," I say. "I live with loggers and farmers in Minnesota. Everybody's getting screwed except the guys in suits." But he has no interest in going down this socialist roadway. He's after me.

"What kind of floors you got in your house?" he asks.

"Maple."

"Wood," he says, clarifying my answer to his own satisfaction. "What's the frame of your house?"

"I don't know."

"Two-by-fours. Two-by-sixes. Wood. What about the walls?"

"Plywood, I suppose."

"You suppose. It's wood," he says, pushing me to the place he wants me.

He's made his point, but he's not done. "How about the window frames?"

I give him the answer he wants. "Wood."

He gestures at me with his sandwich. "That's what I'm trying to say."

His manner is getting way too aggressive. "I see where you're coming from," I say.

But he's not to be deterred. He keeps coming forward.

"You think you're going to get that wood if I go out and kiss every fucking tree before I cut it down? You think if I go out and go, 'Oh, that one's too little, that one's too big, that one's too close to that other one, that one's got a fucking owl in it'—you think you're going to ever get your fucking two-by-fours to build your fucking house?"

I want out of this. No magic elixirs here. No little pamphlets to take home and read at my leisure. This has the potential for danger. The containment vessel is starting to leak.

He's looking at me, waiting for an answer. I've got to turn down the pressure.

"You make good sense. Too bad people don't listen to guys like you. They need to understand these things."

He tosses the crust of his sandwich across the road.

"You're fucking right they need to understand these things."

All thoughts of visiting the old homestead are dissipating. I'm in escape mode. This guy's got the same kind of anger as the guy with the gun butt in Washington. A world he neither understands or appreciates is closing in on him from all sides.

Just when I think things are about to reach the breaking point, we hear the sound we've all been waiting for. A truck is chugging its way up the road behind us in the other lane, carrying a front-end loader to remove the slide.

The arrival of the loader breaks the tension and changes the focus. The logger recedes to his good ole boy self. "Sorry," he says. "I get kind of worked up."

"You got good cause," I say. "You should go into politics."

"Fuck," he says, with a sheepish, self-conscious snort.

All around us people are starting their engines in anticipation of the slide being cleared.

"Nice talking to you," I say, and take a quick leave.

I walk hurriedly back through the slop toward the Tuna. I probably should have challenged the man, forced him to examine some of his presuppositions. But he had his tablets, and they were scribed deep. I wasn't going to change his mind.

I sit in the warmth of the Tuna, watching the flakes come down around me. I'm not feeling very good about myself. The cock has crowed three times. I am lukewarm. I deserve to be spit out.

EIGHT

ECHOES

The loader clears the slide in what seems like no time at all. Soon we see cars coming from the opposite direction, headlights on, wipers flapping. One by one, the cars in my line set off. Like it or not, I'm back on the road to the mailman and my old home in Bridge. I'm filled with trepidation. What will I find?

Bridge really never was much of a town, only a sign at a junction where our little side road emerged from the forested hills and hooked up with Highway 42. There was a bar, a store, and a large white consolidated schoolhouse. Nothing more.

The school ran from kindergarten through the eighth grade, drawing kids from the shacks and trailers and hillside cabins of several nearby valleys. After that, the students were bused to the high school in Myrtle Point fifteen miles down the highway. Many children never made it that far. The parents, distrustful of city influences, simply stopped their children's education when they were finished with the Bridge schoolhouse. Myrtle Point had a population of twenty-five hundred.

Will the school still be there? Will the store? Will it all have sunk back into the earth, like the ghost town at the end of the road that exists only on maps? Or will I find a strip mall or a convenience store selling bad pizzas up front and condoms in the rest rooms?

I pass Remote, my favorite named town in Oregon, and one of the most beautiful valleys in this coastal range. Bridge should be only a few miles ahead.

Soon I see it huddling in the distance. Nothing much seems to have changed. The schoolhouse is still here, though it looks as if it's no longer in use. The store still sits back from the highway on its dirt apron, though it has a more modern sign than I remember.

I park on the muddy dirt apron and walk toward the store. The scent of the fir is comforting; the soft earth feels familiar beneath my feet.

Once inside, the presence of the past overwhelms me. I remember the aisles, the racks, the counter spaces. I see the same open-topped wooden box where people used to place letters for the mailman to pick up.

The woman at the store pays no attention to me as I wander among the shelves of Fritos and Hamburger Helper and motor oil. Periodically, when I sense she's not looking, I sneak glances to see if I can remember her face through the changes of the years.

I can't. Either she is someone I never knew, or she has aged into someone I can no longer recognize. Though it's irrational, I'm hesitant to talk to her. I was so much the outsider when I lived here, so much the enemy.

But I must know.

"Say, I was just wondering," I begin. My words feel clumsy, like a hand reaching out for a handshake that will not be returned. "Is Don still the mailman around here?"

The woman looks at me with cold, indifferent eyes.

"I used to live up the road," I continue, trying to justify my curiosity. "The little house past the Gibbs place."

I'm saying too much. I can feel it. Does she remember the hippie who used to live in the rented cabin across the suspension bridge? Was she one of those who quit the route when I delivered it? Was it one of her brothers who dropped the rat in my holding tank?

She closes the shopper she's reading and surveys me flatly. "Don's dead. He died a few years ago."

It hits me like a shock wave. Why it never occurred to me that Don might be dead, I'll never know. I lived here twenty-five years ago. He was my age then; he would have been in his eighties now. But, somehow, in my memory he was like George—static, eternal, frozen in time. His booming voice and crew cut would be waiting for me. His blue Econoline would still be riding these roads, never missing a day, never losing a letter.

"How did he die?" I want to ask. I want to know everything, everything I should have known, everything I should have asked. Did his wife come back? Did he ever get to hold his children again? Did he keep the route? Did he die happy?

But her palpable indifference to my presence stops me. I'm left with the stark, simple, unadorned knowledge: "Don died a few years ago."

He had been like a father to me at a time when I could not reach out to my own father. And I hadn't cared enough even to find out if he was still alive. I'm filled with an unassuageable shame. I feel like the son who left home and never bothered to write.

My God, he was a mailman. I could have sent him a postcard. It would have gone right to him. He would have started his morning sort, and there it would have been, right in his hands. It would have made his morning, made his day, made him swell with pride. He could have showed it to the other postal workers, shown them that he was important in somebody's life. But I was too busy to write.

I'm desperate to talk, but there's no way to open the conversation. She has not brightened at my familiarity with the community or my interest in Don. If she remembers me at all, she doesn't let on. To her, I'm just a prying intruder. She wants nothing more from me; I'll get nothing more from her.

I give her a hollow smile and wander among the few rows of shelves, picking a box of raisins here, a bag of chips there, trying to appear casual, as if this were a normal shopping stop on my travels and not a journey up the dead-end roads of my past.

Once up at the counter I'm tempted to try one last time. But she's ringing up my purchases without speaking to me or looking at me. There is nothing more to be said.

I pay for my purchases and prepare to leave. As I head to the door I notice a rack of picture postcards on a carousel half hidden behind a stack of newspapers. A feeling comes across me. I want something to prove that I was ever at this place.

I grab a card at random. It's a generic "trees and log truck" shot of the kind that's sold at truck stops all up and down the Pacific Northwest coast.

"I'll take this, too," I say. "Do you still sell stamps?"

The woman stares, clearly violated by my knowledge of her store's business practices.

She tears a stamp off a little roll she keeps in a drawer and watches as I place it on the corner of the card.

"Pickup still in the afternoon?" I ask.

"Three," she answers. She'll spare no extra words on me.

I can't help myself. "Who has the route now?" I say.

She doesn't respond.

I take a pen from my jacket pocket, scribble a note, address the card to home, and slip it into the same wooden box that was being used to receive outgoing mail when I lived here those many years ago.

I walk out into the grey afternoon. The atmosphere is hovering between mist and drizzle. I can feel the woman staring at me as I leave.

I drive through the muddy parking area to the junction. My turn signal clicks in time with the windshield wipers as I sit at that same corner where the mailman and I parted almost thirty years before. With a sense of foreboding in my heart, I turn left onto the road and begin the seven-mile drive to my old home.

I drive slowly down the twisting roadway into the fog-laden valley, haunted by the almost unbearable tension between the forgotten and the familiar. It's the little things, the common things, that surprise me—the road turning from tar to gravel, a certain curve, the angle of a particular hill, the rusted carcass of a pickup that has not entered my

memory since the day I left. These are the things that formed the texture of my daily experience and made this place home, and I had forgotten them all. Now they come rushing back, a cataract of images
and feelings, branching off into memories and shapeless yearnings.

This is who I was. This is where I lived.

I don't know what I'm doing here. I don't know who I am here, or
why I've come. All I know is that I'm after something that will tie this
past to my present.

How long the road seems, how deep the valley. The same houses
that seemed so poor and honorable those many years ago now look no
different than the rude shacks that so defeat me when I see them overtaking the landscape around my northern Minnesota home.

Did I romanticize poverty then, or did I appreciate it more because
I was a part of it and understood its struggles better? And is this the
same thing that causes me to remember Oregon loggers as noble,
while seeing their Minnesota equivalents as brutal and crude?

What am I to do with these things? My memory is but a flickering
light in a dark room of possibilities.

Soon I come upon the curve that precedes my old home. Almost
thirty years it's been. What will I find?

The Gibbs house still stands on the edge of the road, owned now
by whom? Old pickups and cars and trailers covered with tarps fill
every open space. Piles of wood and pieces of heavy machinery litter
the property. Even if the owners have changed, the vision has not. Life
is still understood as the accumulation of large, half-operational
objects dedicated to cutting, chopping, and hauling. The whole place
reeks of poverty and despair.

Just past the Gibbs place is the pulloff where I had to park to walk
across the suspension bridge to my house. I can hardly look at the
mailbox that announces its presence. No cars are parked in the area,
so I get out and walk toward the narrow, swaying suspension bridge.
The cables that support it are still wrapped around the same trees and
have dug ever deeper into their trunks. The bridge appears not to
have been updated in any fashion. It still is made of thick planks laid

side by side on a framework of cable, and the planks seem as grey and rotted as they did when I used to walk across them to get the mail.

I look once toward the Gibbs place to see if I'm being observed. Though there are cars and trucks everywhere, there is no sign of movement. I decide to cross and look at the old cabin.

Step by step I make my way along the boards, balancing myself when necessary with the support cables that are strung at waist height on either side of the planking. The bridge bounces and sways, setting up a rhythm that is both familiar and unnerving.

As I approach the other side, I see the cabin. It has been updated, made almost cute. The old rough-cut siding has been replaced by cedar shakes. The bare windows have been framed in with red shutters and now are graced with curtains. Along the front of the house the weeds have been pulled, and succulent plants have been added to form a border. Wood chips have been strewn in curving arcs to create pathways through the grass.

The old barn, where I had spent my days futilely trying to coax a meaningful sculpture out of a block of myrtle, is gone, replaced by a small camping trailer. How did they get that over here?

Behind the house, in the field that backs up against the towering hillside, someone has planted a stand of pine. They seem small and domestic against the thick, dark Douglas fir.

The place feels as if it's tended by a woman's hand; there is a care to the placements and plantings that runs contrary to everything that men around here hold dear. This little cabin is now in the hands of a creator, not a user or a destroyer.

I feel ashamed for the rawness of the life I lived when I was here. I improved nothing, maintained nothing, valued nothing beyond my own ill-formed dreams. I want to skulk away, leaving no trace. This person, these people, are better than I was; they care more than I. The house, with its domestic order, passes judgment on me. If it had a voice, it would scold me. I hurry back across the bridge and head farther up the valley toward the mailman's old homestead. I remember that the valley widened as it approached his house, and this proves to be the case. The hills spread out, leaving pastures at their base. The creek becomes a curving oxbow running through a deep green valley. Large rock outcroppings stick up from the ground, and sheep graze on the hillsides. Mists linger near the hilltops, which are still dark with great stands of fir. I remember the mailman standing on his porch, looking out over this, saying, "It's got to be the most beautiful place in the world." And, in truth, he wasn't far wrong.

I scan the promontories for a cemetery that was supposed to be far up on one of the hillsides. The mailman had pointed it out to me once or twice. Even then, I could never see it, and I had only pretended to take notice as he spoke. Now I wish I could find it. I know he would have wanted to be buried there. But that, too, is lost to me.

Ahead I see the driveway to his home. I can't even recognize the house, but I remember the curve of the drive as it turned upward from the main gravel road.

The house has been poorly painted; I remember it as wood. The shed where he kept his tools has had a lean-to added, and is taken up by bales of hay and a car with a canvas tarp over its hood. Junk vehicles litter the property. Weeds have overtaken everything.

I don't remember it like this. I remember it as the closest thing to a domestic reality I knew while I was here—well-kept and orderly, though with the rawness of man smell over it all. The mailman had once told me that he kept it as best he could, so when his wife came back, she would find it as she had left it.

No wife has come back to this. All I feel as I look at the property is brutishness and ignorance. Its greatest concession to culture and order is a massive white satellite dish staring skyward from a patch of weeds behind the barn.

I'm tempted to go up, to knock on the door, to find out what has happened. I want to know when the mailman died, who was at his funeral, who took his route, where he was buried. I want to peer into the kitchen where he fried those eggs for us at lunch; I want to see the chopping block where he killed the chickens that time he tried to prepare an Easter meal for me and some of my friends. I want all of this, and more. I want everything.

I want to say good-bye.

But I can't. I can't even bring myself to go up the driveway. Instead, I drive slowly along the line of his property. I see his mailbox, bent over, battered, uncared for. It almost makes me weep.

I can't take it anymore. I want to flee from this valley. But I can't leave this way. I must do something. So I stop the car and step out on the side of the road. There's no movement anywhere; no one will see me. I go over to the ditch at the very corner of the property. I bend down, and with my hands, scrape away the weeds and rocks until I get to pure dark soil. I scoop up a handful and put it into an envelope I found in the glove box.

I run back to the car hiding the envelope under my coat, like a man who has just stolen something of value. Once in the privacy of the driver's seat, I wrap the envelope with a rubber band and place it on the seat beside me.

I think of Chief Joseph, the Nez Perce chief who was driven from his homeland in the Wallowa Valley several hundred miles from here. "A man who would not love his father's grave is worse than a wild animal," he said. The mailman was not my father, and this is not his grave. But I know what Joseph meant, and this is close enough.

I need to talk to Louise and Nick. I need it badly. This day has somehow gone severely awry. I've lost my past. I have no courage. My willingness to listen to the points of view of others feels like tepid compromise rather than wisdom. I've betrayed yet another father.

I should be back with my family, binding us ever closer, rather than wandering through memories in a distant, indifferent land. But I'm driving through drizzle on roads that no longer know me, talking to people whose lives have passed me by, calling out to ghosts who have long since fled.

I really can't go home again. I never should have tried.

The phone rings once, twice, three times. Please, answer. One more, and the machine will come on. They should be home by now.

On the fourth ring, the receiver is picked up.

"Hello?" It's Nick's voice. Why is he answering? He usually leaves it for Louise. Has he been waiting for my call?

"Hey, Nick," I say. "It's Dad. How're things going?"

"Dad, what are those Pinocchios you're talking about?"

I'd forgotten my message. Clearly he hadn't. This is a relief. It pulls me away from my aching loneliness and feelings of betrayal.

I explain about George. "He named all his sculptures after a woman, and she didn't like it. She said he was using them to make her nervous."

"You mean, like 'stalking'?" Elementary-school sensitivity training must be having some effect.

"Yeah, kind of."

"What do they look like?"

I describe the sculptures.

"They sound cool."

"They are."

"Do they have motors on them?"

"No."

"Well, how can they be stalking anyone?"

Ah, the blessed literalism of the child. Eugene should consider making him mayor for a day.

"It's the idea," I say.

"That's stupid," he answers.

"I think so," I agree.

It's a good conversation, and just the tonic I need. He's so close to the world, so little affected by memories and ghosts and abstract ideologies. I want nothing more than to be brought up from the hollow spaces where my heart is now residing, and his young voice is my ladder to the sun.

I look out at the darkening hills surrounding me. They've grown taller, tighter, as I've driven south. I feel enveloped by wistful distances. This is not just me getting in touch with memories; this is me getting in touch with the land itself. It's quiet, meditative, sometimes clear, sometimes misty, but always with an underlying cast of blue. No wonder these people got strong; no wonder they looked inward rather than outward, and kept their feelings shrouded and their hearts hidden far from view.

Nick's clear, winter brightness reflects like the sun on fresh snow. I want to climb up to meet him, not pull him into these blue distances.

"So, how's that Shackleton project coming?" I ask. It should be the easiest way to get him talking. There's a long pause on the line. Anyone else would break in and fill the silence with words. But I know better. Nick is an odd duck. He's deep, not quick. Sometimes I think he's picked up some Ojibwe traits from the drinking water around our home: he remains silent until he has formulated his answer, never revealing the process of his thought, only the product. This can make for excruciating conversations full of inconceivable pauses while he weighs the accuracy and sufficiency of his response. This is one of those pauses.

Finally, he answers. "Well, I think it's going very well."

I haven't any idea what went into that assessment, but it's not a sufficient answer to fill the void in the heart of a dad who's sitting at a drive-up phone two thousand miles away in the rain.

"So, what makes him heroic?"

I know it's a teacherlike question, but in teacherlike fashion I've learned I need to give him open-ended questions if I expect more than one-word answers.

"Well . . . he cared about other people."

"Tell me some things he did."

"Well . . ." He pauses to gather his thoughts. "There was this guy who wasn't very good at anything, so Shackleton didn't bring him along. But he snuck on board anyway in one of the crates, and when he came out everyone got really mad at him, and they were going to toss him over-board. But Shackleton asked him more about his life and what his jobs were and why he wanted to come with them. It turned out he was an offi-cial custodian, so they made him the janitor and he cleaned up the ship."

I can hear the wheels spinning, see the paragraphs being parsed for the topic sentences and main points.

"Shackleton sounds like a very kind and reasonable man," I say.

Nick likes this assessment. He brightens. "He was. He always put everyone else before him. If there wasn't enough food for one person, he'd be that person. He'd let everyone else have their fair share of food and he'd take as little as possible. He never tried to leave anyone behind. One time a man fell overboard, and he dove in after him. If there was ever any conflict on the ship, he always had some way up his sleeve to solve it."

"He really was a hero," I say.

"I think so," Nick responds.

We talk a bit more. I can feel the conversation winding down. "Well, why don't you let me talk to Mom for a minute."

"She's at some meeting," he says. "For school. She said she figured you'd call while she was gone." I'm disappointed. I'm really missing my wife.

"I'll call back in a bit," I say.

"That's okay," he tells me. "She said if you called to say you should call her tomorrow at work. She doesn't have classes from ten to noon."

"It's a deal," I promise.

We cover a few other subjects—the behavior of the cats, the social events in his life. It's hard to hang up; I wish Louise were there. But a car has pulled up directly behind me and is waiting for the phone. I say my good-byes and tell Nick I love him.

"Bye, Dad," he says. "I miss you."

I drive away, seeing his face before me and thinking about Shackleton. "He cared about other people. . . . He always put everyone else before him."

Is that what a hero is? And what does that make me, his father, as I drive alone down a rain-slicked highway, seeking answers to private questions a half a continent away from home?

It's long past midnight, now. White-line fever has taken hold.

I push the radio knob, chasing from station to station. The signals rise and fade. Portland, Sacramento, Boise, Los Angeles—voices crackling at me over unseen distances.

I should have stopped at Grants Pass. I'm tired. But this is too delicious. I'm once again the small boy under the covers with the black radio, the young man driving through the star-filled prairie night.

The dashboard lights glow white before me. The motor hums, the stations grab, hold, then disappear into the distant dark. Classical music from Reno. A talk show from San Francisco. Voices, music—fading in, fading out.

Images of George and the mailman and the eggman logger and the store woman rise and fall in my mind. They're like these stations—floating in from their private worlds, forming, congealing, blending into each other, then disappearing into the night.

I should have challenged George and the eggman—told George that Amy had a point, told the eggman that he was tilting at the wrong windmill. But I guess, when all is said and done, I just wave God's sandal in the air. I'll never hit another person with it.

Maybe that's why I no longer belong here. This is a world of true believers, and the only thing I believe in enough to fight for is the truth of the flawed human heart.

That's why I loved the mailman. He understood that truth, and he recognized it in himself even as he recognized it in me. When he saw that lonely young face staring at him from that cabin window, he saw himself. He didn't hate me for who I was; he saw me for who I was—a scared, confused, earnest young man with dreams both adamant and inchoate. I was someone he had to protect and help, not someone he had to convert.

My mind is moving fluidly, grabbing nothing, holding nothing. A snippet of George, a snatch of the logger, a long, low legato of the mailman. It's almost stream of consciousness—intellectual fuzziness seeking a moment of clarity.

Up the hills, around the curves. The car settles down upon itself as I push the accelerator. It grabs at the road; a tiger at full lope, breathing easily. God, how I love this. I must have leapt in the womb when my parents went on drives through the night.

My headlights catch the edge of forest. Not far ahead are the Siskiyous, that last barrier before the long free fall into California. But I don't care. There is no time, no distance; only here, only now, only the lights and the road and the engine and the radio.

How lucky I was tonight. The call to Nick could have gone so wrong. Love can measure the distance, or it can close the gap and warm the heart. Tonight the dice rolled in my favor. How sweet. How sweet.

The great fade is beginning to wash over me. Sleep is drifting down like stardust. I would love to drive till dawn, seeing Nick in my mind, dreaming of holding Louise in this precious night, hearing the eggman, the mailman, and George and Shackleton call out from their muted distances.

But I can feel the pull.

Down, down, gently into sleep. Headlights fanning out like cones in the darkness. So many trees, so many trees.

I'd better stop. I'm getting too tired.

Ahead, I see a sign. "Lodgings. 1 Mile."

I pull off, drive along a winding road through a tunnel of towering Douglas fir. A small, flickering neon "motel" sign glows in the distance. Run-down cabins sit back among the trees; a house with an "office" sign stands apart on a hill.

I walk up and peer in through the calico curtains pulled shut over the window in the kitchen door. Piles of newspapers and brown paper shopping bags full of pizza boxes and beer bottles litter the floor. A rottweiler's nose nudges the curtain, causing me to jump.

A sign above the door says, "Please knock." I rap several times.

"I'm coming, I'm coming," slurs a voice. There is shuffling and movement. The rottweiler mewls and whines. The door opens. A pie-eyed woman with greasy hair stands before me. A reek of urine wafts across, along with the stench of rancid grease. The rottweiler noses at my pants cuff.

"Do you have a vacancy?"

"Hunnerd dollars," she says.

I get back in my car.

I drive toward Medford. My vision is starting to blur. I feel that urge to close my eyes "just for a second." My lids slide downward—an extended blink, really—no more. But it shocks me. I jerk upright. I must find a place to stop; I'm losing hold.

Medford, thirty miles, then fifteen, then ten.

The lights of the city appear before me, a nighttime dream. I take the first exit, not caring where I am.

A motel "vacancy" sign emerges from the mist. I pull in and stumble out, leaving the car running. The first blast of rainy night air shocks me. I shake my head in an attempt to give movement to my thoughts and focus to my eyes.

A sign on the door says, "Please use check-in window. Lobby opens again at 7 AM."

I push a buzzer. A woman with a kindly face emerges from a back room. She's wearing a blue bathrobe and tying up her hair.

She says something to me, but her intercom isn't working. I can barely hear her through the thick, bulletproof glass. She looks warmly at me, like a mother welcoming home a tired child. But the barrier between us mutes our voices and thwarts our effort at human contact.

We're almost yelling. It's an absurd situation. She doesn't want to wake her sleeping family; I don't want to be shouting under an over-lit carport in the rainy dark of an Oregon night.

We share a sheepish grin. This is not the way either of us would have it.

It's a code, this sharing of shrugs. "I see you're okay," hers says, "But I can't let you in. I'm sorry you have to stand out there in the cold."

"I understand," mine responds, "You don't have to apologize." I feel a spasm of Midwestern guilt. I almost shout, "I'm sorry to bother you," but the sound would be a violation of the darkness and the hour.

She tries to direct me to a room, but I can't hear her. She has to write the number on a piece of paper and hold it up to the glass.

I slip her my credit card through a little slot. She runs it through a machine, smiling sympathetically. Our interaction has been reduced to a sequential handling of this small plastic object.

The machine will not accept my card. There's some kind of computer glitch. The woman mouths the word, "Cash?" I check my billfold: thirteen dollars. She smiles and shrugs. I nod and smile. I get back in my car.

Further into the sleepless night. Another sign: "Motel. American Owned." There's anger in the message—anger and fear. Something from the outside is coming in, disrupting, breaking into the dream.

"Night intercom. Press Button. Wait for reply."

I do as I'm commanded. A voice comes on, tired and irritated. A surly man emerges and hands me a key through a slot. "It's all I got. Go see if you want it."

I walk across the rain-slicked pavement and put the key in the door. From the next room I hear drunken shouts and breaking glass. A television is blaring at full blast.

I go back to the window. "The people in the next unit . . ."

He cuts me off short. "Do you want it or not?"

"No, I guess not," I say, and slip the key back through the slot.

"Suit yourself," he says, and turns away.

I'm so tired I'm close to tears. I get back in my car and head off into the darkness.

Suddenly, the night seems different. The cars seem to be following. The darkness feels menacing rather than peaceful.

The signals are changing. St. Helens, the Gorge, are fading. California, big city, are coming in strong.

NINE

TOWARD THE LIGHT

The light shafts in through a grimy window; it must be morning. I have a hazy recollection of a man with tattoos and a ponytail emerging from behind a curtain, of a TV blaring and the smell of frying hamburger.

The room stinks of mildew and stale air. The heater is banging and clanking. On the wall across from me is a painting of two horses running through a storm. A white one is outlined against a dark storm cloud. A black one emerges into the plains daylight. Their manes and tails flow like the wind.

I get up and look around. The shower stall is a cubicle walled off from the rest of the bathroom by a cement-block partition that has been partially covered with tiles. In the shower there is a space that was once a window, but it has been filled in with glass blocks. Silver duct tape forms the seal around the edges.

The shower head is at chest height. The plumbing rattles and groans whenever anyone in another room runs a faucet or flushes a toilet. The mirror over the dresser is a grotesque, ornate Louis XIV knock-off.

There's a TV in the corner on a round pressboard table. One of the rabbit ears is broken off. On the table by the door stands a vase of plastic flowers—daisies, petunias, lilies of the valley.

The wallpaper is peeling; this is the third or fourth layer. It's a crisscross pattern, wheat on a cream background, with a rose in the center of each diamond. This once must have been a family motel; these are a grandmother's sensibilities.

I lie back down and allow my eye to move around the room, examining each detail. There's love encrusted with neglect here. This is a place that once was someone's dream, maintained and decorated with pride, and now is nothing more than a series of rooms rented out to the lonely lost who happen to land here, as I did, by the accident of road-weariness.

I dress quickly and step out into a valley surrounded by forested hills. A deep rain must have passed over last night. The earth gives off a scent of freshness that mingles with the crisp ocean air that has drifted across the coastal range on the fog. It's intoxicating and sweet.

I'm the only car in the lot. If there were other guests, they must already have left. Since there's no one around, I turn on the Tuna and shove an old Bob Dylan tape into the cassette deck to keep me company while I load the trunk. His nasal twang fills the morning air.

> *You've been with the professors, and they've all liked your looks.*
> *With great lawyers you have discussed lepers and crooks.*

I sing along as I retrieve my random belongings from the motel room.

> *But something is happening here, and you don't know what it is,*
> *Do you, Mr. Jones?*

Bob Dylan is not usually my morning type of music, and I'm not quite sure why I'm playing him right now. But the cryptic lyrics and bluesy organ seem right for the day.

I'm sure some of it is a residue from last night in Medford. Something was happening right toward the end, and I didn't know what it was. I felt the whole timbre of my journey changing. Medford didn't have the comforting presence of other southern Oregon towns. It felt aggressive and brash, a sea of neon spilling over the night, laughing and leering like the drunks in the motel room: "You don't like me? Suit yourself. It's not my problem."

My journey had suddenly become charged with an air of implied threat. People were imprisoned in glass boxes for their own protection; signs expressed a xenophobic rage about outsiders. Common civility was outshouted by loutish selfishness.

I know I was tired—too tired—and one should never trust emotions born of exhaustion. But my basic instincts were intact. Darkness was no longer a source of nourishment and peace; instead, it was a hiding place for unseen dangers. The world was made up of partitions and doors. There was a hostility in so many voices. When I hopped in my car, it no longer felt like a magic carpet floating through the landscape; it was a protective capsule hurtling me through alien space. Truly, something was happening, and I didn't know what it was.

But now that's all behind me. Now I'm just a man looking at a map trying to figure out where he is.

I know I'm somewhere between Grants Pass and Medford. I'm staring down the barrel of that thing called California. By nightfall I'll be far across the border. Oregon and Washington will be distant memories.

California is such a puzzle to me. It's a little bit of everything, yet it's a thing unto itself. Susanville has almost nothing in common with San Diego, or Crescent City with El Centro. They're separated by miles and mountains and a hundred cultural divides. Yet something about them each is distinctly Californian.

It's one of those psychic conundrums that confounds the square corners of our intellect, like "What constitutes medieval?" or "What differentiates French Gothic from German Gothic?" You can come up with denotative answers and little checklists, but they never get to the heart of the matter. There simply are distinctions and affinities in life that can only be recognized at a distance and can never be adequately explained. "California-ness" is one of them.

Most Californians I know would dispute this. They'd say I paint with too broad a brush. They'd point to differences between the North and the South, or the L.A. people and the San Francisco people, or the different ethnic groups, or even the residents of Noe Valley and the residents of the Sunset. And they'd be right. But from the distance of New York, or Greenland, or Paris, or Minnesota, Californians all seem to be cut from a common cloth. It has something to do with hopefulness and a willingness to believe in consciousness rather than history as a motive force of human development; a greater faith in the future than responsibility to the past.

When I try to articulate reasons for this, I come up with half-formed ideas like, "Living with the sea to your west puts a sense of infinite yearning at the end of each of your days," or, "They've reached the end of hope and are at the beginning of dream." And such ideas have a certain validity. But, in the end, I'm left with a geopsychic equivalent of the famous Supreme Court answer about pornography. I don't know what "California-ness" is, but I know it when I see it.

The freeway signs tell me I'm approaching Ashland. This is the last stop before I cross the Siskiyou range and catapult down into the other color and other energy that is the "Golden State."

The night has been cold; as I approach, I see that the hilltops are frosted with snow. But down here where I'm driving, orchards sit canted on the hillsides, marking the whole valley with a fecund and hopeful geometry. I feel as if I'm in a Pacific Northwest Grant Wood painting.

I've never paid much attention to Ashland. My various trips between Oregon and the Bay Area were always timed so that Ashland was an inconvenient stopping point. Either I had just climbed the Siskiyous and was roller-coaster giddy to get farther into Oregon, or I was on my way to California, and the looming presence of the Siskiyous represented the barrier I needed to cross before I could exhale and settle into a true "freeway-flier" mode. Either way, Ashland was just a nod and a wave on the side of the road.

In a sense, it's a pity. She's a sweet little town with a college and a world-famous Shakespeare festival. She has always seemed to mix an intellectual civility and an honest logger and lumber heritage. And her proximity to California gives her something of a "border-town" or "gateway" feel, which I always find delicious. Depending on one's mood or bias, she represents a blending of the best of California expansiveness and Oregon introspection, or the first encroachment of that indefinable, banal electric buzz that spreads out from the epicenters of San Francisco and L.A. and threatens to take over the coast, the country, the rest of the world.

But the great magnetic pull of California is tugging on me. I only want to stop long enough to get something to eat. My desire to hurry is amplified by the ominous line of mist that has descended over the tops of the Siskiyous ahead of me. From down here, it's nothing more than an arbitrary visual demarcation. But past experience tells me that, once across that line, the road is gradually disappearing into a soupy fog of snow and sleet. When it gets bad enough, the pass will be closed. If I want to make California, I've got to beat this descending storm.

I should probably make a run for it, but prudence dictates a quick meal and a bit of information. Forewarned is forearmed, and, as I've discovered, I'm no longer a pro at winter mountain roads.

I stop at a gas station and ask the attendant for a restaurant "with a little character." He makes a strange gesture with his lips and directs me to a cafe further up the hill. "You'd probably like it there," he says from beneath his checked wool cap. I'm not sure exactly what he means.

As I get to the restaurant parking lot, I understand. It's a hip kind of half roadhouse, half "redwood and fern" cafe. It walks the same fine line between Shakespeare and chain saws that all of Ashland seems to navigate.

I step forth from the Tuna into air of infinite complexity. The dry, icy breath of a mountain winter commingles with the rich liquid chill of the fog from the Pacific. It's the atmospheric equivalent of some exotic Thai or Moroccan dish that uses unknown spices in unexpected combinations.

I inhale deeply. My lungs expand; my spirit lifts. It's almost enough to make me reconsider the rantings of a group of people I once met—"Breatheairians" they called themselves—who determined that food is unnecessary because all the nutrients one needs are contained in the air. It was a great theory, but few people remained adherents for long.

I devote a few minutes to deep inhalations and exhalations. It doesn't quite convert me to "Breatheairianism," but it does remind me that the yogis are right. There's health approaching holiness in this air.

As I cross the parking lot, the scents from inside the restaurant begin to seduce me. Rich coffee aroma wafts out the door in combination with cinnamon and rosemary and a host of spices I can't identify. It draws me in like a cozy hearth fire.

Once inside, I feel completely at home. People are laughing and talking in a relaxed, working-man's fashion. Except for one booming, discordant voice, there's a good humor and literate civility to the conversational sound. A sinuous instrumental track, with ouds and tablas and a haunting soprano descant, is coming through a series of speakers placed strategically around the room. Waiters in jeans and T-shirts walk by with bowls of fruit and yogurt garnished with sprigs of parsley and other greenery.

I take a seat and survey the menu. It contains the usual eggs and pancakes and other truck-stop fare, but also features multigrain waffles, homemade breads, and tofu scrambles. I order brown rice and vegetables sautéed in olive oil, with seven-grain bread and a glass of freshly squeezed orange juice. It's not so much that it sounds irresistible as the fact that it exists at all. I want to make a stand, in my own way, against the part of me that has gone the way of greasy hash browns and kitchen-sink omelets.

My waiter is a happy, bearded hail-fellow-well-met who wears a plaid flannel shirt and a down vest. He pours me a mug of coffee so dark and strong I can't see the bottom of the cup.

"You have a sense of this weather?" I ask him. "I'm trying to make the pass."

He peers out the window. "I could guess. But you should probably talk to a bigger liar than I am," he says, directing me to a burly bearded man who's sitting at a far table laughing and conversing with several other men. "That's your guy."

The man is booming and thundering; he's obviously the source of the discordant sound I heard when I walked in. I take my mug of coffee and walk toward the group. As I approach I hear one of the men saying, ". . . slippery motherfucker. Damn near took out the guard-rail."

I can see they're all in good spirits. I tell the booming bearded man that he was designated by the waiter as the biggest liar in the place and, thus, the most qualified to counsel a tenderfoot traveler on whether or not to attempt the pass.

He roars with laughter like some big Klondike Mike and shoves a chair in my direction.

"Sit down," he hollers, clapping me on the shoulder. "Where the hell you from?"

"Minnesota," I say.

"Good," he roars. "Then I can tell the truth. If you was from California, I'd send you off into that stuff. Maybe you'd make it. Maybe you wouldn't. Either way we'd come out ahead."

The others join in his revelry. "Hey," one of them says, "I'm from Orange County."

Big Mike claps me hard on the forearm. "See what I mean?"

They're a boisterous bunch, this breakfast crew, made almost giddy by this first taste of winter. They remind me of kids who have been let out of school because of the weather. I'd like to stay with them for a while, but I really need to know if I can get through the pass. The Siskiyous are not so intimidating as the Cascades, but they're mountains, nonetheless.

"Would you try it?" I ask the man to my left. He's been fairly quiet and seems likely to take my question seriously.

He senses my concern. "You got chains?" he asks.

"No. It's a rental car."

This is a source of great sport to Mike. He butts in before the other man can answer.

"A rental car? What the hell? You a traveling salesman . . . knock up some farmer's daughter?"

I take a chance. "Nope. I prefer loggers' wives."

One of the other men jumps on this. He turns to Mike. "So that's the reason your old lady's got that smile on her face."

Mike pounds the table in laughter. "Hey. I'm the reason your old lady smiles at all."

The ribaldry is growing, as is the mist on the hills outside the window. The peaks are now almost completely shrouded in clouds. I peer out at the shifting sky. Here and there patches of blue emerge, only to disappear almost immediately into the drifting, moiling fog.

The men wind down their discussion of wives and begin a discussion about the merits of attempting the pass.

"Shit," says one. "As long as it's open, it's open. I'd make a run for it."

"Don't try it," says another. "If they don't get her open all the way, you could be stuck up there for hours. I've set up there a whole damn afternoon till the storm broke and they cleared the road."

I nod gravely, all the while watching the shifting clouds outside the window.

The conversation goes on, driven by anecdotes and opinions and war stories about successful and unsuccessful winter crossings. Big Mike has just launched into a monologue about the time he went all the way down the other side by memory during a whiteout, when, unexpectedly, the swirling clouds outside our window part, the sky opens, and a shaft of sunlight bursts in and illuminates the table where we're sitting.

Without thinking, I blurt, "Ah. What light from yonder window breaks?" It's one of those stupid comments for which I'm well known among my friends: opaque, situationally inappropriate, and too clever by half.

Immediately, I feel my cheeks flush. What am I doing? Entertaining myself with my cartoon knowledge of Shakespeare? Making some Dylanesque non sequitur in search of meaning? I have this image of Lyndon Johnson snarling about Hubert Humphrey and saying, "It must be something in the water in Minnesota. They don't know how to keep their mouths shut." I cringe inwardly, waiting for the looks of confusion or disgust that Big Mike and his cronies will surely rain down upon me.

But Big Mike looks up and, without missing a beat, responds, "It's the east, tenderfoot, and you'd better get your ass through that pass while the gettin's still good."

All the men laugh. I smile stupidly, like a man who's just walked into his own surprise party. I raise my coffee cup to the men and head back to my table.

I sneak a look back at Big Mike. He's once again laughing and booming and pounding the table. Lumberjack Shakespeare: it's almost enough to make me set up camp and stay here. But it's time to go; my wheels are already turning.

I'm ready to head south, and California is the sun.

The highway is a flurry of activity. Signs flash: "Be Prepared to Stop." "Chain-up Area Ahead." Eighteen-wheelers are pulled over along the side of the road, warning lights flashing, while men in quilted shirts and Carhartt overalls struggle to hook snow chains around their four-foot-tall tires. A sequence of lights from a caution sign is blinking in the distance.

I turn on the radio. Storms are everywhere. Passes are closed; roads are washed out. On the coast, at Port Orford, winds have reached eighty miles per hour.

A car comes toward me covered in snow. Its lights are on and its windshield wipers are flapping. Globs of slush slide roofward across its windshield and spin off into the morning air.

I glance around. Down here there's no sign of snow. In fact, patches of blue are starting to creep through the grey, turbulent sky.

But, farther up the hillside I can see the telltale line of mist that shrouds the hilltops and hides them from view. There's no reprieve at those higher altitudes. Winter is descending with a vengeance and a fury.

I cautiously begin my ascent. For a few miles, everything is fine. Then the sky darkens; the mist increases. The fine spray turns rapidly to a heavy sleet. The roadway becomes slick and glazed. The sleet thickens, and I lose all visibility. My headlights are dim shafts cutting through slashing lines of snow. The entire road has disappeared.

I shut off the radio and try to decelerate. The car goes into a sideways spin.

Panic overcomes me. From the opposite direction a hazy light approaches. It moves quickly, becomes two headlights, then shoots past, spraying slop and snow across the roadway.

I realize I'm in over my head. I don't know this road; I don't know how far the pass is; I don't have chains.

I make the only choice I can. I turn around.

Ever so gingerly I creep back through the swirling whiteness, following the fading tire tracks on the roadway. I can see no more than ten feet ahead of me.

I travel at a glacial pace. There's tension in my hands and arms. I'm gripping the wheel with an involuntary desperation, as if the tightness of my grip will translate into traction on the road.

Within seconds the snow decreases to mist. Piles of wet snow slide off my fenders and windshield. The mist lessens, the clouds part. Ashland reappears, as if through a dream.

The roadway descends. As I round a curve, I can see the line of mist hovering above me. The asphalt is wet and slick, but the sky has broken and the snow is gone. It seems impossible. Moments ago I was in fear for my life. Now I'm on open highway, heading northward, with clearing sky overhead.

I shoot past Ashland, which now glistens, freshly washed, on the hillsides. On the far side of the highway I see the cars and trucks hooking up chains. The line of mist still caps the tops of the hills. Above the valley, the sky is breaking forth in blue.

I check my map and see that the cutover road to the coast is only a few miles back, at Grants Pass. I head back north, intent upon catching it. Soon I'm traveling through rolling snowless hills and orchard-laden valleys. It seems impossible that only miles away there are drivers stuck in a blizzard, in danger for their lives. The distance measured in time is only twenty minutes, but we're worlds apart.

The sun breaks out and dapples the forested hills. I let out a victorious laugh. This is the West Coast at its best and most seductive. I don't have to endure; I can change directions. A few steps backward and I can allemande around a mountain.

Transformation, not perseverance: that's the lightness that I feel. Like the movement from rain to snow and back to sun, it's possible to move effortlessly from one consciousness, one identity, to another. No need to plod mindlessly on a road just because someone has given it to you. Find the right path, the one that works for you.

In some ways it all makes sense: transformation masks, people changing their names, changing their partners, changing their lives daily, weekly; not fighting against an inevitability that stretches in a straight line ahead of them, but seeking the moment of clarity and insight in which a new and better path becomes clear. Even the geography and the climate are freeing me up from the idea of progress, replacing it with a faith in epiphany, apocalypse, metamorphosis.

After all, this is the land of the discovery of gold, of the monstrous shudders of earthquakes—events that alter, in a moment and forever, the psychic terrain on which one lives. It's a world where magical change is possible.

How far this is from my Midwestern life. There we wage trench warfare against adversity and measure our progress in increments and generations. The West Coast's easy willingness to slough off old skins and re-create the self more in the image of our dreams seems a child's fantasy, a playing at the game of life. But here, where one can go from the heaviness of rain to the ethereal lightness of snow in the twinkling of an eye, where the anxiety of a foggy mountain road can change in a heartbeat to the ecstasy of evergreen hills and lapis skies, the truth of transformation seems written in the very fabric of life itself.

I drive forward with an unexpected lightness of heart. The snows are behind me. The world is alive with possibility.

By the time I get back to Grants Pass, the panic of the snow-covered mountain road seems impossibly distant. The sun is out; people are gathering at little outdoor flea markets and pausing for casual chats on the corners. I'm surrounded by the golden light of a crisp Pacific winter day.

The snowstorm has been a tiny cosmic gift to me. Not only has it cracked through some of my skeptical reserve; it has literally set me on a new path. Now I'm aiming directly for the sea, whose great thundering voice has been calling to me since the moment I landed in Seattle. The Grants Pass cutoff will get me there in short order.

I know this cutoff road well. I've taken it many times. It's an old trappers' trail that eventually became the approximate path of the Jacksonville–Crescent City stage route. Now it's U.S. 199—a primary transit route for travelers who want to cut over from the speedway of Interstate 5 to the long, delicious, picture-postcard Pacific Coast highway that winds through the redwoods and along the edge of the sea. I used to take it when I wanted a more leisurely and picturesque route to the Bay Area, or when the weather, like today's, made the I–5 flyway impassable. I should probably have taken it in the first place. But like the snow, that decision's in the past. What's done is done. I'm moving forward into the light.

Grants Pass has always been the true Oregon–California "cusp" town for me. Medford may have the neon California energy, and Ashland may blend the expansive feel of California with the darker emotional hues of the Pacific Northwest, but it's in Grants Pass that I've always felt the deep heaviness of the Pacific rain forest give way to the lavender, pellucid distances of California mediterranean. In the summers when I'd pass here, this was the place where I first felt the sun turn from the bringer of light to the bringer of heat, and the atmosphere transform from liquid mists to sun-washed haze. For me, it's where the land began to speak differently.

This morning, traveling quickly under winter skies, this change in voice is not so easily heard. But, still, Grants Pass captivates me with that relaxed, "island" reality I find so delicious in these nestled Oregon towns. I'd better enjoy it. Once I get to the coast, things are going to change.

Before long, I start to sense that things are already changing, though not in the way I had expected. Both in Grants Pass and along U.S. 199 toward the coast there's a struggle taking place. It's a struggle between the tidy cappuccino shops and river-rafting outfitters, and the junk stores with their rudely carved Sasquatches, piles of bike parts, and pieces of weathered furniture—a struggle not only for money, but for the very soul of the community.

I pass a weathered secondhand store with a hand-lettered cardboard sign in the window. "Need Money Sale," it says. The window in which it sits displays a few old dolls and some piles of *National Geographic*s. In the window on the opposite side of the door, a yellowed wedding gown hangs limply from a dress form. At its base is an old tricycle.

Cars with "For Sale" signs dot the sides of the road, noses facing out toward the highway in hopes of catching the attention of passing motorists. By and large, the cars are not worth much more than a few hundred dollars each. But the sale of one of these junkers could keep many of these people going for months. This is still logging country. Despite the cappuccino shops and outfitters, when the lumber economy goes bad, many of these people are reduced to making a living by hustling, hornswoggling, and horse-trading whatever is at hand.

I motor along slowly, stopping here and there to look at the various wares being hawked along the road. Jellies; rude, blocky chain-saw carvings; burl tables—anything labor intensive with minimal costs for raw materials. This is a road where folks have more time than money.

People nod laconically or stare quizzically at me. It's an interesting mix. There are the "country-western and Jesus" people: beer-drinking men and hard-faced women with bleach-blond hair, beating out rhythms on the roofs of their pickups, cigarettes dangling from the corners of their mouths, and dogs barking from their truck beds at everything that passes. Then there are the placid former-hippies, driving old, worn-out Japanese cars with feathered amulets and talismans dangling from their rearview mirrors. Punctuating it all are the old women in gardens and elderly men in suspenders walking slowly back up gravel drives toward small houses and trailers overgrown with vegetation and surrounded by rusted farm implements.

It's a casual life, a laissez-faire life, a trade-route "live and let live" life, far from the stresses of urban reality. I find it most satisfying after the paranoia of Medford and the stress of the snowstorm.

I come up hard behind an ancient, smoking pickup truck. The driver is a coot wearing a filthy broad-brimmed hat that might have been purchased from the estate of a deceased beekeeper. He's going no more than twenty miles an hour. Pitted car bumpers and chunks of greasy, rusted metal are piled high like body parts in the back of his truck. He grips the steering wheel tightly with both hands. As I pass him, I glance over. He's toothless, wide-eyed, and stubble-bearded. He's yammering and cackling to himself.

I know his type. The hills are full of them. Unless I miss my guess, very soon he'll turn off on some nameless dirt road and wind back into the woods, eventually coming to a stop in front of some tarpaper cabin with junk cars around it and license plates and hubcaps nailed to its walls. He'll spend his nights sleeping under an army blanket on a bare mattress, kept company by a battalion of mangy, nondescript dogs. He eats his meals cold out of tin cans.

Except for the odd trip to Portland and, maybe, a stint in the service during World War II, he has probably never been more than a hundred miles from here. He knows nothing of the cappuccino shops and mountain-bike stores that are beginning to dot the roadsides, and if he did, he wouldn't care.

Soon he'll die and pass, unlamented, to another world. The grasses will grow wild around his house and the dogs will run off and be shot, or be taken in by neighbors, where they'll earn their keep by shredding skunks and raccoons and other nocturnal varmints. His hat and his hubcaps and his car fenders and his license plates will show up on the shelves of one of the weather-beaten junk and secondhand stores. Eventually they'll make their way to the theme restaurants of Malibu or Carmel or Santa Barbara, where they'll be mounted on yet another wall to provide the perfect ambience for an evening of fine dining overlooking the sea.

It's a grotesque train of thought, but probably all too accurate. You can see it on the roadway, feel it in the air. This is a trade route. The people are trolling, and the few Mercedes and BMWs and SUVs parked in front of the junk stores all have California license plates. Already, some of the secondhand stores are beginning to upgrade their image to antique shops; the hometown cafes are beginning to put tamari on the tables next to the ketchup.

It's a template for change, and it's not all change for the better. The spore of California money is strong, and these people are putting their noses to the wind.

I watch with fascination as the cutesy bed-and-breakfasts alternate with the wretched chain-saw carvings and weathered, rough-sawn wooden fruit stands selling jars of homemade blueberry jam. Despite the acrid scent of avarice mixing with desperation, there's still an honesty here. The bed-and-breakfasts may be at war with the secondhand stores, but it's a war between siblings—children sprung from a common land. These are cultural weeds and flowers, grown up from the common humus of the landscape and its people. They're not strategic impositions placed here after a marketing study in some distant corporate headquarters.

Maybe that's why this change fascinates me while the neon strips that dot every city appall me. These changes are organic. No matter how fast they take place, they still bow down to their history and cultural background. These are changes of the people and by the people, not changes foisted on the people. They have a moral authenticity that a McDonald's or a Pizza Hut will always lack.

The sun bathes me as I drive down this curving, forested roadway. A sign on the side of the road announces, "Middle Earth. Population Unknown." Now this is a transformation I'm willing to accept—a change from heavy forest darkness to a lightness of spirit that comes from living under azure skies rich with moist Pacific breezes.

It's a first hint of the "California-ness" about which I'm so ambivalent. If I see a guy dressed as Frodo walking down the street, it makes me smile and lifts my spirits. I know I'll never see such good-humored playfulness back in the Midwest. But if I meet a guy dressed as Frodo who claims he's channeling Tolkien's spirit and is filling auditoriums up and down the coast giving lessons on how to achieve Middle Earth consciousness, I want to throw up and get out of town. And both are entirely possible out here. It's all very strange.

I'd like to go to this particular branch of Middle Earth and see what I'd find. But I'm approaching Cave Junction, and it's almost noon. Louise will soon be at her desk. I'm really anxious to talk to her.

Cave Junction isn't much—just a little country wide spot in the road. It has a slightly glossier and more transient feel than some of the other wide spots, simply because travelers congeal here before taking the turn south to the Oregon Caves. In its own way, it has aspirations toward being a tourist destination. But a little Oregon logging town of a thousand people, deep in the folds of the Klamath Mountains, can't put on too many airs no matter what tourist attraction it abuts. Log trucks still rumble through the streets, and gas stations are still little pulloff establishments with men sitting in front of the buildings, watching the cars go by.

I notice this because I'm on the lookout for a pay phone, and the first one I see is at the edge of the apron of one of these stations. A log truck sits impatiently at idle while its driver chats casually with the station proprietor, who is, indeed, rocking back and forth on a wooden chair by his front door.

The diesel rumble of the truck makes the possibility of a phone conversation problematic, so I wander into the station in hopes that the logger will soon finish his conversation and drive off. As is sometimes my habit—I don't know why—I leave my car door partially open. It's probably the residual effect of years of carrying armloads of junk to and from waiting cars, and not wanting to go through the extra step of placing everything on the roof or the hood while I perform the inconvenient task of unlatching a door. It's also a habit that reflects the rural character of most of the places I have lived for the past several decades. The average city dweller would be appalled at this lapse of good judgment, especially when it became obvious that I not only leave the door open, but that I often leave the keys loosely inserted in the ignition.

I'll automatically revert to my urban caution and paranoia when I get into the Bay Area. But here, in the Oregon hills, it seems both unnecessary and premature. I stick to my homegrown habits. So it comes as a surprise when the station attendant shakes his head and says to me, "You're a pretty trusting fella," as I emerge from the darkness of his station.

He gestures to my open door. "I wouldn't leave my car like that if I were you."

"Car thieves? Here?" I ask, feeling vaguely like a motorist who's been warned by the police for some petty stupidity like not using his turn signal or not wearing his seat belt.

"You bet," the man says.

I guess I should have assumed that tourist areas are transient, and that Cave Junction is starting to draw enough visitors to lose its sleepy, trusting character. But I figured he and the truck driver would serve as witness enough to deter any potential thief.

"The perils of tourism," I say.

He shakes his head. "Ain't the tourists," he says. "It's the prison."

"Pelican Bay," the log-truck driver chimes in.

I'm sorting out dusty information in my brain. Pelican Bay. The bad California prison. Maximum security. *Sixty Minutes* exposé.

Lockup. Inhumane treatment. The worst of the worst. It's pretty fuzzy, but a picture is emerging.

"Is that near here?" I ask.

"Crescent City," the man says.

"Ain't far enough," the log-truck man adds.

I've been following my progress down 199 in my road atlas. Crescent City is still fifty miles away.

"You get trouble all the way up here? What? Escaped inmates?"

The attendant shakes his head. "Nobody escapes from that. It's the families. Move up here to be close to the prison."

I'd never thought about that, I tell him.

"Nobody ever does," he says. "That's why I got out of Crescent. I was making good money. But they put that prison in, turned the town into a stink hole. Now it's coming up here. You don't lock your car at night, you got no car in the morning."

"And you think it's the prison?"

"Fuckin' A right it's the prison."

The conversation doesn't interest the logger. He's been through it all before. He says his good-byes, hops in his truck, releases his air brakes, and rumbles off down the road.

With the logger gone, the attendant is in command. He leans back in his chair and puts his hands behind his head. The sun is bright and surprisingly warm. Despite the distant threat of Pelican Bay, the whole town seems "Mayberry relaxed" to me. I sit down on a log next to the man and stretch out my legs. I haven't been out of the Tuna since before the snowstorm on the pass.

"What do you think of that Bonneville?" he asks.

"Nice car," I say. "It's got road manners. You know, most American boats, they're good for up where I live—northern Minnesota, near the North Dakota border. Straight line for thirty miles. This thing really sits down on the curves."

"Yeah, always liked Ponchos," he says. "Weren't worth a shit for a few years. Little ones are still trash. That four is an eggbeater. But that three-eight . . ." He shakes his head like a man remembering a fine wine.

This is a conversation I love. Cars are one of my secret passions. From nineteen-dollar-and-forty-three-cent Fred to my current Mitsubishi station wagon, I've had a succession of cars that would beggar the imagination of the rational man. I once counted, and the number came up somewhere on the far side of sixty. I once even flew from Minnesota to Florida to shop for a used Cadillac when I had a hankering to ride around in a living room.

Louise has accepted this, and has almost taken a little shine to my eccentricity. One day she came home and noted that she could feel the suspension difference between her little Honda and a friend's Toyota. It made her both proud and appalled, she noted. But, she had to admit, it was kind of fun.

"If Pontiac would just stop covering everything with those plastic side panels, and give up trying to make their sheet metal look like human muscles," I say.

The man laughs. I've got a better sense of design metaphor than he does, but he knows exactly what I'm talking about. His forte is engines. "I used to put Carter four barrels on everything," he says. "Advance the timing, fuck with the shift points. I had a GTO. That car was a bat out of hell. It was when I lived in Crescent. There are cops still looking for me."

"Pelican Bay for you," I say.

He laughs heartily. The sun is cascading down, filtering through the pines. The rich scent of cedar is everywhere. A group of whippet-thin bikers goes by in formation, soundless except for the shishing of their chains as they pedal. I nod, the attendant waves. The bikers raise their hands in passing salute, then are gone. It's a forest idyll, West Coast style, and I'm feeling light as a coastal breeze.

The attendant begins to launch into a discourse on the proper tuning of a Pontiac's exhaust, but another car drives in to get gas. "Well, better help this fella," he says. "Got to put on my Chamber of Commerce smile."

I push myself up from the log and do a long house-cat stretch, then go over to the phone booth to call Louise. I'm still thinking about

Pontiacs and mulling over the simple but obvious truth that prisoners' families move to the towns where the prisons are located. It seems like Sociology 101, but for some reason it's never occurred to me.

I dial her office number and close my eyes while the phone is ringing. The sun caresses my face and the ambrosial cedar air tickles my nostrils.

She answers after the second ring. I can hear a computer printer chirring in the background.

"Hey, stranger," I say.

"Well, well, well," she answers. "I thought I was going to have to start looking for a new husband."

"You could still do that," I say.

"Don't tempt me," she laughs. She's in good spirits, but I can tell by the tone in her voice that she's harried. "Where are you?"

"Halfway between Middle Earth and the worst prison in America, breathing God's nectar for air."

"Sounds like California."

"Not quite, but right on the border. Cave Junction, just out of Grants Pass."

She shifts gears. "Have you found me a new job?"

"I wish. But I've seen some interesting places."

"Eugene?"

"It still has a hold on me," I tell her. "Bach festivals and stalking Pinocchio dolls."

Nick has obviously recounted some garbled version of my George story, and she begins laughing out loud as I tell her the specifics of the sculpture-stalker wars.

I ask her about her day and how things are going. I want to find out about this edge in her voice. I'm still feeling guilty about being gone; I want to know if some problem is compounding because of my absence. It turns out she's caught in a vise between a vicious university administrator and strident students threatening lawsuits. And, yes, there are a few problems with the house. The heating system isn't working right. Is there someone she should call, some vent she should be opening? I do my best to analyze the problem at a distance and give her my best "all thumbs" counsel on some course of action she might take. Neither of us really wants to talk about it.

"So, what are you finding out?" she asks.

I tell her a little about the mailman and my old home, but that's a private sorrow from a different past and not worth excavating at a time like this.

What I really want to do is tell her about this seductive sense of possibility that's begun to wash over me. But the timing seems wrong. What would I say: my consciousness is opening up? My spirit is lightening? Such language doesn't play well in the icy hollows of the winter North, especially when you're engaged in university political struggles and hand-to-hand combat with recalcitrant heating systems. It's much easier for me to adopt my standard Midwestern critical distance and critique the cultural struggles and environmental battles that are curling the edges of reality around here. But I don't want to go there. I'm feeling lifted by this lightness of being, and it seems somehow overly analytical and mean-spirited to focus on the shadows that are moving across this sunlit ground.

I need more time to frame a decent answer. What I should say, I don't want to say. What I want to say, I feel I shouldn't say. It's Romans 7 turned on its head. I decide to leave it alone and go back to my stories about the drive up Mt. St. Helens and the snowstorm outside of Ashland.

We talk for almost a half hour, catching up on housekeeping matters and, generally, finding ourselves across the distance. Her easy laughter—the thing I love most about her—fills me with longing. But, for all that love and longing, the one chasm I can't bridge is the distance between these blue, sunlit Oregon winter skies and the grey, cloudy reticence of a Minnesota November. Despite her easy banter, Louise has no dance in her right now, only the businesslike march into readiness. She is already preparing herself, spiritually and intellectually, for the descent into winter darkness.

I want to fly to her, pull her out, save that laugh. Yet who am I? A guy with a credit card and a rental car. A New Age St. Paul who's almost been knocked off his horse and can't decide whether or not to hold on. What do I know about reality?

The conversation ends on a good note. Nick is happy. Her classes are going well, and, despite the administrator and the complaining students, she has some interesting projects under way with a few other faculty members. The home is buttoned up and ready for the Big Blast. There are no tiny specifics turning the thumbscrews on me.

"I really miss you," I tell her.

"I miss you too. But I'm glad you're doing this."

"You really mean that?"

"Yes. I want you to get that distance out of your eyes."

It is just the right touch, a perfect balance between loving concern and moral challenge. A perfect Midwestern comment.

"Twenty minutes to California," I say.

"Kiss your good sense good-bye," she answers.

"Good sense drives a K car. I'm driving a Bonneville."

"What's a K car?" she laughs.

We leave things there. I've touched home, and it felt good. It was a true Minnesota moment: a little shy on wings, but solid on the earth. I have to remember: people there don't fly and swoop like ravens; they prowl the earth like wolves and bears. It's a good thing to keep in mind as I make my way south from Middle Earth.

Just past Cave Junction I see a road sign pointing toward Takilma. To most travelers it would be just one more marker indicating one more small town somewhere back in the hills. Every state has thousands of such places—small vestigial concentrations of population that are off the main thoroughfares and off the cultural radar of any but those who live there. People pass them by without ever taking notice. They're dots on a map and nothing more. But Takilma rings a bell with me. It was a mythic destination for a lot of old Bay Area hippies during the sixties and seventies; a mecca of disaffected utopianism where people went when they were out of money, out of dope, out of hope, and out of options. Pooling their few dollars, selling a few goods, they would pile their indeterminate number of children, dogs, and friends into their old Rambler station wagons or pickups or VW buses and clatter north, leaving a trail of blue-black exhaust smoke behind them. Once in Takilma they could live a blissful, unhassled, almost feral existence.

Years ago, on the recommendation of some friends, I had spent an afternoon there and slept on the side of the road before continuing to some now forgotten destination. It was considered a kind of safe harbor for transient longhairs navigating the stormy seas of redneck reality.

Even in those days I remember it as a "leave me alone" kind of place where people had come in order to root around in whatever kind of philosophical or cultural or psychic reality they chose to inhabit. Outsiders all, they were able to pursue their own private visions in a cultural diaspora of their own design. To the ends of the roads they'd gone, where they lived in chicken coops and huts and school buses and cabooses and lean-tos made of polyethylene and deadfall, until they could build the geodesic dome or A-frame or Japanese temple or ashram or longhouse that constituted their dream of back-to-the-land counterculture bliss.

In those days tepees dotted the hillsides and the sounds of flutes and drums could be heard across the land. The roads were alive with dogs and children and people waving their hands to ask for a ride or stopping passing cars only to hand a joint through the window. It was in no manner unusual to see someone dancing blissfully in the sun, tossing flowers, and behaving like a character in a Maxfield Parrish painting.

The place I see now bears little resemblance to that memory. Somewhere along the way, the gritty, skin-of-the-teeth survival reality of the area overtook the dreams. The lean-tos and the school buses remain, but few of the grand cedar-shaked temples and domes ever got completed. There are no dancers. The only figure I see is a white-bearded man weaving uncertainly toward me on a black balloon-tired bicycle.

He churns by me, a deranged sourdough. Thirty years ago he was probably one of the school-bus seekers passing joints and sharing bowls of lentils. Now, thousands of acid trips later, he's as insane as the old man yammering in his pickup. From opposite ends of the cultural spectrum they have arrived at a common place of inner demons, non sequiturs, and disconnected realities. The hills have claimed them both.

I watch him make his way down the road. He's hooting and singing. His bike has been hand painted with a brush.

The whole area now has the look of a hippie Indian reservation, full of abandonments and half completions. The scowls of the locals that greet me as I drive past say, "You're not welcome. We don't know you. You don't belong."

This is no longer a haven for the itinerant disenfranchised; the residents have taken on the suspicions of the basic rural indigent. Their mendicant lifestyle has been reduced to a pauper's huddling inside of half-finished huts. The old school buses sit, more per square mile than anywhere you might wish to see—abandoned carcasses of Day-Glo '60s dreams. It is eerily similar to the squalid, shack-and-trailer reality I've just left on U.S. 199. After all, a school bus on blocks is just a mobile home that made a stop in the '60s. But somehow it seems more disquieting. In fact, the whole reality seems disquieting. What was once a destination for anarchic utopians has now become a forgotten outpost, atrophying and inbred as surely as any Appalachian community, fueled by marijuana instead of moonshine, and harboring a desperate need to protect its petty illegalities against the encroachment of a newer world of SUVs and espresso bars and real-estate profiteers.

More even than the junk-shop owners and purveyors of mason jars full of jam, these people are dinosaurs. They thought they were the advance guard of an unstoppable cultural movement. But their land bridge collapsed behind them. Now they're trying to make sure no one builds another bridge to reach them.

I feel a bit ashamed and voyeuristic cruising through these weedy back roads in a shiny, white rental Bonneville. As in Eugene, I want to cry out, "I was one of you. Don't you recognize me?" But they don't, nor should they. I have gone over to the other side. A Bonneville is just three or four notches below an SUV, and it's a heck of a lot further away than that from a paisley school bus sitting up on blocks.

It's confusing and a bit frightening. We've all become what we had feared. They, rude and suspicious rural indigents carrying rifles and living in huts. Me, a rental car–driving, home-owning, credit card–carrying member of the middle class.

We were all going to transform the world, but the world transformed us. The ground we stood on shifted, and we each, in our own fashion, slid down some unnoticed slippery slope toward an unexpected, but perhaps inevitable, conclusion.

On the surface it seems so simple. Age, circumstance, and economic realities ground our common ideals into grist, and we each reconstituted them in the way best suited to help us survive. But in truth, despite our common cultural origins, the old hooting sourdough is closer kin to the yammering cackler in his pickup truck than he is to me. And, in my self-deprecating and cautiously watchful manner, I'm closer kin to the Ojibwe who walked the forests and paddled the rivers around me than I am to these squint-eyed hippies with whom I might have once shared a joint or a meal or a pipeful of hashish.

Cultural proximity? Maybe. But maybe it's something deeper. We have all been transformed, but we have also been claimed.

Something has, indeed, happened, Mr. Jones. Our lives have been painted in the colors of the land.

TEN

LOST DREAMS

The ocean appears in through a "V" in the hillsides—an impossible horizontal in a world of diagonals and verticals. The fog sits above the distant horizon line like a roll of cotton, ready to spread across the land. It will arrive early tonight. At least the storms they were trumpeting have stayed north by Port Orford.

The sky has lost the blue luster it had back in Cave Junction, but it remains hospitable. I've decided to give myself another big dose of nature. And to this end I've devised a plan. I'll spend several hours by the sea, then highball it directly to the great groves of towering redwoods down at Avenue of the Giants.

But first, I have a little unfinished business. I want to get to the bottom of this prison issue and what it really means to the people of Crescent City.

Crescent City is just as I remember it—low, windswept, and destitute, huddling in the far northwest corner of California. Despite the brightness of the ocean light, it has about it an unrelenting drabness. Everything seems washed out. Even the impervious plastic franchise signs seem dull and have the appearance of rude survivors.

The sea has no sense of romance or majesty here. It rumbles and rolls murkily behind artificial seawalls. In 1964, as a result of the great Alaska earthquake, it formed into a great tidal wave, breached those walls, and washed through the streets of the town. Hundreds of residents were killed, and the town seems not to have recovered.

There's a bone-weariness about the place, and it feels spiritual as well as economic. Trash gathers along the road in scrubby bushes bent almost horizontal by the wind. The highways are flanked by crude displays of redwood burls and driftwood sculptures. The small downtown seems to have been battered into submission by the wind and the sea and the grey winter drear.

It's the perfect place to put a controversial prison—isolated, poverty-stricken, with no political clout. This is a classic political play: find an area with exactly these characteristics and put distasteful societal detritus there. Buy the sympathies and silence of the local residents with massive infusions of cash and the promise of a great rise in the general standard of living, make rosy projections about the influx of jobs and money that will take place, minimize the social and ecological disruptions that will result, and never, never, acknowledge that it's the powerlessness of the community that's the real reason for the choice of this location. Sometimes it works; sometimes it doesn't. It depends on the politics and economic desperation of the community.

From what I can tell, Crescent City is divided and ambivalent about the prison. Most people give me a hooded stare when I ask them about it, then answer with that careful evasiveness of someone who doesn't wish to express a strong opinion on something controversial. A few have been forthright. One man gave voice to my own thoughts, saying, "They're treating us like a garbage dump, putting all the shit they don't want here." A clerk in a drugstore was more resigned. "Well, I guess it's good for the economy," she said, "and, what with the state of logging and fishing, we can sure use that."

My favorite observation came from three old men outside a bank. They were probably retired sawmill or fisheries workers who now meet every day to drink coffee and pass the time. After they had made various innocuous comments like, "Don't seem so bad to me," and "Don't seem to cause much trouble," one of them piped up with his true feelings. "You know," he said, in a loud, conspiratorial whisper, "we damn near had Charlie Manson. Wouldn't thata been something!" Upon hearing the unspeakable voiced, the others started nodding and clucking in vehement agreement. They knew what Pelican Bay meant to them.

I'm tremendously ambivalent about prisons in general, and this one in particular. I once worked as a writer for the Governor's Commission in Minnesota, and I was in close contact with everyone involved in the criminal justice system—police, courts, corrections, prevention and rehabilitation specialists, and even the prisoners themselves. What I saw admitted of no easy answers. Prisons were inhumane and did nothing to rehabilitate anyone; yet there were legitimately bad human beings out there who would slit your throat for a nickel. Anyone who thinks the issue is clear-cut and simple should walk into a prison and see how it conspires to snuff out the goodness and hope in decent men who have made mistakes in their lives. Then, when they think they've got everything figured out, they should look into the cold, empty shark eyes of one of the men who dismembered his girlfriend with a butcher knife because she wouldn't have sex with him or poked out the eyes of a baby with a scissors because it was crying during a football game. If they still have a clear answer for me after that, I'll be willing to listen. Until then, I'll retain my ambivalence.

Still, from what I can recall, Pelican Bay seems to set new standards in psychological brutality: prisoners in solitary confinement or jammed two to an eight-by-ten concrete cell; no windows to let in daylight; an hour and a half of solitary exercise per day in an empty, roofed, concrete exercise area little bigger than a living room; constant video surveillance; lights burning twenty-four hours a day; and on and on.

The corrections people claim it's a necessary response to inmate violence; a clean well-lighted place in which to warehouse the most incorrigible and unmanageable of the prisoner population. Its opponents see it as a twenty-first-century descent into the high-tech penal dark ages, guaranteed to make men crazier and far more vicious than they were when they went in. All I can say for certain is that it gives the lie to any belief in rehabilitation, not to mention the possibility of transformation that I have felt floating in the air around me.

On the streets of Crescent City the concern with Pelican Bay seems to be less about its capacity for rehabilitation and transformation than about its mere presence. As one woman tells me, with Zenlike clarity, "Before it came here we had nothing. But at least we had that." She's in her mid-thirties, pushing a baby in a multicolored jogging stroller.

"I used to think I was a liberal," she says. "But there's a big difference between being poor because you can't find work and being poor as a lifestyle."

"What's that have to do with Pelican Bay?" I ask her.

"It's the families," she says, echoing the concern of the man in Cave Junction. "They move up here to be close to the men. They don't work. They want welfare. Their kids are out of control." Unconsciously, she reaches down and tucks the blanket tighter around the tot in the stroller.

"Then there's the crazy ones," she continues. "Jailhouse romances. They meet the guy on the Internet and think they're in love. These men are cons. They'll say anything. What kind of woman falls for that? Then they move up here to wait."

I'm confused. I thought Pelican Bay was the end of the line, a sort of Crescent City of prisons, perched bleakly on the edge of the earth.

"No, no," she tells me. "There's regular maximum security too. These guys get out. They have some job training. Some of them stick around. How many shoemakers do we need? Pretty soon their friends are coming up from Oakland and Fresno and L.A. You see these Cadillacs driving through. You know they're dealing dope again, or at least using. I just want to get out of here."

"Where do you want to go?" I ask.

She rocks her baby back and forth. "I don't know. I just don't know."

I feel for her. I live in a place that people don't seek out. I understand about the virtues of emptiness and being ignored. If you make your peace with it, you have a freedom other Americans lack. You're not on the radar screen; you can pick and choose the shape of the reality around you. But when government comes calling with a fistful of dollars, the whole equation changes.

A few years ago, a small town near us in northern Minnesota made a deal with the state to become a dumping ground for hazardous waste. It was going to be big business. All assurances were given that technology would make it safe. The town, which was dying, was to be given a new infusion of life: a new library, lots of money, new jobs, and so on, and so on. The town weighed the options and was ready to sign on the dotted line. Had a local Indian leader not used his political clout by reminding officials of the votes the tribe was able to deliver to candidates who supported its agenda, our little pine-studded reality would have been the repository for incinerator ash and toxics from everywhere from Nebraska to Illinois. The kids would have had a nice library—and maybe brain tumors to go with it. Thankfully, our savvy local Indian tribes saved the land for those of us whose ancestors had taken it from them.

But there were no Indian tribes or anything else around here with enough savvy or clout to stop Pelican Bay, and, by this woman's account, it's already leaking its toxins into the community.

Her concern is both touching and heartbreaking. Though Crescent City is bleak and desolate and wounded by nature and the economy, it has nonetheless become her home, and she loves it. But now its greatest virtue has become its greatest liability. Its isolation and lack of cultural and political importance have made it the perfect dumping ground for California's most toxic human waste.

I commiserate with her, then start to leave. But the floodgates have opened. She wants to unburden herself. "They don't understand. These men are locked up and they have everything done for them. They get out, they get a girlfriend, and the only thing they know is being waited on. The first time she says no, or doesn't have dinner ready on time . . ." She pantomimes slapping someone. It's a sad gesture, so unnatural and unthreatening in the way she performs it. It

just underlines the helplessness of a woman in the face of male violence and anger. "I just want my little girl away from here."

It seems almost a plea, as if I'm supposed to help her or have some
answer.

I wonder what her story is—if she has a husband, if maybe she has
more firsthand knowledge of these cons than she'd like to admit. But
I don't want to ask. Her plaintive confession has created too much
intimacy already. I feel uncomfortable staring in at her raw and frightened emotions.

"Thanks for talking to me," I say. It sounds foolish. The only more
foolish thing would be to offer some Pollyanna comment about how
things are sure to get better. They're probably not, unless you're a
Chamber of Commerce booster or a local merchant.

She gives me a smile that would fool anyone who hadn't just listened to her heartfelt outpouring.

"You've got a beautiful daughter," I say. She nods once; her smile
broadens.

I drive away, watching her push her brightly-colored baby jogger
down the dingy washed-out streets of the town she once loved. "This
place is going to lose her," I think. And she's what they need: someone who loves this place and cares. Her loss will be bigger than they
know. With her will go a portion of the town's spirit. In its place will
be a large infusion of cash and the possibility of Charlie Manson.
That's not much of a trade.

I head out of town thinking about my own situation. I feel like a
man with a hangnail who's just met a person with cancer. I worry
about Nick growing up in a world of hockey and hunting. She's looking at the possibility of her daughter growing up in a town filling up
with paroled killers and rapists. It's Tarique's dad's fear, with a
mother's edge.

I tell myself that maybe she's overreacting. But it's her heart that
is wounded, her sense of peace and security that's been violated. She's
left with the same option I was given by the motel manager who dismissed my concerns about the banging drunks in the next room. "It's

not my problem. Deal with it, or find somewhere else." Motel California has just put a bunch of murderers in the next room, and they didn't even give her a glass box for protection.

The temptation is too strong: on the way out of town I have to drive by the prison. The three old men told me it's "up north a bit. You can't miss it." I drive in that direction, dodging tumbleweeds that have dislodged from the roadside bushes. Soon I see it, surrounded by metal fences and set off behind a stand of pines.

The first thing that strikes me as I drive up is its industrial dreariness. There's no "big house" romance about it; it looks like a series of grey concrete boxes.

It's the logical extension of Hannah Arendt's banality of evil—the banality of incarceration. I've been in prisons. I played basketball in San Quentin, did crime commission business inside the great walled monoliths of Minnesota's state penitentiaries. They're terrifying—frozen screams made into architecture. But at least they have the dark heartbeat of men hungering for the sun.

Pelican Bay has none of this. It's like a giant series of concrete bunkers surrounded by barbed wire and electric fences. Prison as impenetrable basement; prison as crypt.

I tell the guard at the gate that I just want to see what the infamous Pelican Bay looks like. He's ready for me. This is California—PR is job one. He hands me a brochure explaining the prison and launches into a well-prepared speech. Built in 1989 to house the most dangerous criminals. Protects the other inmates. Newest technologies. Brings eighty-four million into the local economy. It goes on and on.

I can't keep my eyes off the building. It's like the cooling tower and containment vessel at Kalama—silent, concrete, housing something unseen but lethal. Yet it lacks the sense of *mysterium tremendum* that the nuclear plant contained. Incarcerated human beings simply don't elicit the same sense of terror as radioactive rods. In fact, the real terror is in the thinness of the line between inside and outside. A mall,

properly retrofitted, could probably do the same job. No windows to
the outside, no sunlight, no clocks. Just a place to do time, but with
nothing to buy.

I try to engage the guard on a human level. He's a most pleasant
and forthcoming man. He took this job, he explains, because it gave
him a chance to get his family out of the city. Crescent City is great.
He loves the hunting and fishing. Most prisons where he might have
been stationed, he says, are in places you don't want to live. This one
is smack in the middle of the outdoors. All his friends at other institutions are jealous.

I push him a bit on the prison itself. But either he doesn't spend
much time inside or he chooses not to talk about it. For him, it's just
a necessary but unfortunate part of human society. He's just doing his
job, and he's damn lucky to have landed in an outdoor paradise.

He asks me about my family. I tell him about my wife, my son. He
gives me a little pin to give to Nick. It slips out of my hand and falls
on the ground. I don't tell him, and drive away.

A mile down the road I stop at a small gas station and store to get
some batteries for my cassette recorder. The proprietor is conversing
with a friend when I walk in. Maybe it's my imagination, but I feel as
if they're looking at me strangely as I wander among the shelves. I
find the batteries and bring them to the counter.

"Prison been good for business?" I ask offhandedly. He retreats to
that hooded distance I'd seen among so many of his townsfolk.

"It's all right," he says.

I try to pry open the conversation. "It's a tough call," I say, hoping
to take a measured neutral stance. "Helps the economy, but changes
the community."

"That's about it," he answers. There's no emotion in his voice.

This man won't crack. There's no sense in trying. But I'm in a
funny mood.

"Hear you almost had Charlie Manson," I offer.

"That'll be three oh five," he says.

I walk back out to the Tuna. I glance over at the cars parked by the side of the station. All the doors are locked.

One of the strange quirks of California cultural geography is that the coastal area north of the Golden Gate is identified less by its cities than its counties. In their own way, they are like the old city-states of Italy: people relate to them and are shaped by them, almost more than by any larger political divisions. You're not from northern California. You're from Humboldt County, or Mendocino, or Sonoma, or Marin.

Del Norte, the home of Crescent City, is a thing unto itself, defined almost in opposition to the others. To the Del Norte folks, there's an incremental increase in something effete as you go south, and they want no part of it. As far as they're concerned, the ladder of descent into California's shaky "woo-woo" reality begins at the Humboldt County line and descends through the dope-growing haven of Mendocino into the rich, big-mansion faux-country snobbery of Sonoma, before it reaches its absolute nadir in the Brie and Mercedes reality of that most effete and disgusting of all counties, Marin.

The other side of the Golden Gate is a different planet, and not part of the equation. But these northern counties are somehow tied together, like Tuscany and Umbria. The Del Norte folks want to make sure that the cultural seawall between them and those other northern counties is never breached. They know what a tidal wave can do.

Despite my desire to make it to Humboldt, I'm still in Del Norte when I come upon the beach I've been seeking. It's a great arcing cove, with huge surging waves rolling ceaselessly onto the shore. I remembered it somewhere in the back of my mind as one of the places where the sea was most dramatic in its thundering presence.

I park the Tuna on the side of the road and walk toward the water. The waves are booming in the distance. They rise, drop, explode against the earth. Behind them the sea rolls with the rhythmic thunder of its winter voice.

I cross the sand toward the breakers, intent on getting to their very edge. To see them from a distance is not enough; I need to feel them surge, drop, lick at the toes of my boots, then exhale as they flow back into the wintry sea.

A wave crashes hollow in front of me, moves shoreward, laps at my feet, then recedes. Another, then another. They come with hypnotic regularity, washing the sand to dark and leaving with a singing hiss. Mussels, starfish, crab shells emerge only to be reclaimed by the next rolling wash of surf. I stand beside this great grey vastness, drinking in something deeper than memory—something amniotic, annihilating; half lullaby, half dirge. Seabirds wheel and screech above me. Their voices cut like glass.

In the dim distance, grey with silver highlights, the far line of the open sea glints and gloams in half light. It's a haunted illumination, unacquainted with the passage of time, heralding nothing, marking nothing. My breathing calms: I feel the sea rising and falling within me. The salt spray on my tongue has the taste of blood, of passion.

I begin to weave imperceptibly. Inner and outer are beginning to merge. I move with the rhythms, flow with the tides. Smells as pungent as love, as dank as death rise from the waters that course around my feet. Out beyond, where the sea is unbounded, the roll goes on, an endless roar that has no source. Only this wall of breakers, rising now, then falling hard before retreating, brings the awesome power into human scale.

I exhale a breath that seems to come from the very center of my being. All the prisons, all the human tragedies, all the strip malls and culture wars and human dilemmas are gone, washed clean.

I sit on the sand, cup my hands around my knees. The coming of the fog is in the air. The chill is deep; it wraps me in its shroud. That distant line of light, that promise of meaning out beyond the horizon, is like a light from another room, another land, another time.

I lie down, pull my jacket tight around me, and close my eyes. Louise and Nick float before me, and I am at peace.

I awake wet and cold. The fog has moved in; its mist has settled over everything. How long have I been asleep? I'm shivering from the damp.

I run to the Tuna and turn its heater up full blast. I have to get dry. This shiver will cut too deeply.

I stop at a gas station to change into some dry clothes. The kid working there smiles when I ask for the rest-room key. He sees the pants and sweatshirt under my arm. He knows what I'm about.

I fumble with my clothes, with the wet, with the cold. I'm breathless, dizzy, still hypnotized by the sea. I wonder if I breathed in rhythm with its rise and fall while I was asleep.

Once dried and warmed, I hurry back to the Tuna. No music now. My mind is liquid, my thoughts have no edges. I want to keep this reverie alive in me until I get to the redwoods.

I shoot past Klamath with the golden bear statues on the bridge pillars, past the grotesque Paul Bunyan and the Trees of Mystery tourist trap.

The road climbs into the redwoods, closing down to a single lane as it winds its way among the silent giants of Redwoods National Park.

Memories overwhelm me. There's the place I picked up the mad hitchhiker I told Nick about. There's the spot where two young girls showed me an opening into a grotto with waterfalls and wildflowers and ferns as big as a man.

Up ahead is the grove where I stopped with some friends one time on our way from Oregon to San Francisco. I remember that trip so well. The three of us had jammed into my Nash Metropolitan and were trying to make it to San Francisco to buy a new starter for my car. My friends had come along to help push-start me whenever I had to shut off the engine. It was reason enough to take a week or two out of their shapeless lives.

We had pooled our money and bought a loaf of French bread, a bottle of wine, and some smoked fish at a little market back up the road a ways. The redneck dangers of Del Norte were mostly behind us. This stop was our way of giving thanks for safe passage and the beauty of the day.

We sat in the mystical, filtered haze of this sunlit redwood sanctuary, partaking of our almost biblical repast. Soon another group of travelers came along. We shared the bread and wine and the smoked fish, and we all had enough to eat our fill. The symbolism was lost on none of us.

Such days those were. I'm tempted to stop at the grove as I pass, to try to reclaim that moment. But it's the big trees I'm after, not my memories. I want to get to the Avenue of the Giants. There the highway is farther away from the groves. I'll be better able to hear the whispers of the great redwoods as I stand beneath them.

Still, the heady, fragile innocence of those bygone days calls to me. We were all so full of hope; we had so much more faith than fear.

I think of Nick and the world he's growing into. How much less embracing, how much more threatening it seems. Every action carries a caution. Fish is tainted with mercury. Wine wrecks your liver. Sex kills. Drugs destroy chromosomes. Don't pick up hitchhikers, beware of strangers. Drink wine and drive, and you're likely to kill someone.

How, really, did we survive? Were things really that much simpler then? The only threat we saw was from society, never behavior. Were we unconscious? Or were we simply naive and pure of heart?

There was such a vast network, and such a vast web of dreams. People traded cars with strangers on the side of the road. You met someone hitchhiking and moved in with them for a month. You could live for weeks on only a few dollars and the luck of the road.

Was it only youth, or was there something greater taking place? We'll never know, for it all turned to dust in our hands. Maybe, at a great enough distance, some chronicler will be able to put it all into perspective. For now, it's locked in the memories of those who were part of it. Like the light at the edge of the sea, it's unreachable, unfathomable, an illumination from another time.

I fly past Arcata, slow through Eureka, where the highway turns for a few miles into city streets. Here the memories darken, and I'm overtaken by the nightmare side of those youthful days.

I remember trying to sneak through this town at night in my Volkswagen bus. In the cities, that vehicle was a statement. In the country, it became a target. Every pair of headlights that pulled in behind me was a danger; every pickup that slowed as it passed was a threat.

I see a small restaurant where I once stopped for a late-night cup of coffee. A group of men at a table began harassing me as I entered. It was the same tired stuff: "Is that a boy or a girl? Hey, pussyface, want to give me a blow job?" Such jeers and jibes were common fare. But here on alien soil, the dark violence of the words was a palpable threat.

I sat at the counter while the waitress ignored me, until finally her message became clear, and I snuck out as unobtrusively as I could. Through the window I could see the men rising quickly from their seats as I drove away. I took a few turns and hid in an alley, then sat in cold terror almost until dawn as their truck drove slowly up and down the nearby streets. Whether they were looking for me, I'll never know. But more than one of my friends had been followed out of some town by locals and had been run off the road and beaten. And all of us had heard stories of long-hairs who had been killed or had their cars stolen or set on fire.

And the police were no help. Often, they were worse. They would follow, harass, pull you over for nothing. If you said the wrong thing, had the wrong hitchhiker with you who carried a stash of dope or started mouthing off, or if you simply got the wrong cop, you were a candidate for jail, even prison. In Texas, people were being given twenty-year sentences for a single marijuana seed, and word was out that the police conveniently kept a bag of seeds with them, in case their actual search came up empty. For all we knew, the practice was common in other places as well.

We were fugitives in our own country, and we had nowhere to turn. All we had was each other and our dreams. Small wonder that we formed together into traveling bands and knew of safe houses, safe communities.

That's all ancient history now, an impossible reality from an impossible past. Except for those dinosaurs still bunkered in the Takilmas of the world, life has moved on. Cities like Eureka seem as benign as kittens. The guys in the pickups wear beards and smoke dope. The old hippies have lost their teeth and found Jesus, or have cut their hair and are the schoolteachers and city council members. People who were hawking candles on a street corner are now running shops in the mall and selling crafts from Third World countries through the Internet. Others are getting rich selling stocks in brokerage houses. A dealer's a dealer, and the more things change, the more they remain the same.

After all, this is America, not Palestine or Bosnia. The animosities do not run deep; the cultural fissures and fractures are shallow. In a decade, a generation, children mingle, take their parents' idiosyncrasies, and stir them into the hodgepodge of postmodern reality. The Gap sells bell-bottoms, and Young Republicans hold '60s hippie parties. Wars of cultural values get reduced to style statements and Friday night keggers.

On a whim, I decide to stop at that same cafe for a cup of coffee. I want to set foot in this place in the daylight, to see what changes thirty years have wrought.

The inside is hardly recognizable. If it were not for how indelibly the location is etched in my memory, I might not believe I was in the right place.

A pleasant young waitress wearing three earrings and a head scarf comes up and takes my order. Another waitress is frothing a cup of milk on a cappuccino maker. Young men in ponytails lounge around reading the *San Francisco Chronicle*. A family is happily sitting at a table eating ice cream sundaes. Their children are playing with plastic action figures.

Over in the corner I hear a couple of old-timers talking. An Oklahoma twang still permeates their accents. They might well have been the guys in the pickup those many years ago—flat-topped refugees from the dust bowl who arrived here as kids in their parents' overloaded stakebed trucks and learned from their youthful experiences that outsiders were to be terrorized and brutalized.

It's so ironic: wave after wave of immigrants, each turning a steely gaze to those who came after. From the disgruntled gold miners, to the loggers and fishermen, to the dust-bowl refugees, to the dopers and hippies, it's been an endless parade of American dreamers, come to seek their fortune in this hard land where giant trees rise in the mist and the sea pounds ceaselessly against a ragged shore. And, more often than not, each wave met with a resistance that ranged from ostracism to violence.

But little by little, outsiders become insiders. Now, the generations all sit together in this little cafe—a peaceable kingdom—people of the north coast, shaped by the trees and the sea and the challenges of life here in these rugged rain-drenched hills.

It pleases me to think about this as I look around at the mélange of folk warming themselves on hearty soups and heavy breads on this chill California winter day. I always loved this north coast, despite the dangers it presented me on my youthful journeys. There was some-thing to the meeting of land and sea, and the harsh demands of the weather that appealed to my sense of drama and moral responsibility. It always saddened me that when I passed through here I was reduced to the status of prey.

Now that veil has lifted, and I feel at home. These northern coastal towns shine forth for what they are: sturdy, no-nonsense bastions of hard-living, big-dreaming, "leave me alone" iconoclasts, happily dis-tanced by several hundred miles from urban centers and their soft-hands realities. In that way, they're not so different from my northern Minnesota home, except for the scale of the dreams that come from living amid three-hundred-foot redwoods and facing out on the thundering sea.

"Nice cafe," I say to the waitress in the scarf as I pay for my coffee.

"Thank you, sir," she says. "Enjoy your stay in Eureka."

I walk back outside into the misty air. I shouldn't have stopped; I'm filled with longing. The warmth in the cafe was more than phys-ical. There was something familial about the place, something you never quite get in a big city, even in a neighborhood hangout. It has to do with forced proximity—like brothers and sisters who share a common bond about which they have no choice. It made me yearn for home.

Near the Tuna, a family is piling out of a giant forest-green Chevy Tahoe. It looks big enough to carry the entire Oakland Raiders football team and all their gear. But it contains only four people.

They look different from the folks I saw in the cafe—better dressed, more pressed and creased, wealthier, more urbane. The woman has long, straight, dyed blond hair, beautifully cut. She is heavily made up, but tastefully so, like someone who makes her living off her appearance. The man, who is wearing a pullover cashmere sweater and deck shoes, is saying something about stopping to pick up some skis back in Atherton. The two children are seated in the back—one, a young boy in a car seat, the other, a girl of about twelve.

I know Atherton. My short stint at Stanford had me driving past its hedged confines every day on the way to school. I don't believe I ever spent any time there, but I knew it was the fenced and hedged bastion of old wealth in the South Bay.

I assume that, like me, this family is just traveling through. In fact, I'm about to engage them in conversation, maybe say something about Stanford or Kepler's, a bookstore I liked to frequent in nearby Menlo Park. After all, despite our obvious difference in economic status, we're fellow travelers with a common geographical bond, and I'm suddenly feeling lonely and far from home.

Then I hear the woman say she needs to run back to the house for a minute to pick up some papers before a three o'clock showing. I look at their bumper; there's a sticker for Zane Middle School in Eureka. I check the license-plate bracket: Sunnyvale, a few miles south of Atherton. Things start to fall into place. These are probably Peninsula folk, moved north, and the woman is probably involved in real estate.

The man says something; the woman laughs and touches him lightly on the sleeve. I withdraw into myself and move toward the Tuna. The idea of engaging them in conversation suddenly seems intrusive. They appear to be a loving family, out enjoying the day. They don't need the involvement of a solitary traveler.

I watch them get out of their gargantuan high-tech vehicle, wearing their designer high-style clothes, and walk happily into the cafe. I'm filled with conflicting emotions.

On one hand, I envy their togetherness and am warmed by their obvious love for each other. That could be me, with Louise and Nick, if I were back home rather than gallivanting up and down some distant coastline.

But on the other hand, they seem even more alien on this landscape than I do. People in insular places develop a deep, indefinable sameness that is often only recognizable when set against outsiders. Maybe it's that they all wash their clothes in the same water, or all develop a common carriage in the face of a common climate, or all set their eyes in the same fashion as they stare at a common horizon—I don't know. But a close observer can almost always tell a local from an outsider. And these people, locals though they may be, look as if they don't belong here. They still have the brightness and bearing of wealthy city folk.

They're as different from the other people in that cafe as I was when I stopped there thirty years ago. And it's a fair analogy. The counterculture, of which I was a part, was the last great wave of immigration to arrive on this coast. These people are part of the newest wave: wealthy transplants who struck gold in the stock and real-estate markets of Los Angeles and the Bay Area, and are coming north and buying up land, seeking their own personal sanctuaries.

I knew I would see this further south, but it surprises me to see it here. Humboldt, I assumed, was still terra incognita to people from the Bay Area. Perhaps these folk are the more adventurous. Perhaps they have some prior connection to this place, or are just willing to roam farther afield. Or perhaps cybercommuting has had a greater effect on demographics than I had suspected. Or perhaps these are just the new forty-niners, mining the real-estate market and selling the choice nuggets to their wealthy friends back in the city.

Once again, I'm tremendously ambivalent. These people have every right to be here; they are, in their own way, just the next wave. But unlike the previous waves of immigrants who brought with them values that challenged and disrupted—and ultimately blended with—the local culture, this new generation, freed by wealth rather than driven by poverty and a search for opportunity, often has no interest in the local culture at all. They don't need it. In fact, they can skate over the top of it. What they don't have they can purchase and have delivered, or seek out on weekend junkets to the bright lights of the city environments from which they've come.

The attraction to them of a place such as this is less what it is than what it is not—that it's not Los Angeles or San Francisco or Sunnyvale or Atherton. They bring with them a desire to avoid, to escape—to place down, fully formed, a lifestyle they had developed but were in danger of losing to intrusions.

This family has chosen Humboldt. It could probably just as easily have chosen Tahoe or Sedona or Friday Harbor. It's a picture in a magazine, a ratings sheet in a Chamber of Commerce brochure on school rankings. Their money comes from elsewhere, and their contribution to the community will be in the money they spend, not the labor they contribute. This is less a search for a new beginning than it is a lifestyle adventure.

I don't like myself for thinking this way, and it is exactly the kind of jaundiced analysis I had hoped to avoid by going straight to the redwoods. These are clearly loving people and a caring family, and I really have no grounds for making the assumptions I'm making. But I've seen this so many times. It's happening everywhere, even in our little corner of northern Minnesota. There will be a buzz among local contractors, a sudden unavailability of the best tradesmen, and a bit of sleuthing will reveal a hunting lodge the size of a small hotel being built on a pristine point of virgin white pine on some secluded local lake. Further research will reveal a "retirement" or "summer" home being constructed for a candy tycoon from Chicago or a wealthy wheat farmer from the Dakotas, or a new log chalet being built for a family that has decided to get out of the rat race and has visions of an idyllic, rural enclave from which they can cybercommute to their work in some distant city. They will come in, show up at a few local art events or lectures at the university, then disappear into their forest fortress, which will ultimately serve as no more than a base for their far-flung lifestyles.

Even if they want to be part of the community, their wealth insulates them from the daily struggles and rhythms of the people who make their lives on the land. They are as buffered from us as the prisoners at Pelican Bay are buffered from the people of Crescent City, but the walls are of their own choice and their own design.

What I wonder is whether the land will ever claim such people? Will this loving SUR family ultimately be shaped by this rugged coastline of twenty-foot seas and three-hundred-foot redwoods? Or will they be able to insulate themselves with wealth from the influences of the land on which they walk?

Once again, the Lakota chief Luther Standing Bear whispers to me. It is, he said, a long time before men are able to divine and meet the rhythm of the land. One must be born and reborn to belong. Our bodies must be formed of the dust of our forefathers' bones.

Will these new immigrants be able to do this? Or are they the final untethering of the link that has become ever more tenuous since our forefathers, committed to subduing the earth, conquered the peoples for whom each rock and tree had a spirit and a name?

I don't know. And I wonder.

And I wonder even further if, perhaps, my roots in my Minnesota soil, where my son is being raised up from the dust of his grandfathers' bones, are not perhaps something of infinite value, even if they seem at times to be constricting and untenable. Transformation may, indeed, be possible. But perhaps it needs to have its roots in the soil.

I leave the family and the cafe and head out toward the Avenue of the Giants, a small paved road south of Eureka that winds through a

majestic thirty-three-mile stand of redwoods hundreds of feet high
and thousands of years old. It's a Potemkin village—a false front of
old-growth trees just wide enough to trick the unsuspecting tourist
into thinking that these giants are bountiful and protected. But I'm
not here for the politics; I'm here for the spirit of the place. Years ago
I spent a night sleeping on a picnic bench under the sheltering canopy
of these great trees. I don't believe I have ever, before or since, experienced the sense of peace and protection I felt as I awoke beneath their
towering, whispering branches.

The "Avenue" is inland from the sea; the fog's advance has been
slowed by the intervening hills, and the waning day is still bathed in
sun. As I approach, the giants rise in the distance. I drive toward them
slowly, like a man approaching a shrine.

I'm humbled by these great trees and their silent eloquence. They
seem apart from us, another race. I drive slowly, almost solemnly,
along the thin ribbon of roadway that winds beneath them. Even so,
my automobile feels intrusive and presumptuous.

In the distance I hear the groan and whine of a log truck as it nego-
tiates the highway I have just left. The thought of these giants severed
and stacked upon the back of a truck seems an inconceivable violation
of the natural order. Despite my sympathy for the economic plight of
the loggers, here their arguments leave me unmoved. Maybe it's just
that I need a mighty voice before I'm able to hear. But these trees are
living presences, and to kill one would, quite literally, be a crime
against nature.

Still, I know that many of the loggers love these trees and are
proud to say so. They simply see the issue as one of beauty and eco-
nomics. If there are enough trees left to provide people with an experience of beauty, they feel, there can be no harm in cutting a few to
help a family survive.

Yet when you stand among these giants, the issue ceases to be one
of beauty or economy and becomes one of spiritual presence. You
sense them as individual beings, with individual spirits that are sacred

and inviolable. More so than with smaller trees, you are aware that to kill one is to take a life, to remove from the earth something that has lived and breathed and conversed with the sky for thousands of years.

I can't believe the loggers don't feel this and bow their heads before this knowledge, as well. Perhaps they do; perhaps it's just easier to do the math of translating three hundred feet of virgin redwood into board feet and multiplying by dollars than it is to listen to the deep voice of one of these solemn beings. Or perhaps they simply reject the spiritual argument, the way someone rejects the Hindu argument for the protection of cows while people are starving.

Still, I sometimes wonder if the problem isn't more complex, if it doesn't have its roots in our very language and the way it teaches us to see the world. We're so inclined to subsume individual things into broad, general categories. It takes a poet or a crazy person to name, and know, an individual tree; to invest it with life and character and personality. And most of us are neither poets nor madmen.

Yet in other times it wasn't this way. Here in California there were once over a hundred and twenty languages spoken, some extending only for a few valleys or miles in either direction. When a language is small and spoken by few, it claims the specifics around it with a passion that larger linguistic groups never know. Each tree can have a name, each rock and grove a history. And when things are named, and not merely identified or categorized, they can be addressed personally. The world is alive, sentient, watchful, and listening. You need no omniscient God to punish or reward you for your acts. It is the trees who see you, the creeks who hear you, the birds and the animals who watch your every move. You are part of them, and they of you. Your responsibilities are mutual and intertwined.

If only the loggers could, for a moment, return to this understanding. If only they could call these trees by name, know them as individual living beings. But that truth, if it exists at all, is guarded by old hippies living in tree houses and loosely-wired new agers full-gossamer fantasies. It is no longer guarded by people who carry the moral authority to speak of and for these great beings.

I'm afraid the only people who truly have that authority have been swept almost out of existence by the succeeding waves of immigrants to this coast. They have been made the keepers of the casinos rather than the keepers of the trees, and when they speak, it's in our own imperfect language. Only those old hippies and new agers even bother to listen.

I look for a spot to stop. I could pull in at one of the main groves, but I want to find a pulloff that seems to have no purpose. Usually, these mark the entry to a private place, known only to a few.

I drive slowly until I see a small path, hardly visible, leading off from the side of the road. I park the Tuna and enter into the forest. The trail weaves and winds through bracken and moss and tangled growth.

My foot can barely pass through the humus and the rot. Twisted roots grab at me; groping tendrils touch my legs. Ferns with boughs as big as eagles' wings block my way.

All around me froglike sounds cry out. Water moves beneath me in unseen pathways. The dankness drips, and greens as dark as lizard eyes reach out to touch me. Beneath each spongy step is life immeasurable. This is new earth, formed by the commingling of liquid and decay; a living ground, woven of death and birth so closely bound as to be inseparable. Life springs almost instantaneously from the muck.

I inhale deeply. The air is alive and moist. I'm standing in the lungs of the earth. All around me I can sense the breathings of this ancient race, indifferent to my presence, unconscious of my time, with a musk unforgettable and sweet.

Eventually, the path opens into a hidden sanctuary ringed by giants towering to the sky. I enter quietly into its heavy darkness. Dappling shafts of sunlight shoot down like messages from the gods.

I'm tired, breathing hard. I lie on a fallen trunk and stare skyward in awestruck humility. The tops of the trees move majestically in the wind. They seem more conversant with the clouds than they are with me.

So much rushes across me: cathedrals, witches' covens, druidic rituals—our struggling human attempts to make contact with the divine. I recall the echoing silence of the cathedral in the small German town where I once lived. Its towering Gothic arches were but pallid imitations of these forest grottoes; the solemnity of its stained glass was but the domestication of this holy filtered light.

As I lie here, I can't help sensing how much like we humans these great beings seem, with their feet on the earth, their heads in the sky, their arms stretched out in solemn supplication. I can almost hear them breathing as I rest beneath their towering boughs.

Life seems so simple as I rest here among them; their lessons for us humans seem so clear: "Find your place, accept it with grace. Grow roots before you grow branches. Give shelter, shade, and nourishment to those who seek your protection. And in your passing, leave the earth richer for those who follow."

Far above, the wisps of fog are starting to make their way among the treetops. A branch moves slightly, and an arrow of amber light streams down to touch my hand. The light plays upon my fingers, then withdraws. I feel honored and chosen, as if I have just received a blessing or, maybe, a message.

The Avenue of the Giants ends at Phillipsville, and I'm forced back onto the freeway. I'm not ready to return to the venal reality of vehicular bustle, so I decide to stop at Garberville, the next small town to the south, to consider my options.

I remember Garberville well. It was once the ultimate war zone between the loggers and the hippies. It was close enough to the Bay Area to attract an influx of middle-class kids who had been raised far from the economic necessities of logging. Yet it was far enough from any population center to have a local populace that had been there for generations, living off the bounty of the forests and distrusting anything urban and intellectual.

When the hippies started coming, the battle was joined. To the locals, it made no difference whether these new longhairs were tie-dyed airheads who mouthed disconnected half-formed platitudes while dancing in the redwood groves, or hard-core ecological ideologues who had been battle-tested on the streets of Oakland and Berkeley. All were outsiders, and they all, in some fashion, threatened the only way of life these people knew. The result was a line in the sand, and all who chose to live here were on one side or the other. It was far more dire than the confrontation between the loggers and my ilk in the Oregon hills. Here, the trees were bigger and the stakes were higher. You could hear the heavy breathing of the Bay Area, and money, not poverty, fueled the fires of the confrontation.

Upon entering Garberville I see that the whole calculus has changed. Interspersed with the idling log trucks and old hippie pick-ups and station wagons are Ford Explorers, Jeep Cherokees, Porsches, and BMWs. Most of them have license-plate holders that carry the names of Bay Area dealerships.

Two college-age kids in baggy shorts with mountain bikes strapped to the top of their Suzuki Samurai are tossing a Frisbee in the street. Their car stereo is foomping out some insistent and assaultive rap tune. Middle-aged women in logo-covered athletic gear are coming and going from little faux general stores. A man in an L.L. Bean windbreaker is delicately arranging some wrapped item in the trunk of an Audi. The whole place feels like a resort town where people with too much wealth have come to play.

I don't like it, and I want to get out. I preferred the stark political confrontations of the loggers and the hippies. At least something beyond self-gratification was at stake.

I decide to head out in search of the place near here where I had once spent a night many years ago. My memory is hazy, but I recall a winding, bumping dirt road with campfires burning on the hillsides and houses made of salvaged windows fitted into structures crafted of tree trunks. I remember being led by kerosene lantern to a room in an old cabin, and waking in the morning to see a tall, gaunt man rising naked from an army sleeping bag, surrounded by five or six women, again all naked, in varying degrees of pregnancy, nestled together in a welter of quilts and sleeping bags like puppies in a bin. He was the leader of this particular family, had a Ph.D. in Chinese history, or so I was told, and had given up a college teaching position to pursue some personal obsession with arcane Vedic texts. I don't expect to find him; nor do I want to. I just want to see how far reality is from the gauzy images of my recollection.

The rich nectar of manzanita tingles in my nostrils as I wind down the curving lanes that cut into the coastal hillsides. I have no idea where I'm going, but I'm enjoying the drive. Soon I break into a clearing that contains a little crossroads store. It seems vaguely familiar.

A heavy middle-aged woman with wild salt-and-pepper hair is struggling to pull a loom out of an old Chevy Celebrity station wagon crammed to overflowing with assorted weaving paraphernalia. Her contortions reveal dark hairy legs and worn-out Birkenstocks beneath her faded ground-length skirt. Thirty years ago she was probably some young hippie chick dancing in the fountains of Golden Gate Park or curled up in that jumble of sleeping bags and quilts in the gaunt man's hovel. Now she is perilously close to becoming a bag lady.

Two men wearing felt broad-brimmed hats and sporting scraggly grey beards down to their waists stand in front of a bulletin board reading a poster about cosmic consciousness. They are serious and taciturn—something between Z.Z. tops and granola rabbis.

Directly in front of me a wild-eyed man is rocking on his toes and making little spider movements with his fingers while emitting a variety of meaningless yips and shouts. His beard too is long, pubic, and untrimmed. No one is paying any attention to him.

A man on a bicycle—near relative to the sourdough in Takilma—proceeds up the road pulling a wagon piled ten feet high with black trash bags. He is hunched over, exerting mightily, making little progress. I feel as if I'm a million cultural miles from the yuppie crossroads that appears to have evolved in Garberville.

Suddenly I hear a rhythmic thumping from the canyon behind me. The Samurai with its whooping stereo squeals around the corner and pulls in beside me. One of the baggy-shorts guys vaults out and runs into the store. The other leans back and pops open a beer. He doesn't shut off the stereo.

The spider-fingered man cocks his head quizzically. The granola rabbis turn slowly and stare. I drive away as quickly as I can. In some abstract way, I'm feeling hunted.

The road drops deeper into the coastal folds. It follows the over-grown ravines where it can, rises up over the hilltops where it must. One minute I'm on a sun-drenched hillside resplendent with Med-iterranean vegetation. The next, I'm passing through the dark solem-nity of the towering redwoods. It induces a strange Manichaeism of the spirit to move so quickly from light to darkness and back to light. But I'm feeling better. I seem to have left the Samurai and its whomping stereo far behind.

The road gets narrower and less passable. I pass by yards full of junk cars, Coca-Cola signs, peace signs, barber poles, rocking chairs, and engine hoists. This is outpost reality with a doper's edge.

As I turn a corner I come upon a flattened car body tied upon a giant rock. I'm mystified and amazed. Great effort was required, but to what end?

Art? Perhaps, in the postmodern craziness where effort with a pur-pose equals artistic creation: "It will be a juxtaposition of the eternity of a boulder with the transience of contemporary culture, and instead of having the boulder crush the car, we will have the car, metaphori-cally, crush the boulder."

Humor? Perhaps. "Far out. Let's go to the junkyard and get one of those squashed cars and chain-hoist it up on that giant boulder. Then we'll tie it with ropes. That will blow people's minds."

Drug-induced obsession? "That was my favorite car, man. It got me out here. I always want to be able to see it. You know, like Roy Rogers had Trigger stuffed and put in his bedroom. I'm going to have my Rambler crushed and put on that rock."

I drive by slowly, unable to fathom exactly what it is I'm seeing. An old hippie carrying a rifle eyes me suspiciously as I pass.

Eventually I reach the rutted terminus of the road. From here it deteriorates into personal pathways and private marijuana patches. Prudence dictates that I go no further. I back my way into a clearing and turn the Tuna around.

I navigate my way back up through the hills toward Garberville. I feel like some sort of cultural troglodyte returning from the underground.

Soon I'm back at the town center. The boys in their Samurai are there, this time with a collection of young girls in bulging halter tops. A log truck is idling on the side of the road. Its diesel rumble is the equal of the whooping subwoofers of the Samurai. On its back are several forty-foot-long redwood logs as big around as pickups.

I fill my car with gas and contemplate the dark harmonics of the various stereos and engines that are pulsating around me. While I'm fueling, a tall, angular man with deep, intense eyes comes out from the service station. He looks at me for a minute, then nods, crosses the street, and climbs into the log truck. The air brakes wheeze, the gears engage, and the truck moves slowly down the tree-shaded roadway. I stare at the butt ends of the great amputated redwoods as they disappear from view. I know it's crazy, but I can't help but think that the driver looked exactly like my hazy memory of the Chinese Ph.D. rising naked from his harem and his pile of sleeping bags.

ELEVEN

FORK IN THE ROAD

It's way past midnight. I'm in a dingy motel room near Garberville. I'm having a hard night. The day was too much about dislocations and artificial impositions. It makes me question the wisdom of this whole enterprise. The prison, the family in Eureka, the implied solution of new-growth trees to the destruction of old-growth forests all seem like metaphors I ignore at my own peril. Do I belong here? Do we belong here? Would I not simply be trying to transplant the shoot of our family into unfamiliar ground?

What if it didn't take? What if we became a failed transplant? Would we then become rootless—American tumbleweeds able to find rest only in the homogenized sameness of American consumer culture? I don't know.

After all, everyone at one time is an immigrant, whether you came during the dust bowl, during the '60s, or eons ago across the Bering land bridge or in reed boats along the seacoast. All those people didn't descend into superficiality and banality. Maybe I don't trust enough in the transformative power of the land. Maybe it's not about roots, but about risk.

But I can't ignore the reality of Garberville. It was an ominous foreshadowing of inevitable change, and a spiritual diminution I could not endure. What had once been a forest crossroads was now a miniature traffic jam. Stereos were pumping, car doors were slamming. Vehicles rolled endlessly up and down the once quiet main street.

I could hear no wind. I could hear no waves. The immensity was gone. The eternal roll of the sea, the whisper of trees brushing against the sky, all those things that make this land what it is, were subsumed. A roof had been put over the top of things. The big gods were gone. Everyone was at a party.

Now I'm lying in my bed, at the south end of the great redwood forests, listening to a clock tick off the minutes of a night that will not end. I'm tired and weary, ready to be done with this travel. I'm sick of being here. I long to sleep in my own bed.

I guess I shouldn't be surprised that this feeling has come over me. I knew it had to happen; I just didn't know when. It surfaces in every journey—an ineffable weariness of spirit that dampens the sense of adventure and reduces every day to a repetitious sameness. The mission grows dim; the spirit of discovery grows stale. You just want to be home.

Here, in this dreary motel room on the south end of the redwoods, that moment has come to me. I'm unsure of myself, unsure of my purpose, and lonely to the core for what I've left behind.

I roll over in my bed and stare at the evil little clock. It's one of those antiquated models with little cards that flip over every time a minute changes.

Ca-chik. Two twenty-five. Ca-chik. Two twenty-six.

Maybe I should call Louise. This room at least has a phone. But what good would that do? "Hi. This is me. Yes, I know it's twelve-thirty. No, nothing's wrong. I just wanted to hear your voice."

That's just what she needs—a peripatetic husband seeking long-distance solace in the middle of the night. When we were young and our hearts were bleeding for each other every minute, such a call would have been a tortured balm: "Oh, yes, I love you. . . . I love you too. . . . I wish you were here. . . . I wish you were here too."

There would be some of that now. But we're older, more accustomed to separations. Wiser heads must prevail. She doesn't need my uncertainty, at least not in the middle of the night. Instead, she needs my confidence, and the solace of the knowledge that I'm taking care of business on my end, so she can take care of hers without the added burden of having to prop me up emotionally. Better to wait until the light of dawn, when the outside world puts limits on the borderless fears and fantasies of late-night thoughts.

So what am I to do? I can't sleep. The room has no television. I don't want to read. My mind is a weapon that has turned against me. There's really no escape.

Ca-chik. Two forty-one. Ca-chik. Two forty-two. God, it's Edgar Allan Poe and the telltale clock.

Let's see. A hundred and fifty miles to the Bay Area. Maybe I could just drive down, forget about looking around, and fly out tomorrow. I could say I got sick. Or I could do something revolutionary and tell the truth: "I just got tired. I wanted to see you."

No, that won't work. The hollow gaze would too soon return to my eyes, and everything I had left unresolved would just come back to the surface. One too many green-teethed men in big pickup trucks, another tragic old woman with a lamp for sale, and it would all start again. Temporary spiritual weariness is not an adequate reason to curtail this journey.

I roll onto my back and stare at the ceiling. My mind wanders crazily. I begin to think about the pioneers and settlers who crossed the great western plains to this coast. What must it have been like for them when this spiritual exhaustion hit?

How must they have felt to wake up one night halfway through the journey and think, "No. It's over. This is enough. We're stopping here. We're not going on"?

I imagine those who chose to stop, standing somewhere along the trail, watching as the wagon train pulled away, while they stood with their family, their possessions, their hope, and a great emptiness in their hearts, wondering if their decision had been right, and if those who had chosen to go on were not perhaps braver, stronger, and wiser than they?

How did they know if they had made the right choice? Did it gnaw at them forever? Does it gnaw at their children now, generations later, passed down through the blood and some collective unconscious, whispering to them as they stare at the sunset on the western horizon? Is that what drives those of us in the middle to doubt the finality of our place on this continent?

It's the burden of the settler: those who push on are always cast as the heroes. There's an unspoken sense that they are the more courageous and more adventurous and that their willingness to forge ahead is a sign of strength lacking in those who remain behind. Alan Ladd rides off, the dumpy dad stands there with his shovel and his ax, while Mom and the kid look longingly at the figure departing into the sunset. "Come on, there's work to do," says Dad, and they all buckle down to a life sentence of hoeing potatoes.

No, you don't quit in mid-journey, no matter how good the soil or how noble the enterprise. You need to go to the end, then make your choice to backtrack if you so desire. You make it willingly, voluntarily, with full open-eyed awareness of what you have chosen, and what you have chosen to leave behind.

Yet there's the other side, the dark side. Every traveler knows that the indefatigable pushing, the urge to continue despite all rational arguments to the contrary, is often nothing more than the blind action of someone crazed and intoxicated with the sensation of movement.

Stories abound of families enduring the sufferings and travails of the great journey to the Oregon territory, only to have the husband insist on continuing, alone, to the south and the California gold fields. When he had left his home back east, the promise of his own more fertile land had been enough. But months of traveling had somehow unhinged his sense of destination and supplanted it with an uncontrollable urge to movement.

Maybe that's our great American curse. No matter how natural the stop, no matter how completely it fulfills our needs, there remains a sense of irritability that claws away, saying, "Is this all there is? Can

I expect nothing more?" It's as if the internal gyroscope still spins, even though all external circumstance cries out for stoppage and rest.

Maybe the farmer with his ax is the real hero. Maybe Shane is nothing more than a pitiful clown, the perpetual adolescent, who nowadays goes from woman to woman instead of from town to town, never able to make a claim on a person or a place or a life, obsessed with himself and his cheesy heroic isolation.

After all, even Odysseus returned to Penelope. It's only Jesus and the cowboys who seemed obsessed with always going over the next hill.

I pull the pillow over my head. I can't let this go on. Now I've brought Jesus into the argument. My hinges are clearly coming loose. I don't know whether I'm a man longing for rest, a gyroscope spinning out of control, a father abandoning his family, or a hero in search of the Grail.

I jump out of bed and look out the window at the rain. The redwoods stand, mute and indifferent, in the whispering fog. The Tuna sits in front of the motel, beckoning.

I turn on the light, grab my map, and begin staking out routes and computing distances. A quick shower and I'm back on the road, heading off over the next hill, no longer sure if I'm running from something to something, or simply circling like a bird too cowardly and uncertain to land.

The storm has made its way south. The rain beats viciously on the windshield as I motor through the night. This is a true Pacific winter storm—the water comes in sheets and the wind shakes the car in shuddering gusts. It's the kind of night described in cheap novels as "fit for neither man nor beast." And this description is embarrassingly apt, because right now, I feel like something between a man and a beast. My dreams are shaky, my memory is faulty, and the darkness is filled with fears and phantoms. I'm driving like a maniac, trying to get away from the man who inhabits my skin. I just have to make it till daylight without making any big decisions. Then the morning light will put things back in focus.

But ahead, just a few miles away, a big decision is demanding to be made. At Leggett the road forks, and I'm going to have to decide whether to turn left and slingshot my way south into the Bay Area on U.S. 101, or turn right and take the curving, coast-hugging drive along Highway 1 through Mendocino, Point Arena, and the other coastal towns.

Normally, this would be a simple choice between beauty and expediency. But tonight nothing is simple. I'm a man beset by demons and ghosts, and Highway 1, for me, is a road haunted by demons and ghosts. I've got to decide whether I want to do battle with them, or whether I just want to pass them by.

It all goes back to those days at Stanford, when I had first come out here to go to school. I was young, confused, and desperately unhappy. But it wasn't just Stanford and its wealthy suburban setting, though that's what I told my family. It wasn't just my life of crabbed note taking and listening to professors drone on about theories of soteriology, though that's what I told my friends. And it wasn't just living in overpriced rental housing with students who were so competitively obsessed that they flirted with suicide if they didn't get the highest grade in the class, though that's what I tried hard to make myself believe.

No, it was a girl—a beautiful, simple, waiflike girl I had left back in Minnesota.

She was my first love, and I loved her with that purity of heart you get only once in your life. We were God's chosen ones; in our presence the angels wept with envy.

But I was also a young man obsessed with God, and therein lay the rub. For reasons as complicated as the constellations in the sky, I had come to believe that the only route to spiritual fulfillment was through the dark and icy passages of solitude and asceticism. There was no such thing as finding God in a warm embrace or seeing human love as a mirror of the divine presence. Human love was weakness, a snare to draw the eye downward from things of the spirit to things of the flesh.

This was no twisted psychological ploy to avoid human intimacy; it was me taking the measure of my own spiritual purity and commitment to God. I walked haltingly in the giant footsteps of Jesus, St. Paul, the Buddha, and St. Francis. I scraped my knees on the stones before St. John of the Cross and Thomas à Kempis. Self-transcendence, not self-realization, was my goal. Human love, I believed, would turn me from that light and I would be left with the false, illusory warmth of human hearth fires. Yet, in my heart, I wanted nothing more than to feel that love and sit by those fires.

Into this titanic youthful struggle had walked that sweet, innocent girl, and I immediately turned her into the dual embodiment of both perfect human love and a perfect spiritual snare.

I loved her, I hated her, I embraced her, I pushed her away. We dreamed, we laughed, we fought, we wept. But, always, we came back together. It was one of those awful relationships with tearful separations and joyful reunions, desperate cross-country drives to throw ourselves into each other's arms, and then the slow, agonizingly familiar crumbling of our dreams into bickering and recriminations.

She had stepped into the front lines of a man doing battle with God, and she was a casualty of war. The great, brutal irony was that in her simplicity, she possessed a spiritual purity far beyond any that my spiritual ragings could ever achieve.

If I had been Francis with Clare, or Abelard with Héloïse, perhaps we could have scaled some spiritual heights, for, in many ways, she had the spiritual purity of Clare or Héloïse. But despite my dreams of spiritual elevation, I was no Francis or Abelard; I was a yearning, aching, Kerouac-reading, cross-country-driving, blues-listening, Yeats- and Eliot-quoting, tortured young man who kept Dostoevsky by his bedside and raged at the heavens for all the blind, crippled, poor, and friendless who lived in lonely suffering on this cruel and incomprehensible earth. She, on the other hand, simply loved and accepted.

A friend of mine, less inclined to spiritual interpretations of things than I, once put it succinctly and pithily. I lived life like a wolf, he said, while she lived it like a golden retriever puppy. And this was the chasm we simply could not bridge.

In the last analysis, I could not love her and live in the world, just as I could not love her and be the type of spiritual seeker that at that age I believed I needed to be. My love for her was a betrayal of my austere, solitary love for God; my life with her was a betrayal of my existential, analytical relationship to the world. Either everything I was had to go, or she had to go.

Eventually, I determined—we determined—that she had to go. I left for Stanford with tears in my eyes and a hole in my heart. In the famous words carved in the hearts of all parting lovers, if it was meant to be, it was meant to be. Our time apart would reveal all. I would test myself against the intellectual rigors of Stanford. She would weave her Penelope's shroud and wait to see if I came to my senses.

But Stanford did not work out. I was hungry for God and being fed philosophical theology; I was aching for love and sleeping alone under a pile of blankets on the floor of an overpriced suburban rental house in Palo Alto. On weekends I would drink myself silly on tequila or Windsor Canadian, or get in my rapidly deteriorating Volkswagen bus and drive north to San Francisco and wander the streets watching happy couples go arm in arm into clubs and cafes. Once or twice a month I would have a spasm of academic guilt and stoke my brain full of enough methedrine to do a hundred hours of work in the course of an evening, and would produce impacted, convoluted prose that my professors mistook for unformed, but trainable, intellectual brilliance. In this way, I kept my head above water, though it was obvious to anyone who cared enough to notice that, in fact, I was drowning.

Eventually, I, too, realized I was sinking, and if I didn't do something, I would come to a bitter, maybe tragic, end. I switched gears and determined that my decision had been a mistake: it was not my pure-hearted, distant lover who had to go; it was everything else I stood for that had to go. I would make the call and arrange for her to come out, then slowly unravel the mess I had made of my life and put together a life the two of us could share.

Enter Highway 1, the road I'm now approaching. This one-hundred-and-fifty-mile coastal drive was the place where I was going to find the answer. On my weekend jaunts north from Palo Alto, I had often crossed the Golden Gate and driven over Mt. Tamalpais to the small seaside towns of Bolinas and Stinson Beach. There I found people like me, living the way I wanted to live. They were not accursed and stultified intellectuals. They were artists and eccentrics and cranks dreaming big dreams and living artistic, eccentric, and cranky lives within earshot of the sea.

On long weekends and holidays I pushed even farther north on Highway 1 and found even more congenial settings—places that seemed idyllic, even magical, in both their locations and their lifestyles. Olema, Point Reyes Station, Bodega Bay, Mendocino—little weathered-cottage towns sitting on shelves of land thrusting out into a cobalt sea, with window boxes full of flowers, cafes smelling of fresh breads, and shops of artisans crafting stained-glass chandeliers and carving carousel-quality black-walnut rocking horses.

People would smile at me as I walked down the streets, invite me to their houses, do my astrological chart, ply me with brown rice and dope and homemade wine, tell me arcane and convoluted theories about human consciousness that, for reasons I can no longer recall, seemed infinitely more logical and valuable than the theories of soteriology and eschatology I had left behind in the academy.

Suddenly it all seemed so simple. My girlfriend and I would come to one of these towns and find some little weathered house overlooking the sea. She'd garden and sew, I'd carve and write, we'd make love to the sound of the surf, then wander hand in hand to one of those small cozy cafes where people who looked like us, thought like us, and shared our vision of a simple, idyllic life would welcome us with the warm embrace of easy friendship.

I'd forget T. S. Eliot. I'd forget the magic mountain and Raskalnikov and my beatnik boddhisatva vision of allowing myself no happiness until all others were in heaven before me. Instead of struggling with Yeats and his rough beast slouching toward Bethlehem, I'd simply join the ranks of those who had moved into the new Jerusalem. We'd sit around bonfires at the beach, smoking joints with gentle-hearted, intellectually unencumbered people.

And it almost worked. She quit her waitressing job in Minneapolis and bought a ticket west. We spent weekends walking the streets of these little coastal towns, placing "Cottage Wanted" ads on bulletin boards, meeting residents, sitting on rocky promontories overlooking the sea, and sharing excited conversations about how everything was going to be fine when we finally got the chance to live this life of magical innocence in this magical land of artists and visionaries.

As should have been obvious, our dreams were doomed. Nothing had changed about either of us. I was no less obsessed with God and the icy regions of spiritual asceticism; she was no less affirming and intellectually disinterested. We fought, we cried, we made love, we made up. We did everything but get it right.

Eventually, I made her so miserable that out of grief and a desire for solace she went to another man, leaving me to loathe and flagellate myself and to wallow in a pit of spiritual desolation so deep I thought I would never emerge.

And so this road—Highway 1, the road that had been our road of hope and fantasies—became, instead, my road of broken dreams. While she was struggling to put her life back together in the arms of another man less twisted and tortured than I, I continued to drive north from Stanford in my Volkswagen bus, coming to these little towns and sitting hollow-eyed in the seaside cafes, watching men like me with beautiful, vibrant women and happy children, and wondering what dark stain was on my soul that would not allow me to give myself wholly to such simple, joyful human pleasures.

I walked the seaside cliff tops at night, cursing and begging God, as the indifferent ocean crashed and roared far below me. The lights in the houses flickered on the hillsides, and I would imagine the love inside them, the warm nights, the shared morning cups of coffee, the children and the laughter. Then I would climb back into my van, curl up in the damp in my old army-surplus sleeping bag, and read

Narcissus and Goldmund or Kazantzakis's *Last Temptation of Christ* until I fell into a cold and tearful sleep.

Now Highway 1 looms again.

Do I really want to drive down this road of golden dreams, on a cold and dreary morning, and wander into shops alive with ghosts and a young man's demons? Every place I've visited so far on this journey has proven that memory is a cruel mistress. And this is not a journey about my past; it's a journey about my family's future.

Psychologists might stroke their beards and smirk knowingly about denial and avoidance. But I prefer to say, simply, "When I was a child, I thought like a child. Since I've become a man, I've given up my childish ways." Water flows where it will and seeks its own level. We grow and change, and some things we simply leave behind.

I now find deep rest in the arms of a very different woman, and I love her with all my heart. She has a mind that challenges me, interests that expand me, a sense of humor and a delight that buoy me, and a strong, courageous sense of self that humbles me. I love watching her grow and make her way through the world.

She leaves me room to carry on my love affair with God, and for that I love her all the more. The young man who wanted to be subsumed into God is now thankful to simply brush against the holy. The man who looked on human relationships as snares now honors them as the ultimate gift of a loving and present Creator and, instead of shaking his fist at God, now drops to his knees in prayerful thankfulness. Louise is the woman who made this possible, and I am at peace.

Still, that road not taken beckons, and it will beckon forever.

The headlights catch the sign for Highway 1. It flashes brightly through the dark, its arrow pointing off toward the right. My muscles urge left; my muscles urge right. In a split second I make and remake the decision a hundred times, a hundred ways.

Reason, emotion, wisdom, knowledge, memory, hope, honor, regret—all do battle in the twinkling of an eye.

The turn is coming; I have to choose.

I slam on the Tuna's brakes and slide to a stop on the gravel shoulder. I should have thought of this earlier.

Years ago, in *Yojimbo,* one of my favorite films, I saw Toshiro Mifune perform an act that has impacted my life ever since. At the end of the film, in order to decide which direction to go in his life, he picked up a stick and threw it high in the air. It spun, came down, bounced once or twice, and settled. He walked over, aligned himself with it, and headed off in the direction it was pointing.

That, for me, was the true definition of faith. God isn't helping basketball players make free throws. Scraping my knees on the stones and petitioning him for light isn't going to give me answers. He's made me a free man, equally cursed and blessed with the gift of free will, and the closest I believe he will come to giving me an answer is allowing me to believe in the strange, inscrutable wisdom of the universe.

This stick in the air is my claim on that belief.

I step from the car. The air is chill; the sky is still dark. The rain has let up momentarily. A blast of blustery wind rushes across me, causing me to shiver. On the side of the road I find a stick about as thick as my wrist and a foot long. I stand before the sign and toss it underhand as high as I can in the air. It spins lazily, reaches its zenith, and comes back toward the earth almost directly before my feet. It hits once, bounces on the wet gravel, and comes to rest. I walk over and stare down at it. Then, with a smile on my face and a song in my heart, I walk back to the Tuna, put on my turn signal, and aim left onto the long, loping roadway of U. S. 101.

God spoke clearly: there's no gain in chasing ghosts when what you hold in your arms is enough.

TWELVE

PERFECT MARIN

Once I made the decision at Leggett—or rather once the decision was made—things got easier. I guess I'd been hit by a double whammy: I knew I was about to leave the comforting immensity of nature and descend into the jingle-jangle of urban culture, and I knew I was driving toward a dangerous and seductive part of my past. Neither was particularly appealing, and when you add in the spiritual fatigue and the dampening presence of a Pacific winter rain, small wonder that self-doubt had begun to creep in and overwhelm my sense of purpose. But there's an urban animal inside of me as well, and he's a pretty resourceful creature, well able to adapt to the rhythms and smells of street life when the occasion demands. All I needed to do was accept the fact that it was time for him to come out.

It was a conversation in Laytonville that really set him free. I had outdriven the rain and had stopped at a convenience store to clear my head and shake myself into consciousness. I was still lost in the trees and the memories and the winsome recollections of lost coastal dreams. Some young Chicano kid in a raked, red '50s Chevy pickup truck started talking to me in the parking lot. He had that California lightness and lilt in his manner that said, "My life may not be much, but at least I'm having fun."

We got talking about cars we'd owned. He showed me the new upholstery job he had just completed on the interior of his truck—red and white leather, with a matching tuck-and-roll dashboard. By the time he pulled out of the lot with his glass packs rumbling, I was less offended at the noise he was making than I was appreciative of the statement his vehicle made.

"Have a good one, man," he shouted.

"You too, man," I shouted back.

I knew right then I was going to be fine. For the moment, at least, culture had trumped nature, activity had drowned out mystery, and self-doubt and uncertainty had been replaced by the urban excitement of endless possibility.

I rummaged around in my tape box and found a compilation I had made off a bunch of old LPs that sit moldering in my garage. A healthy dose of Al Green and Carlos Santana later, I was one-handing it down the highway, tapping out rhythms on my dashboard, and singing along with every song.

Now I'm on the north end of Sonoma, entering into the salmon run of traffic down the freeway stretch of U. S. 101 toward the Bay Area. San Francisco and my old haunts loom ahead. I have no fear of ghosts there. Everything there is a ghost—every street corner, every stop sign, every shop. In a very different way from yesterday afternoon when I was listening to the ocean, I feel as though I'm coming home.

Though last night was tough, I'm glad it happened. It forced me to examine my motives as well as my modus operandi. Louise was right: these are my demons, and I have to do battle with them. Now it's clear that these demons are not the demons of my past. It is not who I was that I need to confront; it's who I want to be.

Ever since my stop in Eugene, I've been harboring the unspoken conviction that I would probably visit a bunch of old friends when I got to the Bay Area. Like someone who has broken a New Year's resolution, I took all bets off the table when I visited George: I had broken my commitment to do this journey without visiting acquaintances, so promises I'd made to myself no longer carried any real authority.

Since then I've been making mental lists of who I might contact. Any of a dozen people would be happy to see me, and a simple phone call would result in an invitation to stay the night or the weekend, a welcome respite from the rolling loneliness of the road. Now, having wrestled the memories up there at the junction of Highway 1, I realize my focus should not be on what it is that I left, but on what it is that caused me to leave. And it wasn't my friends who drove me out; it was something in the character, in the *geist,* of the place.

If I truly want to find that something, I've got to forget the seductions of past good times and let the lives of strangers speak to me. I've got to find people who live here, listen to their stories, and see how this crazy, seductive place has shaped their various characters. I have to do what I do best: talk to folks and get them to tell their stories. If I choose well, I should be able to put together an ideogram of meaning that will tell me something about the shape of life out here. Maybe I'll see some of what drove me out; maybe I'll see some of what's calling me back. Maybe I'll find my ram in the thicket.

I decide to start in Marin, partly because I'm entering the Bay Area from the north, and partly because I've always felt that, in some ways, Marin is the epitome of Bay Area culture. It's also where I had my first real introduction to Bay Area life thirty years ago.

I had driven off from Minnesota with a few names and the phone numbers of one or two shirttail acquaintances who had moved here from their Minnesota lairs.

Upon arriving, I called one of the numbers in hopes of getting some grounding in this huge, amorphous place. In keeping with the spirit of the times, I was immediately invited over and welcomed by a pack of breezy, easygoing folk. Almost before I had time to get everyone's name straight, I was piled into a car and spirited off to a party in Mill Valley. I didn't know what or where Mill Valley was. To me, there was San Francisco and a bunch of bit players—the Midwestern notion of the city as center and everything else as subordinate suburb.

As we drove across the Golden Gate Bridge, I began to get the sense that maybe this was not a monolithic world expanding in concentric circles from a single urban epicenter. San Francisco was being left far behind, and in front of me were verdant green headlands with houses perched precariously on towering hillsides. My friends were singing and passing joints—a practice that filled me with dark terrors of Turkish-like prisons and permanent incarceration. But I wasn't in Kansas anymore; I was in Rome, trying to do as the Romans did. So I smoked and passed and sang and laughed.

I really knew I had left Kansas as soon as I saw the rainbow painted around the opening to the Marin tunnel through the hills on the north side of the bridge. Such a bit of foofery would never have been tolerated in the Midwest. It would have cost too much money and, besides, our parents didn't need rainbows around their tunnels. Why should we?

Soon we were driving up twisting hillside roadways unlike anything I had ever known, through vegetation unlike anything I had ever seen, to a redwood house unlike any I had ever visited, to a party filled with a group of people unlike any I had ever imagined.

I was used to basement gatherings with cheap wine, red lights hanging in the corners, the heavy sweetness of marijuana in the air, and old blues on the record player. Things were intimate, intense, claustrophobic, with an edge of hysteria and paranoia. Everyone was always between twenty and thirty, and a wary eye was kept toward anyone who might be underage, overage, or an outsider.

When I stepped out of the car at the Mill Valley party, I stepped into a world with no boundaries. People were hanging out on decks that blended into the succulent, flowering foliage. Music was wafting through the hills. Children were running around, laughing, and shouting. People were openly passing joints to strangers, including the children. People who seemed ancient to me—men and women with crow's-feet around their eyes and flowing white hair—were sitting naked in a hot tub along with teenage girls and boys. New arrivals were casually disrobing and climbing in alongside the others.

It was inconceivable to me—at once both terrifying and fascinating. This was the openness I had dreamed of when I had packed up and left the stultifying confines of the Midwest. But when my friends pulled me toward the hot tub, my life flashed before me. In a haze of embarrassment I stripped naked and walked across the deck like Adam being expelled from the garden in a medieval painting. Before long I was sitting in the froth, touching naked shoulders and hips with people I didn't know, feeling strange legs against my own and unseen hands brushing against my thighs.

I woke up the next morning, curled up on the deck, with birds singing above me, manzanita and eucalyptus tickling my nostrils, and the sight of one of the white-haired women from the hot tub wearing a flowing, flowered muumuu, smoking a long ceramic pipe full of hashish and cooking up a breakfast of vegetables and chapatis for the twenty or so of us who were draped around her house in various configurations and various degrees of undress.

This experience set an indelible stamp on my ten years of living out here, and it seems only fitting that I should start my journey back into the Bay Area in the place where, in some ways, everything all began.

But I don't want to underestimate the other reason for starting here, and that is the very character of Marin itself. I understand all too well what it is that the rough-handed laborers of Del Norte so despise about this place. People here spend more on shiatsu for their dogs than some of the loggers make in a year. But if you're able to look past the wealth and excess, or, better yet, if you're able to see the wealth and excess as abundance and possibility, this is the Bay Area at its idyllic best. It's the life I would like to live if I had all the money in the world and were suddenly lobotomized of all guilt and sense of social responsibility.

As I have often told my friends in the Midwest, Marin is the litmus test for American culture: either the revolution will start here, or this will be the first place leveled when the revolution comes. It's just a matter of which revolution you believe in—the revolution of consciousness or the revolution of economic justice.

This morning, however, those issues are not even on my intellectual radar. I'm blasted on loud music and freeway rhythms. Redwoods and oceans and loggers and workers are all in the past. This is rock-and-roll highway, and I'm getting my fix.

Down the great serpent of a freeway through San Rafael and Corte Madera. God, how I love this landscape. The quality of light and the ambrosial gentleness of the air make it almost irresistible.

If geography is destiny, Marin has been dealt about as good a hand as you can get. It's separated from the busyness of San Francisco by the open waters of the Golden Gate; its western edge is washed by the sea, while its eastern shore lies soft against the San Francisco Bay and Napa Valley. In between lie the fecund, rolling hills of the most open, least populated land in the entire Bay Area. These hills are large enough to create broad vistas for the eye, but small enough to create a sense of intimacy and gentle enclosure for those who live in their hollows. Life is carried on with a sense of graceful ease.

It is truly a unique place—so unique, in fact, that many of the wealthy people of Marin have left their inheritances to the county in hopes of maintaining and augmenting the Marin way of life for future generations. And it is a way of life. But it's more than hot tubs and naked parties—it's an entire worldview characterized by a fundamental belief in the perfectibility of the human character and the birthright of everyone to a life of abundance. To those of us from the outside it may seem naive and arrogant. But give yourself a couple of days among the rich nectars of manzanitas and the crystal blue of a sky washed by the sea, and it's hard—indeed, almost impossible—not to fall under the spell.

Right now, I'm happy to be under that spell. And, in homage to that first visit to Marin thirty years ago, I've chosen Mill Valley to try to entrance me.

Mill Valley sits nestled in a valley at the base of Mt. Tamalpais, a high rounded peak whose gentle curve reminded the Indians of a woman's breast. That visual image speaks well of both the sense of nourishment and the incipient sensuality that runs like an electric current through the entire experience of life in the North Bay.

Though I can't quite reconnect with that sensuality, any more than I could retrace my path to the house of that party, I can sense its tingle as I drive toward the town center.

I make my way through the rather ugly clot of supermarkets and banks that form the outskirts of Mill Valley, until I arrive at the town square. It's a large, tree-shaded area centered on a veranda filled with tables and benches. I park in one of the metered spaces that abuts the veranda and wander off to examine the little shops that line the surrounding streets.

It's now late morning, maybe ten thirty. Women in designer exercise suits and cotton sundresses and Birkenstocks drive up in front of the shops in their Volvo wagons and Mercedes, run in, grab packages, and drive away again. Young people who should be in school are playing hackysack under the manzanitas. Men in creased chinos and soft loafers sit at tables drinking cafe lattes while talking animatedly on cell phones. Everyone is busy, but no one seems to be working. Even the shopkeepers have a holiday lilt to their manner, laughing and joking with customers and stopping to carry on conversations about personal matters while other customers wait, without irritation, for their chance to be served.

At first I have a tough time settling down. My pace is wrong. Though I thought I had relaxed into a laid-back freeway-flier mode, I find I've still got a motorhead. My transactions and interactions still speak of a desire to be done with things and get moving rather than to go with the flow and take full enjoyment in process and interaction.

I tap my fingers and exhale theatrically as the woman ahead of me at a coffee shop buys a quarter pound of four or five different coffees, always answering the clerk's question, "Is there anything else?" with, "Yes, I'd like to have a bit of that over there," and then demanding a full explanation of where it came from and what its history is. She's on

a shopping expedition, and she's undertaking it with the care of someone about to embark upon a trek across the desert. But I just want to
get a roll and espresso and sit down. Yet it's clear that by feeling this
way, in some fundamental sense, I'm missing the point.

Also, I'm feeling singularly out of place. Everyone is dressed for
appearances, no one for function. At the pace of my travels, I'm only
several days removed from the truck stops of Oregon and Washington, where my clean hands and baggy jeans betrayed the bour-
geois nature of my lifestyle. Here I'm inappropriate in a different way.
The cut of my jib says department store rather than designer shop,
and although that was a sign of city softness to the Oregon loggers
and truck-stop gun toters, it marks me as a rube and a geehaw in this
setting of wealth and personal image.

Then, there's the bothersome memory of the Mexican laborers I
saw squatting by a drainage canal in San Rafael just north of here
when I pulled off for gas. They were laughing, smoking cigarettes,
lolling on the grass. I asked the station attendant what they were
doing, and he said they came there every day and waited to be hired
by Marinites who need a shrub removed or a garage cleaned or an old
appliance hauled away.

I must have betrayed some sense of disapproval, because he
quickly elaborated on his observation. "Hey," he said. "They get six,
eight bucks an hour. How much you think they'd be making in
Sonora or Ensenada?"

I suppose he's right, but they cast a shadow over my enjoyment as
I stand in line waiting for a three-dollar espresso in this garden valley
where hundred-thousand-dollar incomes provide you with a marginal
middle-class life and million-dollar houses are as common as the manzanita on the hillside.

Eventually my time in line comes. I order a shot of espresso with
just a little bit of steamed skim milk. "You mean a skinny macchiato,"
the young girl says, obviously trying to educate me as much as to clarify my order.

"Whatever you choose to call it," I say, resisting the temptation to observe that I thought Skinny Macchiato was a pistolero for the Gambese family. But even with my restraint, my voice sounds snarky and irritated.

I feel I should apologize, but she has shrugged me off with a smile and gone off to create my pedestrian drink.

"Wet or dry?" she shouts over to me.

I've never been quite clear on this "wet" and "dry" distinction, and, like a person who has never learned the difference between megs and RAM on a computer, I feel I must hide my ignorance. I developed my espresso habit twenty-five years ago in Italy—long before my current waitress was even born, and long before Americans had parsed and dissected coffee drinking, and elevated it into a marketing science. There you got what they made, and it was damnably good.

"Uh, wet," I say, and step back into the shadows.

By the time she finishes making my drink I have had to make four or five on-the-fly decisions: Wet or dry? Cinnamon or nutmeg? Cocoa? Chocolate sprinkles? Added flavors? Here or to go? Large cup or small? And a few I can't even remember. I've been occupied staring at the various coffee-bean selections and trying not to make any sociological connections between the Mexican varietals and the men squatting and smoking near the drainage ditch a dozen miles up the road.

She hands me my personalized, customized, wet, cinnamon but not too much, skinny macchiato. I give her my best Minnesota grateful smile and take a sip. It is, indeed, tasty.

"Next time just ask for a skinny mock," she says.

"I'll remember that," I say.

I make my way out to the veranda. I once again feel as if I'm at a party where everyone knows something that I don't understand.

I take a seat at a table near a man who's reading a *New York Times*. He's young, perhaps early thirties, trim, tan, with a calm and intelligent look about him. I can easily imagine him in an Armani suit sitting behind a great oak desk with the Manhattan skyline behind him, though here he sits in an open-collared white shirt—very well tailored but very relaxed—and wears a pair of triple-reverse-pleat taupe pants that break once at the instep of his woven tan loafers with white tops. A tasteful gold bracelet hangs loosely around his wrist and he wears no socks. A cell phone sits at the ready on the table next to his latte. He smiles and nods at me, and gestures toward the sections of the *Times* that he's already finished.

"Thanks," I say, and pick one up. He does not appear to have taken me for a vagrant in my grey T-shirt and blocky department-store jeans. I think I'll take the chance and talk to him.

I self-consciously wipe the milk foam from my mustache and consider an appropriate opening comment. I could mention some story in the *Times,* but that seems too political. I suppose I could ask him for directions or make some comment about the local sports teams, but those seem too contrived and forced. As I'm mulling over my options and looking around the veranda for some conversational touchstone, I have one of those tiny epiphanies that sneaks up and hits a person during the course of a day: I realize that about half the people occupying the tables on the veranda are men.

Plying, as I do, a rather idiosyncratic craft that has about it no particular hours, I'm usually acutely aware of the sensation of being a man wandering through stores and shops at an hour such as this, when most able-bodied and gainfully employed males are engaged in their workaday activities. Oftentimes I feel compelled to look as if I'm in a hurry between destinations or involved in some fictitious business task. It's an absurd and bizarre sense of cultural paranoia, but one that persists. Here, I realize, there is none of that. Men, women, school-age children, and everyone else is out and about, involved in leisurely tasks, at ten forty-five in the morning.

I decide this is a good place to start the conversation.

"You know, it always shocks me to see so many men sitting around and not working in the middle of the day," I say. The second it comes from my mouth I know it sounds wrong. But he takes no offense and seems to draw no unintended conclusions from the comment.

He puts down his *Times* business section and smiles. "What makes you think they're not working?" he responds.

"Well, there just seems to be a general sense of leisure," I say, scrambling to get back on level ground.

"Leisure and work aren't incompatible," he responds. "That's a bit of a fallacy." I can sense the authoritative tone of a closet ideologue.

"I'm from the Midwest," I answer quickly. I figure that such an admission will reduce me to the status of quivering hayseed and thus remove any residual sense of confrontation from my initial comment. "Work is religion back there."

"And religion is work," he ripostes.

It's a nice touch and causes me to laugh. "I know what you're talking about," he continues. "I'm from Ohio."

I should have remembered: almost everyone here is from somewhere else.

"Minnesota," I say.

He nods knowingly. "Been there a couple times," he says. "Pretty state. Couldn't take the winters, though."

I give him a "What are you going to do?" shrug. He shrugs back. Our common Midwesternness has established a small but solid bond.

"I understand what you're saying," he says, gesturing to the assembled coffee drinkers and cell-phone users. "It blew me away when I first came out here, too. Here I was, in one of the most expensive places in America, and people are relaxing in the middle of the day. 'Are they doing it with mirrors?' I said. 'Are they all so rich that they don't have to work?'"

Across the veranda two forty-something women who look like infomercial actresses are greeting each other with elaborate hugs. The histrionics are breathtaking. I try hard not to stare at them.

"Gradually I figured it out," he continues. "People here do work. It's just that they don't work in the way that I was taught to work. I mean, I don't know what Minnesota was like. But I grew up in a mill town. I thought work meant busting my ass at something I hated. It was something out of the industrial revolution. You know, guys with lunch pails going to work before the sun was up and standing at smelters all day. Forty hours and a paycheck, overtime if you're lucky. You want more money, you work harder, work longer. If you do a good job they move you up, add a nickel to your paycheck. Two weeks vacation. Retire at sixty-five, buy an RV, kick off at sixty-six. That's how it was for my dad, for everybody around me. It was a real linear concept—work and earn and spend and pay. Work and earn and spend and pay. Dollars for hours. More hours, more dollars."

I've hit the jackpot: a Midwesterner who's gotten Marin religion. I want him to keep talking. "So how's it different out here?" I ask, gesturing toward the tables of men talking on their cell phones. "They don't look like they're waiting for the night shift."

"You're right. They're not," he says, taking my flip comment with the utmost seriousness. "Work's different here. It's about creation, about achieving critical mass, where you've created so much that the life spinning around you comes together centripetally and keeps itself going effortlessly and without your help. It's a completely different way of thinking."

"Certainly different than mine," I offer. "I've always looked on work as labor. The only issue is the kind of labor."

He sits back and smiles, as if he's found an apt and willing pupil. The honey-rich morning sun gleams on his gold bracelet.

"Let me tell you a story," he says. "When I first got here, I went looking for a job the way I was raised. I looked in the want ads. Went to interviews. I was operating from a really negative paradigm. Start at the bottom, work your way up.

"Then one day I was at a friend's house. His kid—maybe seventeen—had just gotten out of school for summer vacation. I asked him what he was doing for a job. He said he didn't do jobs.

"I couldn't believe it. 'I don't do jobs.' I wanted to kill the little bastard. Turns out, he and a friend were taking their cars and going over to the Oakland docks and picking up sailors who just came into port and driving them around for a hundred dollars apiece. The sailors liked it because they could go where they wanted, the kids got good money—better than I was making. That blew my mind. Here I was with this real bust-ass job and these high-school kids were making hundreds of dollars a day, and to my mind they weren't even working. They were just having fun driving around and getting paid for it."

"Nice work if you can get it," I say.

"That's almost exactly what I said," he responds. "And you know what my friend said? He said, 'Work is about meeting needs, not about doing time.' Bam! It was like I'd gotten hit by a bolt of lightning. It changed my whole life. I wasn't meeting anybody's needs—I was doing somebody else's time."

He leans closer.

"See, everybody needs something. You just need to see what people's needs are, then figure out how to fill them."

I nod appreciatively. He sits back and steeples his hands, confident he has made his point.

"I work in films now," he continues. "Nothing big. Documentaries, promotional pieces. It's complicated. I arrange financing, organizing, do a kind of underwriting. What I'm really doing is getting people together who have mutually satisfiable needs. Someone wants to make a film, someone else wants to invest some money, they want the deal to be tight. I get them together and make it tight. I do it by connecting everyone with the people they need. I take my cut and the deal gets done and the film gets made."

He stops suddenly, as if he's forgotten something. "By the way, I didn't get your name," he says.

"Kent," I tell him, assuming, in true California fashion, that a first name is good enough.

"Dave," he responds, holding out his hand. "Good to meet a Midwestern brother." We shake hands, then he continues.

"Anyway, Kent," he says. "This is how America should be. But right now we're too much about creating wants, not meeting needs."

He looks at me earnestly. "What do you drive, Kent?"

Now that he knows my name, he intends to use it.

"A Mitsubishi," I say, forgetting, for a moment, the belugal rented Bonneville that's parked a few feet away from us.

"See," he says. "You understand. But the American car companies, they have a tough time getting it. That's why they're all in trouble. That's what messed up my old hometown. They were telling us we wanted all these big clunky pieces of steel on wheels, when what people needed was something small and efficient and comfortable. The Japanese saw that and met that need. Germans too. All of them. The American car companies couldn't figure out what was going on. Here they were turning out these big shining pieces of shit, and no one would buy them. They were just victims of their own bad imagery. They were projecting these images out there of big, clumsy sofa cars. That's what you want, they said, and they invested all their psychic and financial energy into selling that want. Meanwhile, the Japanese were meeting people's needs. People just told the American car manufacturers to fuck off."

I'm not sure where he's going, but I'm fascinated. He reaches out and taps the table in front of me.

"See, Kent, what you need to understand is that the American economy is a machine, and it works in a certain way. Either you beat on that machine until it opens the door a crack, then climb in and let it grind you up, or you figure out how the machine works and become its operator. These people sitting here"—he gestures around the veranda—"they're the people who know how to run the machine. You see them and you think they're not working. It's because you think working is being in the machine. That's bad imagery. You're looking for the people who are inside the machine being ground up. They don't live here. They live in Oakland or Vallejo or somewhere."

He steeples his fingers again and rocks them back and forth several times. It's a vaguely Japanese gesture. "That's why a lot of people are down on Marin. They say it's only a place for rich people. But money is only a measure of worth, and you're worth as much as you think you're worth. If you think you're only worth four dollars an hour, then that's what you're worth. If you think you're worth a hundred dollars an hour, then you're worth one hundred dollars an hour."

I can't resist: "Even the Mexicans down by the canal in San Rafael?"

He doesn't skip a beat. "Even the Mexicans down by the canal in San Rafael. If one of those Mexicans decided he was the absolute best yard cleaner, and he cleaned better than anyone else, did all the little things that other people don't do, and he put that idea in his head and told himself, 'I'm going to do this with a level of excellence that no one has ever done, and I'm going to be worth a hundred dollars an hour,' then he could get one hundred dollars an hour. I know he could. I know people who'd pay him that if he could show them he was worth it. But he'd have to do yard work so much better than everyone else that he believed he was worth one hundred dollars an hour. That's the test. He'd have to be able to believe it, so other people would see his belief and buy into it."

He picks up a leaf that has fluttered onto the table and begins rolling it delicately into a tube. It is a practiced gesture, suspiciously like rolling a dollar bill into a tube for snorting cocaine.

"See, Kent," he says, rolling the leaf between his fingers, "most people in America are like these Mexican laborers. They still think that labor is what matters. Hey, people who want to do labor in America, they're dinosaurs. Because there are people out there who will do labor harder and faster than you do for thirty cents an hour in some other country. That's why those guys left Mexico. They didn't want to work for thirty cents an hour. So what good does it do you to run a sewing machine at four dollars an hour or seven dollars an hour when there's some Mexican who will do the job for thirty cents, and just as well?"

He's not making the strongest possible case for NAFTA, and I'm tempted to bring that up. But that's the thinking of a groundhog. It's fraught with negative imagery.

"Our economy now is based on abstracts, not labor," he says. "Peace of mind, time, things like that. Those are the things I trade in. I don't do anything my clients couldn't do for themselves, but it's not worth it for them to invest their time and the psychic energy in doing it. Our lives are so compressed and fast now, we have so much to do, that nobody has enough time to do everything. Your time is so valuable that it would be a total mistake for you to invest it in things that I can do faster and better. I'm actually saving you money when you use my services, because you're not going to have to invest any time or energy into it. When I'm done, the deal is done. It's that clear, that simple."

I have to admit I enjoy this guy. He's perfect Marin—open, affable, and completely confident in his belief.

"Listen, Kent," he says. "I know I'm really going on here. But this is important. You'll get what you put your energy into. That's the truth. That's the physics of life. Like, if you get up and say, 'I've got to get a job,' and the mental image behind that statement is, 'I've got to find some horseshit work where I go there at eight in the morning and work my ass off until dark,' then you'll end up going to work at eight in the morning and working your ass off until dark. Because that's what you visualized as success, and that's where you'll put your energy. What you need to do is change your idea of what work is.

"It all has to do with consciousness, about visualizing what you really want. Everyone has it in them, but people block out their dreams.

"What do you think the people say when they hear me talking like this back in Ohio, Kent?" he asks.

"I imagine they laugh at you," I say, wishing I had the Dale Carnegie chutzpah to append "Dave" to the end of the sentence.

"Exactly," he says, and points at me like a teacher acknowledging a promising student. "They just laugh. But laughing at something is just another way of closing yourself off to its power. They're sitting there with their lunch buckets waiting for the mill to reopen and they're laughing at me."

He leans closer. "You know, Kent, bad luck, bad karma—those are just excuses for continued failure. They're just different ways of telling yourself, 'I'm not good enough. I don't deserve that.'"

I'm expecting him to take my hands in his and hold them like a preacher.

"Kent, I'm telling you. If you believe that, it's true. It becomes like a mantra for your subconscious. 'I don't deserve to have a nice house. I don't deserve to be rich. I don't deserve to have a beautiful family and a good life.' What you're doing is saying that your life isn't what you want, but that it's out of your control. It's the universe. It's your karma. It's your parents. It's your race or your sex. It's the steel mills shutting down or the auto plant closing. Whatever. They all come down to the same thing. Excuses for failure. Ways to get off on your own unhappiness.

"I wish I could take everyone in Ohio, Kent—everyone, everywhere—and just for one minute have them dream of the life they would really like to have. Just sit back, close their eyes, and imagine the world they would really like to live in. No war, no hunger, no poverty . . ."

"No Mexicans," I'm tempted to interject. But that's the same kind of cynical attitude that almost had me asking if "skinny macchiato" was a capo in the Gambese family. I take the wiser course and hold my tongue.

". . . people sharing with each other. It sounds naive, but if we all had the same script, it would come true. There are enough resources. There's an abundance of creative energy. It comes down to distribution and connection."

The activity around us is increasing. The lunchtime crowd is starting to assemble. He can sense it too. He drives his sermon toward a close.

"If we can dream it, we can make it," he says. "That's the truth. In fact, I see signs of it already. There's a big consciousness shift taking place on this planet. We've already seen things happen that we didn't think were possible. Look at the fall of communism. That was an energy force that had gotten so powerful that it controlled governments. It had armies. It totally controlled people's lives. But when energy was withdrawn, it disappeared. Its life was totally propped up by an incredible daily infusion of negative energy. When that energy was gone, it was gone.

"Or the Berlin Wall. People thought it would be there forever. It was like a mountain or some natural land form. But when the negative energy that held it up was withdrawn, the wall came down almost overnight. It was like it died from exhaustion and fell over. Twenty years ago it would have taken all the armies in the world fighting on both sides to deal with that wall because so much was invested in it. But when that investment was gone, all it took was a few people with sledgehammers.

"What I'm trying to tell you, Kent, is that we all have Berlin Walls in us. We're raised to defend them and we fight anyone who wants to tear them down.

"See, things require energy to survive, and negative things don't create energy, so we have to keep investing new energy in them to make them survive. That takes a lot of work and a lot of energy that could be used for other things. If we stopped investing energy in the negative, the barriers in our lives would fall like the Berlin Wall.

"I know it can happen. It happened to me."

He sits back, both exhilarated and exhausted. I sit back, impressed and almost converted. I doubt he has ever had the opportunity to expound his philosophy so fully before.

There really isn't too much else to say. The conversation has come to its natural conclusion. We exchange a few more pleasantries, and I stand to leave.

"Well," I say, "I guess I should be going. I've taken up a lot of your time."

"Hey, my time's my own," he says. "Remember?"

"Got it," I say.

He winks, makes a little cluck, and shoots his finger at me, as if to say "Bingo."

I have to spend almost an hour in the nearby bookstore until he finishes his coffee and newspaper, so I can sneak back and climb into my big, shiny, American-piece-of-shit Bonneville without being seen.

On a whim, or driven by some inner discomfort, I swing back through San Rafael to where I got my gas. The Mexicans are still there, sitting by the drainage canal. Apparently no one needs a shrub transplanted today.

I'm unsure of how to approach these men. I don't know if they speak any English, or if any approach other than to procure their services will be seen as a transgression on their space. I park the Tuna and walk across to where they're standing. They're laughing and joking among themselves and don't make much effort to approach me to see if I'm offering a job. All their conversation is in Spanish, so I'm not sure what they're saying. Perhaps it's, "This guy is dressed like shit. He doesn't have any work." Perhaps it's, "Here comes another stupid gringo. Let's kill him."

But the public nature of our meeting rules out any precipitous action on any of our parts, so we greet with a simple openness and casual good humor. Some of the men don't speak any English and keep their conversations among themselves. One of the men, whose English is broken but serviceable, is quite affable and forthcoming.

Yeah, he's looking for work. But he doesn't know how long he'll stay. He just came up here from Greenfield. Some of his friends told him about it. They said he could make pretty good cash. The work is easy. Marin people don't like to do anything, so they pay you for simple shit, really easy. He can't believe they don't do it themselves.

He pulls out his wallet, shows me his family. They look as though they're right out of central casting. There's his wife, three boys, two girls, and an infant. The man stands proud and erect at the back of the group. His wife, looking thirty-five going on eighty, stands next to him holding the baby and smiling wearily. The oldest daughter, about seventeen, looks sultry. His eldest son, who's probably fifteen, has the ramrod stiffness of a young boy trying to act the man, while the younger boys are hair-tousling cute, and his younger daughter has the innocent purity of the child chosen to play the Virgin Mary in the church pageant. They're all scrubbed and combed and dressed in pressed white shirts and blouses. They're standing in front of a dusty brick building.

"That's my cousin's house in Michoacán," he says. "He owns it."

I ask him where his family is.

"They're in Greenfield," he answers. "My wife's picking in the strawberry fields."

I ask him who takes care of the baby.

"Oh, she goes to the fields with her. My other kids, they all go to school." He says it with the pride of the immigrant.

He points to the sultry daughter. "My Julisa, she's going to quit school, though." He makes a large arcing gesture in front of his belly to indicate pregnancy. "Then she can take care of the rest of them."

It confirms almost every nightmare vision I have of migrant life.

"Do you like America?" I ask.

He grins broadly and rubs his thumb back and forth along his forefinger in the universal gesture indicating money.

"Is it good for the kids?"

"Cruz, and the little ones, there's no one there when they get home. He gets headaches a lot. From the fields. I worry about him."

I have visions of Nick breathing pesticides and hanging out unsupervised after school with a gang of teenagers.

"I want them to grow up here," the man says. "To learn English. Make themselves better. That's why I come up here, too. It makes me learn English. In Greenfield, I just speak Spanish. I want to know English better to help them with their homework. I was good in math."

I never would have thought of such a thing. I assumed his reason for being here was all economic. But, here, at the core, is one more of those hidden truths of uncelebrated fatherhood—a man leaving his family to learn the language better to help his kids.

"Hey, I wish I could hire you for something," I say, "but I'm just traveling." I'd like to give him some money, but it seems too weird.

He points out at the passing cars. "Mercedes. Jaguar. Someday . . ." He taps his chest and winks.

I say good-bye, offer to go to the Safeway and buy him some beer.

It seems like a male gesture of friendship rather than an act of noblesse oblige. But he declines.

"No good if I want to work." He makes the money gesture again.

I get back in the Tuna and head toward the Richmond–San Rafael bridge. I really liked this man and wish I could have helped him. I'm almost tempted to go back to Mill Valley and look for Dave to see if he could hire him to move a shrub. But Dave would probably be gone, off doing deals. And I'm not sure that this man would appreciate being told to visualize success. But, then again, maybe that's exactly what he's already doing.

THIRTEEN

FAT POCKETS AND A BIG RIDE

Money for crack, money for crack."

". . . Give me some money, man. Don't make me go to one of them church food places. I ain't eating that shit. That's fuckin' vegetarian."

". . . You got a cigarette, man? I got a gun."

I'm walking down Telegraph Avenue, the mythic Berkeley street on the south side of the U.C. campus. I could have chosen a hundred other streets. After all, I went to grad school here for eight long years after my hiatus in the Oregon woods, so these streets are as familiar to me as the streets of my current hometown. Though I'm honoring my commitment not to excavate my past, I did stop at the Graduate Theological Union on the north side of the campus to peer into a building where one of my first serious sculptures was once installed.

The sculpture was an overlife-size depiction of John the Baptist I had done as part of my Ph.D. thesis. I had carved it, stroke by stroke, with hand chisels, from a twelve-foot trunk of black walnut, and had invested it with all the anguished urgency of a young artist creating his first major work.

I had hoped it might still be installed there. All art is, on some level, a self-portrait, and it would have given me a solid, tangible, reified vision of who I was in those youthful days. It also would have told me if, perhaps, there was something in my younger self that I have either refined or lost. It seemed a safer way to catch a glimpse of my past than to walk the streets with the ghost of an old girlfriend.

But the sculpture was gone. I knew it had been purchased by an Orthodox archbishop from San Francisco—I had received payment years ago—but for years afterward I had gotten irritated telephone calls from the administration at the Graduate Theological Union asking me when it was going to be removed. I was two thousand miles away, with neither the interest nor the wherewithal to address the problem, so I just ignored the calls and figured the archbishop would get it when he wanted it.

Apparently someone—archbishop or otherwise—had finally come along with the chain hoists and tools of mechanical advantage necessary to move the piece. No janitor with a pickup truck could have hauled it away. At any rate, it's no longer there. Someday I'll have to find out where it went. But the universe takes care of works of art and sends them where they're supposed to be. For now, all its absence means to me is that it has a new home and that I'll have to look elsewhere for spiritual self-portraits.

So I've turned my attention to Telegraph. It's not that Telegraph has any special meaning for me or will offer me any special insight into my character. But it has always been the destination for youthful émigrés whose counterculture visions run toward the political and the radical. It seems the logical place to go when you're looking for a glimpse into the current state of the California dream, Berkeley-style.

I wend my way among the hawkers and vendors and panhandlers. Astonishingly, I recognize a few of the street denizens. They were here, pushing the same shopping carts, jabbering the same unintelligible poetry, twenty years ago. A half-ton piece of walnut can disappear without a trace, but two decades of social change can't budge these people from their chosen corners.

What strikes me the most is that the street has a much different character than it used to. It's angrier, dirtier, less celebratory, more confused. Even the panhandlers are different—their tone is more aggressive, more desperate, like guests at a party who are starting to come off their drunks, or patrons at a bar after the lights are turned up at closing time. A burr of indignation lies beneath their petitions. Someone, or something, has betrayed them.

I'm struck by a comment a policeman on Telegraph and Dwight made when I told him how astonished I was at the vile and degraded condition of People's Park. "Telegraph used to be full of people who took drugs," he said. "Now it's full of people who forgot to take their drugs." It's Reagan's dream of emptying out asylums, and now the streets are our Bedlam.

Up ahead I see two boys in their early twenties sitting on the side-walk in front of the Cafe Med, one of my occasional haunts during grad school. They're talking to a young girl who is holding a tiny white puppy. She's clutching it like a baby.

One of the boys catches my eye. There's something indefinably lit-erate in his manner. His hands are long and delicate, like a pianist's. He watches and nods while the others speak, and answers with calming, measured prose. The girl is crying about something, and the other boy is twitching and scratching himself inside his sweatshirt. The boy with the long hands takes the girl's shoulders in his graceful grip and moves his face close to hers. He speaks to her gently, like a father counseling a child. She nods and sniffles. He gives her a protective, comforting hug.

As I approach, he pulls himself away from her and steps toward me. "Money for floor space?" he says.

This is new to me. "Floor space?" I ask.

He measures me: Is it worth humoring a tourist for a few pennies? "Yeah," he says. "Floor space."

I reach in my pocket. I've still got a handful of bridge toll change. "Explain," I say, pulling out some coins. He glances over at the sob-bing girl and his twitching compatriot. They watch him expectantly.

"Well," he answers, "a bunch of us rent a motel room for the night if we can get enough money. I got to get my part, then I get floor space."

"How much?"

"Depends on the room and the number of people. Maybe three, four bucks if there are ten of us."

"Why don't you go to the homeless shelters?" I ask.

He winces. "Full of crackheads. Like really whack. I stayed there one night, but I swear I'll never stay there again. I got robbed. First night."

"Mean streets," I offer.

"Tell me about it."

"I'd rather you told me about it."

The twitching boy butts in. I've stayed around long enough to indicate that maybe I'm good for a touch. "You got a smoke, man?"

"No," I answer. "That stuff will kill you."

Sensing a sermon, he moves away quickly. The sobbing girl follows, clutching her puppy. I'm left face to face with the literate boy.

A heavy shower has begun. The street vendors are rushing to cover their racks of tie-dyed T-shirts and trays of jewelry. We step back under a canopy. The proximity is slightly uncomfortable.

We measure each other. He's young and handsome, but wary. His black hair hangs greasy and stringy down to his shoulders, and he has a wisp of Fu Manchu beard that clutches in single strands on his chin. He's wearing a dirty grey Guatemalan pullover that's worn through at the elbows. I can smell him even at the distance of several feet.

His pants—filthy chinos—drop limply from his bony hips and trail down into frayed cuffs that splay out over laceless tennis shoes. There is no sense that any of these clothes are his. They have the irretrievable dinginess of clothes picked from a lost-and-found box at a laundromat.

He stands next to me with his shoulders hunched and his hands dug deep into his pockets—a latter-day James Dean. "Well?" he says, as if I'm some aging pederast who's going to ask him for sex.

"I'm not out for anything," I say, in answer to the unspoken question. "I just want to hear your story."

He eyes me cautiously. I need to answer all his questions before he asks them. "I want to know what it's like on the streets these days," I tell him. "I used to live here."

Still, he says nothing.

I tell him the policeman's story about how Telegraph has changed. He smiles.

I decide to go further. "You interest me," I say. "There's an intelligence in your eyes. You don't seem to be 'standing on the corner rapping at the moon' kind of crazy."

He smiles again. "I'm a little insane, and I like to smoke some pot. But, yeah, I know what you mean. I'm not like that."

I open my billfold. There are two tens and a handful of ones. He watches carefully as I examine my money. I pull the two tens out enough so he can see them. "I buy you dinner, you tell me your story, I keep the ones for gas and tolls, and the rest is yours. I don't need to know your name. Meal's over, I'm out the door, and we never see each other again."

He hunches his shoulders and stares at me. All his decision making is interior. A long pause, then, "Okay, but no Chinese." A wave of agitation flashes in his eyes, reducing him for a moment to a frightened child. "I got kind of a bad stomach, you know?"

"No Chinese," I say.

The sun shower has passed. The street vendors and panhandlers are hustling back to their posts. I gesture to the street. "You pick the place."

He hesitates, then says sheepishly, "I mean, like, will this be part of the twenty dollars?"

"Nope," I tell him. "That's yours."

Relieved, he leads me to a tiny falafel and pita restaurant. He orders a full meal and, in between almost frantic bites, begins to tell me his tale.

"I'm an artist and a writer," he says. "I got a big problem with staying in one place for too long. I sit around and I start . . . you know, there's no more of what I'm looking for, you know? No more experience, if you know what I mean. You've been there, you did it, you experienced it, and there's no more inspiration. It gets to the point where the faces change but the attitudes are the same. And every town you go to, everything's a little bit different, you know?"

"Oh, I know," I tell him.

"And so I get a house and I make money and I pay my bills and I pay my rent and I do whatever, and pretty soon I start feeling miserable, so I ditch my lease and I go on the road, end up somewhere like this where I've got no money and no house and no nothing, and I owe tons of money back home."

"So why here?"

"I'm struggling to find a place where I can stop and be comfortable for a while. I figure anywhere I can go with no money and be treated well and feel comfortable, that's a community I would want to contribute to.

"You know, if I show up at a place and everyone's an asshole and no one can understand that I'm hungry or cold, that I need somewhere to sleep . . . or even if they don't give me money or nothing, if no one will stop and talk to me and even give a shit about me at all, then I don't want to live there because I don't want to have money and meet those people again and have them be all, 'Hey, how you doing?' knowing full well that they really don't care."

He has wolfed down the falafel and is glancing toward the menu.

"Eat up," I say. "It's all on the house. Whatever you want."

"You sure?" he says. "I mean, this is costing you a lot of money."

"It's all relative," I answer.

"Maybe I'll get something else when we leave, if that's okay?"

"Happy to do it."

He smiles broadly.

"I'm from Madison," he continues, "so I feel pretty at home here. Madison's a little like this. But you know, it's wintertime there, and it seems like every time I get settled in, well, it gets wintertime and I've got to go again.

"Berkeley sounded like a good place. It's a little crazier than Madison. I guess in the past this was a real good town where people understood the problems there are with living the kind of life I'm liv-ing. But it seems like no one cares now. I don't know what happened. Maybe there were just too many folks for too many years. People got fed up."

"So how bad is it?" I ask.

He reaches into his pocket and pulls out a handful of grubby change. He moves it around in his left palm with his right forefinger.

"I amassed a dollar five today," he says. "Just trying to make sure I eat enough. There's this place down the way and they're remodeling, knocking out a wall, making it into a storefront, you know? I asked them if they needed any help. They were rude. They told me, basi-cally, 'Hell, no.' It's like I can't get a job or work. No one wants to give me a job. They just want me to leave. But they won't give me a job or money so I can go. I guess they want me to walk, carrying all my stuff. They want me to think, 'Fuck, I hated Berkeley. I'm not going back there.' I mean, I guess that's the deal.

"You know, they just passed some laws regarding loitering with the intent to panhandle or sell drugs or just basically loitering at all. Whenever the cops go by, they tell us to move on. This morning I bought some breakfast at the Cafe Intermezzo. Well, not breakfast, but some bread and some butter—and sat out in front. There were like five or six of us sitting on the sidewalk and leaning against the wall and the police came and made us move. And I'm, like, 'Well, why?'

"'You're trespassing.'

"I was eating food I bought in that fucking store, and they're bust-ing me for trespassing."

He points to a sign in the window of the restaurant where we're sit-ting. "No Loitering or Trespassing," it reads.

"That's how it is," he says. "Every store window has a 'No Trespassing' sign. And that's for outside. Like if I'm just standing there. Even if I go inside and buy some food, if I'm standing there and a police car drives by, they'll pull over and tell me to go somewhere else.

"It's not like I'm walking into a restaurant and asking people for food off their plates. I know people who do that. That's just lack of respect. I mean, they could at least wait until the person is done. There's a cafe down the way where at any given time you can go in and grab a half a sandwich and a big bowl of salad off a table when no one is eating it. That same sandwich shop, I was there a couple of months ago, and I would say they were probably giving away a hundred pounds of food a day. You know, just people walking in, 'Hey, you got any orders that are messed up?'

"And the employees were real cool and understood the situation and I think maybe they started messing up stuff on purpose, like putting the wrong stuff on a sandwich or putting the wrong stuff in a salad. Because pretty much everyone around was going in there at least once a day and getting a sandwich. That was a great lunch. You didn't have to sit out on the street and deal with the bullshit quite as long, because you knew good food was coming. I mean, you know, when you get free food at one of those feeding places, it's, like, 'free food,' you know? It's not very good stuff."

"So where to now?" I ask him. He seems to have appraised his circumstances fairly accurately and doesn't harbor any more fantasies about the free and easy life in Berkeley.

"From here I figure I'll go to Hawaii. Hopefully work on some kind of freight ship. I was hoping to come up with a few hundred dollars to take an airplane, but that doesn't seem very much of a reality. Maybe in the city. But in the city there's nowhere to sleep. It's a bigger hassle than this. Stuff goes on, and sometimes you've got to be part of it or you'll get killed, you know what I mean? It's crazy over there, man. Just crazy.

"I can see how it pisses people off, being hit up for money and stuff. But it's like, 'Hey, give me a shot.' I really don't understand the attitude that makes people not want to give someone a chance. I mean, for me to go into a place and offer to run around and grab nails and haul around two-by-fours and stuff—I mean, offering to spend my time doing something I feel is pretty much almost a criminal waste of my talents, for me to offer to do that and to have the guy say, 'Fuck you, man,' is like, 'Wait a minute. I'm lowering myself to get a chance to better myself, and I can't even do that.'

"You know, I'm stuck out here. I don't have a musical instrument, I don't have any art supplies, I don't even have paper and a pen. You know, I can't do anything out here, really. Then you go into a place and you ask them for work and they treat you like you're asking them to give up their left arm. You ask them for a quarter and they act like you're asking them for their left arm.

"I know no one owes me anything. But at a certain point in time . . . I mean, we all owe it to the world to help the world, whether that's buying me a hamburger or kicking me, I don't know. I don't know which is more of a help to me. I guess from their point of view, why the fuck can't I help myself? And I'd like to. But you get down to a certain point and you've got no place to move. At a certain point you're at the end of the line."

I look across the table at his sad, literate eyes. I see the same eyes the mailman saw as he watched me peer through my window waiting for answers in the mail. I guess I don't need any walnut sculpture to catch a glimpse of my youth.

I wish I could do something for this kid—maybe buy him some art supplies or a ticket to Hawaii or go talk to the construction crews that won't even hire him to carry two-by-fours. But none of those would solve anything. He wouldn't last two days carrying two-by-fours, and he'd probably just hock the art supplies to get floor space. He's wrestling demons right now. Whether he knows it or not, he's a seeker, and until he figures out what he's seeking, a beach in Maui wouldn't be a whole lot different from a street corner in Berkeley; it would just be another, albeit warmer, stop on life's journey.

How much I like this kid. He's the polar opposite of Marin Dave. Life for him is questions, not answers. Dave would just tell him to show those workers that he's the best two-by-four carrier who ever lived. The kid is wondering why he, or anyone else, should have to carry two-by-fours when there's an artist in his soul.

I don't have an answer. I guess the only answer is that somebody has to carry those two-by-fours, and, to some extent, it's the luck of the draw. Do what you can to make sure you don't get the short straw, but respect and honor those who do.

All I can think of is the smug, secure philosophy professor at Stanford who tried to counsel me as I wriggled in my skin and tried to figure out what to do with my life. "I've never known anyone who was so adamant about something so inchoate," he'd said. He was right. And it applies to this boy as well as it did to me. He wants something from life, but he doesn't know what it is. And until he gets it, he'll drift, windblown, from town to town, pointing fingers at police and restaurant owners and construction crew bosses, thinking that all he needs is some art supplies and a break, when what he really needs is a clear path to walk.

"You know, you're a sensitive guy," I tell him. "You're a dreamer, but your dreams have no shape."

It's an innocent comment, the surface skim of my deeper ruminations. But it sets him on alert. He gets a pained look on his face, like someone who's just tasted something bitter and unexpected. "Say, you're not a minister, are you?" he asks.

"No, I'm not a minister," I tell him.

"Good," he says. "I don't like ministers."

I can't resist. "But, you know, we're all ministers," I tell him. It's almost a direct quote from a professor of mine at Graduate Theological Union. "You. Me. Everyone else. It comes with the territory of being human."

I'm cutting too close to the bone; he wants out. He starts moving nervously in his chair; will I renege on my promise to give him money?

I want to set him at ease. I pull out my billfold and give him the two tens.

"Do you want to get something else before you go?" I ask.

"Nah, I guess I'm full," he says. He just wants to get away.

I reach out to shake his hand. Tentatively, he reaches across the table and offers me his hand in return. His grip is so soft I can barely feel it. This is not a kid who can carry two-by-fours.

"Thanks for talking to me," I say.

"Yeah," he responds.

"And you know what?"

He looks at me quizzically.

"I like your ministry. You do a good job with your friends. I can see it."

He smiles weakly and sidles out the door. Before I even know it, he's disappeared into the passing crowd.

I'm surprised I gave him that "ministry" speech. It was a bit out of character. I'm not like Marin Dave—I'm disinclined to wield God's sandal so blatantly and overtly. I guess those words just popped out of the deep background static of my memories from my time here in Berkeley. I can still see that professor, sitting in the midst of his seminar of wide-eyed, hopeful, confused graduate students who were about to be released on the world. I can hear his quiet measured tones: "It doesn't matter if you're going into the ministry or not. You're all ministers. You can't escape it. Don't try to run from it; just find it and claim it. That's all that life is, for anyone. Finding a ministry and claiming it."

It was one of those defining moments for me. Like so many other young theological students—especially here in Berkeley—I'd been looking for a priesthood—a singular truth I could dispense to others that would transubstantiate their lives. I never found it. All I found was human need and yearning, and an ever increasing awareness of its presence in all of us. And that hadn't seemed like enough. My professor's simple comment had aligned my compass: I really didn't have a priesthood; I had a ministry. My task in life was to lift those around me, to protect the weak and comfort the lonely. It wasn't heroic; it wasn't the stuff of legend. But it was God's quiet work, and it was enough.

I guess, subconsciously, I had hoped to pass that defining moment on to my young friend on Telegraph. He reminded me so much of myself in my younger days. And the way he had comforted the girl with the puppy had touched me. I couldn't have reached her; her parents obviously couldn't reach her. But he could reach her, and he did, with a touch and a hug of infinite gentleness.

I should have pushed him a little harder despite his discomfort. "Forget the two-by-fours," I should have said. "Your hands are made for people." But he's gone—two ships passed in the night, blinked their lights, and moved on.

I drive toward Oakland. Something is forming in my mind.

The light is fading. I've taken up a post behind a chain-link fence in the flats of Oakland, where I'm watching a group of young black men play a game of pickup basketball. I feel strange and more than a little nervous. I know this place. I used to play ball here twenty-five years ago. I was the only white guy and my game didn't fit with street ball, but I came anyway.

I liked Oakland. It was tough, but it wasn't mean. It felt like a black town, but that gave the residents a sense of pride and civic ownership. I was an outsider here, but I wasn't the enemy. I was just off my turf, and I had to play by the rules.

As was the case with Telegraph, something has changed, and I don't know how much of it is me and how much of it is the streets. All I know is the dynamic is different now. I'm an outsider in a different way. I'm not the white auslander whose presence elicits a kind of tacit approval, and even a quiet respect. Now, something about me is the enemy.

I try to get a feel for the source of this odd sensation. Is it my increased age? Is it because these streets no longer are my home, and my status as a stranger in a strange land has increased exponentially? Is it because the culture has changed, and the sense of celebration and possibility that lived beneath all the muck of poverty has been smothered and replaced by a sense of decay and betrayal, and I somehow represent that betrayal by the very fact of my middle-aged whiteness?

I can't tell. All I know is I'm not welcome here. No one is looking at me with even the slightest sense of approval. The groups of young black men—that most basal of terrors for the white middle class—are hooded and brooding. They wear oversized Oakland Raiders sweat-shirts and giant pants that hang down on their buttocks. They walk past me with a sense of arrogant conviction, pointedly throwing candy wrappers at my feet, all the while conversing with those hard chopping gestures, as if the wrists are broken and the speaker is try-ing to bludgeon his point into existence.

I stand my ground and stare blankly. There's no sense pretending to be casual or anonymous. My presence is noted and I'm being assessed. I hear the phrase "white motherfucker," followed by harsh laughter. Hands are slapped, fists are piled one on top of another.

I remember reading once that the jackets with sleeves down to the fingers and all the chopping bent-wrist gestures originated as a way to conceal weapons. Now the style is residual and probably means nothing. Still, these outfits give me pause. The boys see me looking, and they hold my gaze until I look away.

This is a strange feeling for me. These are my old streets. These are the same bent rims, the same chipped backboards. I've lived in black neighborhoods before. I may not be free of racism—after all, I'm an American, and race was programmed into me at an early age as a cutting-edge distinction in my understanding of humanity—but I do know that on a one-to-one level, I don't carry much prejudice within me. In fact, it was my transparent fascination with black street cul-ture, and my appreciation for all that it contains, that originally brought me to these streets so many years ago and has always made me choose racially-mixed neighborhoods whenever I've resided in cities.

Here none of that matters. Something has reached critical mass, and it is not Marin Dave's economic juggernaut of self-perpetuating wealth.

The boys stare out of their hooded sweatshirts like cobras. What are they thinking?

In some odd way, my solitariness gives me power. My presence here makes no sense, and that causes them to be wary. A cop? A narc? A white guy trying to buy drugs? There has to be a story, and the possible dimensions and ramifications of that story are my shield. I'm protected by the power of their imaginations.

Nonetheless, I realize I've probably made a mistake. A park with a basketball hoop is a man's place, but it's my whiteness, not my maleness, that's the defining factor in my presence here. The maleness of the setting only lethalizes the tensions of race and class.

I want to leave, to climb into the Tuna and get out of here. The expressway is only a mile away. I could be on it in a few minutes. I could sort out all the implications of my reactions in the security of my speeding automobile. But I can't bolt now. I'm being watched. I've got to represent.

I see an old battered bench a bit back from the court. Paper bags and bottles are littered around its base. A man about my age is sitting on it. He has on a fatigue jacket and his hair is cut in a fade. Vietnam, maybe. Perhaps our generational link will be strong enough to bridge the racial divide. Or perhaps he's a junkie stoned out of his mind, and I'm walking into the box canyon of all box canyons.

I approach warily. I have no other reasonable course of action.

As I get closer the man looks up at me. I feel a flush of relief. It's clear he's no junkie. He gestures to the open spot next to him on the bench. I sit down, anticipating an interrogation about why I'm hanging in this neighborhood. But the man has taken me for granted. To him, I'm just another guy watching the young fellows play their game.

"See that dude?" he says, pointing to a young man with arms that look like bowling balls stuffed in nylon stockings. "Had scholarship offers all over shit." He pantomimes drawing on a joint. "Up in smoke."

The kid is hollering, "Give me the rock. Give me the rock." He grabs a rebound, weaves his way back out to the perimeter, and hoists up a shot. It clangs off the rim.

I take a chance. "Shot's kind of flat. All in his arms," I say. "He'll lose it when his legs get tired. Bad geometry."

The man smiles. He has gentle eyes. "You a coach?"

"No. I just like the game. Used to play here when I was younger. I'm just passing through."

He emits a low chuckle and smiles broadly. "You played here? You're awful white."

"Didn't matter," I tell him. "No one ever threw me the ball anyway. Think I might have touched it twice in a couple of years."

"Got to make your own game."

"Hey. How was I supposed to get a rebound? White legs."

He knows what I mean, and he appreciates the humor. He extends his hand to me, palm up. I self-consciously give him five. He gives me five back.

I'm feeling more at ease. I'm connecting with this man, and my involvement with him may provide me with the buffer I need to protect me from the cobra boys.

"Yeah, things've changed around here," he answers.

"No one drove up to me with the Welcome Wagon," I say.

He smiles again. "Ain't no more Welcome Wagon. Someone stole the wheels."

We talk a bit about the bus stop across the street where I remember that a little boy picked up a package and had his hand blown off. It was some kind of a bomb placed there by a random nut. The whole town was outraged. Funds were set up at banks; the papers followed the progress of the boy's recovery.

"Wouldn't happen today," the man says. "Kids getting snuffed all the time. Old news."

I point to an apartment building rising in the distance. "Isn't that where Huey Newton used to live?" It's an idle question, spurred by a hazy memory back in my brain. But something in it touches him. A winsome expression crosses his face.

"You do know this shit, don't you?" he says. "Yeah, Huey P. Newton lived there. Huey P. Them was good times." He gestures around the park, toward the young men on the court. There are ten in the game, about twenty more waiting to play. All of them are old enough to work.

"Look at this. They been here all day. All of 'em. No motherfucking jobs. Don't even try. Back when Huey was here . . ."

He turns to me from his seat on the park bench. The memory has opened up something deep inside him. Beneath the gentleness, I see a great weariness in his face. The edges of his hair have turned white, as has much of his beard and mustache. "See, them was my days. I was down with them, man," he says. "Angela. Bobby. We was doing something. Now it's all 'gangster, gangster, gangster.' All these kids want is fat pockets and a big ride."

A shot ricochets off the rim and bounces over to me. I resist grabbing it and throwing it back. One of the players runs by and scoops it up. He stares at me for a split second, then goes back to the game. I can see some words pass between him and a few of the other players.

The man continues. "It's that crack cocaine doing us in, man. It's stealing our youth. Makes the little brothers crazy. Gives the cops an excuse. They catch you with that, put you away till forever. Cocaine? That's the white-boy drug. They don't do nothing to you. Doctors, lawyers, they do that shit. Slap on the wrist. You check the laws. You'll see what I'm saying. You want to do hard time, you do crack. You want to do free crime, do blow.

"Then if the little brothers don't get caught, they terrorize the community. Drive-bys, stickups, snatchings. Gangster bullshit. It's tearing us apart, see what I'm saying?"

I don't know whether he expects an answer or not, so I just nod.

"Back in my time," he goes on, "Huey P. Newton and the Panthers, they gave us young folk a way to do something other than commit crimes on our brothers and sisters. See, these kids ain't nothing but petty criminals. They got the bad-ass look and that gun thing, but they ain't nothing. They call themselves gangsters. But take away all the colors and shit, and they're just petty thieves and stickup men. Ain't nothing high about that.

"In my day the Panthers showed another way. We didn't have to rob and kill. We could do something for the community. We started schools, day care, helped the old folks, kept on top of the cops. We don't have that anymore. What we got is crack cocaine and drive-by bullshit, you see what I'm saying?"

It's a conversational crutch, a cultural tag line, but I feel I need to respond. I nod again.

"I seen it all come down, man, in my time," he continues. "I saw the bad shit almost happen and the good shit almost happen. So I know there's a dream. These young-ass gangsters don't know nothing about the dream. They think being bad is enough. So they kill their black brothers and Whitey looks on and says, 'Yeah, another nigger bit the dust, man. That's cool.' Letting the brothers do the Man's work.

"And the thing is, they're killing for nothing. Dying for nothing. For nothing! That's the shame of it all. We're all going to die, but you want to die for something. Something you built or something you believe. All these young black brothers, they're dying for nothing. For some motherfucking handshake or a jacket or some such.

"All they leave is a bunch of babies. Make some babies, cap somebody, get capped. Another momma crying at a funeral. We need them to be fathers, to build the community. That's why I liked the Panthers, man. They seized the time. They talked about power to the people. They had young people doing something other than shakin' their booty."

He touches me several times on the shoulder, like a man trying to get my attention. In the context, it feels like a tremendously intimate gesture.

"Looky here," he says. "You're talking to me. You ain't gonna talk to them little gangsters over there because they'll shoot your eyes out. They don't give a fuck. They don't know nothing about history. They don't know nothing about culture. They think they're bad, but all they are is ignorant. They see some bullshit, phony-ass movie and they think they're educated. All they got is a bigger attitude. When

the shit comes down, they care more about Michael Jordan than
about Dr. King, you see what I'm saying?"

I nod again. This man makes sad and dismal sense.

"Brother Malcolm, he died for a dream. Brother Martin, he died
for a dream. These kids, they're dying for nothing. Colors and turf.
Then they think they're living large.

"Let me tell you something. The other day I was sitting out on
MacArthur, and up comes this car full of white boys. They drive up to
a young brother, he makes the pass through the window, and the
deal's gone down.

"Ain't nothing going to happen to the white kids. They'll go back
to San Leandro and party. It'll be the brother who takes the hit. Police
will come in here and rough him up and take him away. They'll rough
him up bad, say he was resisting arrest. Another day on the street,
another black man in prison.

"Now, here's the thing. I ain't saying it's right. What the little
brother's doing is wrong, selling that shit. But when the cops come
down hard, beat the shit out of him, get him hard time while the
white boy drives free, then that brother thinks doing wrong is okay,
because he been done wrong. Two wrongs don't make a right, see
what I'm saying?"

This I can answer. "Never has," I say.

"That's my point," he says. "Never has, never will. But that's what
it is. Wrong having babies. Ain't nobody stand-up in the whole thing.
Let me tell you, man, there's a mean motherfucking streak in this
whole country. This whole country. And when that streak comes out,
it comes down hardest on the niggers. If there was someone stand-
up—if the whole motherfucking country was stand-up instead of
mean, maybe these young gangsters would be stand-up too. But it
ain't."

The ball rolls over again. My bench mate picks it up and threads a
smooth bounce pass to one of the players. "You only going right," he
shouts to the kid who catches the pass. "Show me something new."
The kid grins and nods. The other players all hoot and laugh.

"Let me give it to you straight," he says, turning his attention back to me. "I done crimes. I been where these boys are going. And you know what you learn from doing crimes? You learn how to make fear. That's all these young-ass gangsters are doing—they're making fear. They know you white people afraid of them. Black people too. They want that. They want you so full of fear that you lock your doors and shake in your bed all night. That's their power. That's what they think 'Power to the people' means.

"I try to tell them, it ain't no good to spread fear, because fear brings something back on you. It don't help your people. I try to get them to help their people."

"Do they listen, any of them?" I ask.

He shakes his head sadly. "It's a sorry motherfucking time, man. I can tell you that. When the biggest dream you got's in your pants, you ain't going nowhere."

It's a hard comment, and more telling than a direct answer. I think back on Tarique's dad, sitting on that stoop in Seattle and telling me that somewhere there was a bullet with his son's name on it.

"You ever think of leaving?"

It's the same thing I asked Tarique's dad. I know it's a stupid question, but I'm curious. I wonder if a black man sitting on a beat-up bench in Oakland gets the same wanderlust as a white man living on a lake in the northern Minnesota woods. I fully expect a wry shake of the head and a tolerant, accommodating answer worthy of my naiveté. But the man surprises me. A slow smile creeps across his face like the sun across a summer meadow. He looks at me even more closely, as if he wants to know if I really want an answer.

"You want to know?" he says. "You really want to know?"

"Yes, I do," I say, and I mean it.

"I ain't going nowhere," he says. "Somebody's got to care about these kids. Somebody's got to be stand-up and show them some kind of way."

I'm stunned. I assumed there was a kind of vagrancy and dereliction behind his presence. "Is that why you sit out here?" I ask.

"That's why. Every day." He points to a brace on his right foot. I hadn't noticed it. He'd kept his foot under the bench. "I had my time and I did my thing. Now I got my little pension. These kids mostly ain't got no dads. Every once in a while one of them comes over. We talk a bit. Maybe I can set him just a little bit straight."

I'm as humbled as I am shocked. "You're a good man," I say. We sit in silence for a while, watching the game as the day closes down around us.

The man looks at the purpling sky. "You might be wanting to get out of here pretty soon."

"I didn't want to be the one to say it," I tell him.

"Well, I just did."

He reaches out his hand to me. I clasp it tightly.

"Thanks," I say. "I needed you today." He averts his eyes for a moment—the intimate compliment embarrasses him—then he looks back at me. The weariness is gone, replaced by a twinkle.

"You ever want to go one on one . . ." he says, and breaks into a broad grin. We both burst out laughing.

"Score would be zero to zero," I say.

"And it wouldn't be defense," he retorts.

He clanks his braced foot on the ground several times. "I could probably still outjump a white boy."

"Gravity's my constant companion," I say.

The sky is darkening, but I'm no longer afraid. That man has taken my hand in his, and the cobra boys saw it. He's assured my safe passage.

I drive back through the teeming streets toward the freeway. My old professor's words keep playing in my head: "We're all ministers. No sense fighting it. You've just got to find your ministry and claim it."

I work my way upward from the flats toward Grizzly Peak Boulevard, the road that runs along the crest of the East Bay hills.

I feel like a man who's been blessed. I couldn't have dreamed of three more perfect people to shape my day. Sometimes you just have to believe in providence.

There was Dave with his gold bracelet, sitting in confident repose under the manzanitas in the Mill Valley plaza. With his dream of a perfect world, full of possibility and abundance for all, he envisioned the world I would love to see. And for him it was possible, because for him life was simple: envision your perfect self, then climb into it like a new skin. The world is a system; learn to operate it. There is no history, no environment, only the clean slate of pure intention. It's a beautiful truth and a tempting dream. Who wouldn't want to see the world as a place of endless abundance and infinite possibility? But it only works if you stay inside the closed room of the self. Poverty-stricken Mexicans? Wrong thinking. Unemployed auto workers? Negative imagery. No one banging spoons on empty bowls in the Sudan.

I'm afraid, for me, the world is not so easily dismissed. It makes its claims on us in ways we only dimly understand. And, besides, by my lights Dave's got "needs" and "wants" all confused. His rich film clients don't have needs—at least not needs with a capital N—they've got wants. Needs are what those starving people in West Africa have. Needs are what those fatherless kids on the basketball court in Oakland have.

Dave sees himself as an apostle of possibility, but, seen through other eyes, he's just a butler to privilege. What he's selling is a middle-class fantasy, a New Age elixir no different from the lightning in a bottle being hawked by the bright-faced man on the Seattle ferry. To them, the past is nothing more than ballast on our dreams, and the future is anything we want it to be.

Still, I would love to believe Dave; his vision of life is not without virtue. Bad attitudes yield bad results. And no one yet knows what miracles can be wrought by the power of belief and clear intention. But, for me, the self is not a big enough canvas on which to paint a meaningful life. I can project my perfect image of a perfect world, and maybe, just maybe, I can achieve it. But at what cost to a clear-eyed understanding of the world around me?

The truth is, the streets would remain the same whether I

acknowledged them or not. Kids would still be robbed in homeless shelters, Mexican mothers would still take their babies to pesticide-laden fields, lonely old women would still sell the lamps off their husbands' nightstands in order to have a moment of human contact in their solitary lives.

You can't avoid the reality of the world by visualizing it out of existence anymore than you can by moving down the road. Dave had chosen to visualize away the hard side of life; my Berkeley boy had run into it broadside—mean streets, selfish people, a struggle for food, for floor space, for a chance to put a little art in your days.

Both of them, in very different ways, were runners. Both of them were trying to escape from the winter of human affairs. But there are winters everywhere, in every place, in every stage of life. You can't always just move on, just as you can't always dismiss the suffering and injustice in the world as the result of wrong thinking. At some point you've got to stop thinking that the world owes you something and realize you owe something to the world. At some point, you've got to pick a spot and do what you can.

Maybe you'll create great art. Maybe you'll write beautiful poetry. But maybe your calling is simply to comfort a sobbing girl with a puppy or to counsel a fatherless boy who's thinking of dealing drugs. Maybe you'll just make sure everyone gets their mail.

Maybe you don't have easy answers; maybe you don't have five laws or seven truths or an elixir in a bottle.

Maybe you don't have an exalted priesthood, but only a humble ministry.

And maybe, just maybe, that's enough.

I wheel the Tuna along the graceful curves of this roadway that follows the top of these coastal hills. Far below, the lights of the cities are starting to come on. On the bay the tiny ships move like toys over the still waters. In the distance, out past the Golden Gate, the wall of fog is beginning to mass. Soon it will roll its way across the hills, overtaking San Francisco, obscuring Marin, eventually moving across and

swallowing Oakland, Berkeley, and the endless suburbs that stretch
to the north and south along the eastern rim of the bay. The first wisps
will move over my head like phantom fingers, and a chill will fill the
air. The fog will swallow all, and we will all be cloaked in the great
Pacific night.

I look out over the quieting waters toward the Golden Gate
Bridge. What a graceful tracery. Her gentle bow echoes the natural
curve of the horizon.

From somewhere to the south a siren cuts through the growing
night.

I put Bach's *Mass in B Minor* in the tape deck. The hallowed tones
of the Sanctus fill the dusky twilight air.

The lights of the evening are coming on in profusion now. The
whole Bay Area spreads out before me like a bowl filling with stars.
Far in the distance, the Golden Gate lifts her upstretched arms and
holds the setting sun between them, as if consecrating the passing of
this magical day.

Bach sings his praises to the heavens. I know what it is that I
must do.

FOURTEEN

THE CHILDREN OF EL DORADO

D on't ever try to find a cheap motel in San Francisco. It's not as
bad as New York, where I once rented a room on the edge of
the Bronx for thirty-six dollars a night, only to find that the sheets
hadn't been changed and the world's greatest sexual athletes were
performing in the next unit. It was only after several volleys of exactly
the same sequence of screams and grunts and the subsequent mum-
blings of several male voices that I realized a porn movie was being
filmed in that room. Still, it raised some unpleasant questions about
the wet and rumpled sheets in the bed I was supposed to occupy.

My San Francisco room was nowhere near that tawdry, but the
overpowering scent of old alcohol and stale cigarettes made my night
only marginally more pleasant than it would have been had I fallen
asleep under the table in a bar. But for all its deficiencies, the motel
had the virtue of getting me started in the city, where I could begin to
put my plan into place. A few quick phone calls and a visit to a bank
later, and I was once again back on the road.

I want to get Louise and Nick each a present. Nick is easy. He can't
get to stores himself, and we have nothing even approximating a
decent bookstore in my hometown. So I stop at Stacey's and find a
journal written by the man who captained the *Endurance* during

Shackleton's Antarctic adventure. It will take Nick right into the event, if, indeed, he needs to get any closer than he is already.

Louise, however, is more difficult. She travels frequently, she's willing to buy things for herself if she likes them, and she, like all of us, has very distinct tastes. Getting her something she'll like but would never get for herself is a challenge. But it's a challenge I relish. When I get it right, it gives me immeasurable pleasure.

Also, I remember my father's struggling efforts to find presents for my mother. He was not much of a shopper and somehow seemed always to be about a wavelength away from where her tastes were. In his darkest moments, he would make the fatal male error of buying her a frying pan or an iron, thinking her complaints about our current models meant a new one would be an appreciated gift. Witnessing the response, whether direct or implied, had early on taught me that the second three most important words to keep in mind in a relationship are, "No household appliances."

This was underscored by the deep significance my mother has always attached to a velvet-lined, cherry music box my father had once purchased for her, which she keeps to this day as one of her most treasured possessions.

I'm not likely to find a music box for Louise, but I do have an idea of something unique and personal to get her. She loves casual sport coats and jackets she can wear while teaching. Aside from a short and ill-fated dalliance with tailored dress outfits, she has settled on this look, and even when she abandons it out of boredom, she eventually comes back to it as the most reasonable and simpatico personal style.

Unfortunately, the choices we have in clothes in northern Minnesota are as limited as our choice in fresh vegetables, and catalog purchasing has proven spotty as well as being just another variation on off-the-rack garmentry.

What I want is a store with something utterly unusual, unexpected, and West Coast. I pick a spot outside of Stacey's and begin asking women who are wearing exotic clothing where I might purchase something of similar flair. After a few strange glances and hurried escapes, I find a woman who understands what I'm up to. She thinks a bit, then gives me several names. "Start with this one," she says, directing me to a shop some miles away.

The shop turns out to be exactly what I want. It's an unassuming little boutique that purports to have garments from Polynesia and the South Pacific. As I walk through the door, I'm immediately whisked away into a world of bright and joyous colors. Every inch of every wall is covered with garments the colors of exotic fruits and flowers and sunsets. They hang from the ceilings, are spread out on the floor. It's like an oriental bazaar or the boudoir of some Polynesian potentate. The garments themselves are mere excuses to festoon the earth with beautiful colors and fabrics.

"This is beautiful!" I exclaim to the two women who are busying themselves with rearranging and hanging garments. They're on the edge of glazed-eyed—blissed out, like people sated with too much lovemaking or just stepping off a carnival ride.

"Isn't this amazing!" says the older woman, holding up a jacket made of fabrics dyed all manner of purple, orange, and magenta. "It's like a giant flower."

I tell her I'm looking for something for my wife, that we live in a place where, at this time of the year, colors are all blues, dark greens, whites, and browns under an unrelenting grey sky. "Then she needs something from here," she says. "She needs color."

She begins pulling down jackets from the wall and holding them across her arm, like an Arab merchant offering me silks somewhere on the trade routes. Each garment is dizzying and unique. Each prompts a particular story from the owner about why she chose it and what she likes about it.

She then passes it to her younger, shoeless companion, who tries it on over her floor-length gossamer gypsy dress and spins about like a fairy princess. "This one is incredible!" she says. There are no mirrors, only the sumptuous walls and floors and ceilings of color.

"How can I choose?" I say to the older woman. I'm like a man allowed to pick one flower from a tropical garden.

"Oh, you'll know," she responds.

After about a half hour, I do. "This one," I say. It's magenta and turquoise and orange and peach and aqua—a Pacific sunset of a coat, and just what Louise could use to carry her through a bleak Minnesota winter.

"I knew that when you first picked it up," the woman says, "but you had to find out for yourself."

I pay and walk toward the door. "Thank you," I say, staring at the astonishing hues of the jacket I've just purchased. "Thank you. This will really make her happy." And I believe it.

"Oh, no problem," she says. "That's what I'm here for."

I step out into a morning bright with Pacific winter light. The shop owner has followed me to the door. "Color heals, you know," she says, as I leave.

I can't argue with that sentiment, nor do I want to. I look in the bag at the captured Pacific sunset. I need to do some healing myself.

I wander down the streets of this chimerical city that has been so much a part of my past. I was always more of an East Bay person, leaning more to the political than the celebratory. But anyone who has ever spent time in San Francisco knows that it's a place unto itself and that it has a character and an ambience that can seduce even the most taciturn and contemplative mind.

My first lesson in this cultural truth came several days after that introductory party in Marin County, while I was strolling down Market Street. I was glancing about at the various storefronts, and just generally taking in the sights of a new and fascinating city, when suddenly I came face to face with a man, buck naked except for a pair of high-top black tennis shoes, leading a goat on a string. I don't know whether I was more amazed by his mere presence or by the fact that no one was paying him any mind. Word of his very existence in Minnesota would have set social workers, penal officials, and news photographers on red alert across the state.

But after a few weeks in the Bay Area I had made significant progress in redefining my sense of "normal" and probably would have paid no more mind to the goat man than I did to the people with top hats, shopping carts full of balloons, and signs written in cuneiform. As one of my friends put it, "Fellini, not Bergman." For those of us who had spent years in darkened theaters at Janus film festivals, this said it all.

Now I'm back on those Fellini streets, and the goat man and the one-eyed midget and the white rabbit are all still here, now just leavened with a greater sprinkling of people in power suits and hollow-eyed vagrants rattling cups full of pennies.

I drive up through the Haight. San Francisco was not made for cars, and it conspires against them not only through a lack of parking and an unbearable crush of traffic, but by the very geographical configuration of the city itself. Get on a wrong street, and you soon find yourself navigating a transmission-frying grade or a brake-destroying drop or trapped in a no-exit urban box canyon. In an attempt to avoid these pitfalls, I've chosen a straight major street that should allow me some measure of unimpeded passage.

I'm feeling happy and lighthearted. My shopping expeditions have been a success. I'm drunk on the grog of the San Francisco ambience, and I've come to some conclusions in my mind.

I accelerate, decelerate, wait patiently at light after light as the parade of Haight-Ashbury San Francisco goes past me. It's a mishmash of humanity that keeps me attentive and fascinated. Old ladies in long coats. Guys talking randomly to themselves. Black kids with retro Afros wearing headphones and flowered pants. White kids with hair exploding like dandelions out from under baseball caps. Chinese cops on bicycles. Fifty-year-old men in fatigue jackets and long grey beards pushing shopping carts. Guys with no shoes sitting in the doorways of unopened shops, going through old garbage bags, their feet black and filthy and hard as shoe leather. If you can imagine it, you will see it. You need only have the patience to wait until it passes by.

I'm surprised I'm enjoying myself so. I was never a great fan of Haight-Ashbury, even in my most drug-addled counterculture days. There were several streams that flowed together to make up the '60s hip consciousness, and I had arrived by way of the beatnik stream, with its subordinate tributaries of social and political concern. The Haight had been a magnet for those who had floated in on the pastel stream of flowers and rainbows. They were going to change the world by changing their heads, and their airy confusions and LSD moon shots to levels of higher consciousness were only tangentially related to my more populist concerns.

We shared a common taste in music, a penchant for drugs, and a contempt for the Big House constraints of American postwar culture. But when it all unraveled, the fundamental distance between us became clear. What remains here is the dry wash of that psychedelic stream. As the Berkeley boy said from his more contemporary vantage point: it's crazy over here. But when you're in the mood, the craziness is delicious and intoxicating. Today, I'm in the mood.

The traffic moves in three-foot increments. I creep slowly toward an intersection. It's not a pace suitable for an emergency vehicle, but I can live with it. After all, I've got a front-row seat at the circus. What's not to like?

Three feet. Stop. Three feet. Stop.

A woman pushing a purple velvet baby carriage smiles at me from the adjacent sidewalk and quickly disappears down the street ahead of me.

Three feet. Stop. Three feet. Stop.

Then, without warning, even this glacial pace ceases. Everything comes to a dead halt. I crane my eyes to look for the source. At the next cross street I see a bus stalled in the middle of the intersection. It's halfway through a left turn, but can't continue because a truck driver has blocked the street in order to unload some meat to a small butcher stop.

The intersection is jammed. The light changes from red to green to red to green to red. Cars pile up in all directions. The bus driver—black, well-dressed, proud of his uniform—jumps out and runs over to the truck driver, who is sweating and working hard at unloading an impossible cargo in an impossible situation. They begin to shout and gesticulate at each other. The bus driver is frustrated and angry; he's pointing and accusing. The truck driver is screaming in Italian, gesturing first to the shop, then to the sky, waving his hands in a display of wild theatrics.

A passenger jumps out of the bus and begins playing a trombone. People begin clapping. Horns honk, some in time with the trombone, others in long, low blares of rage. People are shouting from their cars, shaking their fists.

A man on a motorcycle screams something and drives up on the sidewalk. People part like the Red Sea. They give him the finger. He revs up his cycle and roars past, knocking people to the ground. Mothers pull children into doorways. Boom boxes are turned on. A man in a clown suit who has been trying to attract patrons to a storefront steps into the street to direct traffic. Dark-windowed cars with suitcase-sized subwoofers throb and reverberate with rap music.

The clown begins to get cars to back up. The trombone player toots an accompanying sound track to each of the clown's gestures. The people on the sidewalk applaud each time a car manages to free itself from the mess and make its way down the street. The bus driver continues to holler, the truck driver waves a meaty leg bone of some large animal. People boo and hiss and shout support to their protagonist of choice.

I shake my head in a mixture of admiration and confusion. Here, in full blossom, is that mix of chaos and carnival that is San Francisco at its finest: life as theater, life as celebration, the Duke and the Dauphin cavorting on the stage of the Royal Nonesuch.

The dour flatlander who looks at this mess and sees infrastructure failure, unbridled population growth, and individual selfishness simply doesn't get it. He's refusing to give himself over to the play, and the play's the thing. It's why I don't belong here anymore: no one's interested in sitting in the theater next to someone who points out the guywires by which Peter Pan is able to fly.

But it is the guywires that I see, the scaffolding that I care about. I'm concerned that the stage fits solidly on the contours of the earth, that it doesn't use too much lumber, that the play's appropriate for children, and that people without enough money for a ticket can still get in. I don't spend enough time applauding the actors, praising them for the panache with which they play their parts. Maybe, just maybe, the guy picking his leathery feet likes his role. If he doesn't, he can just try out for another. After all, miraculous change is possible. Transformation is nothing more than an act of will.

This is the town, this is the place, for such believers. We're not poor players strutting our moment on the stage, then leaving. We're actors and dancers caught up in the fullness of the moment, blowing trombones and wearing costumes the colors of the sunset. Come one, come all, there's a part for everybody, and a new production begins tomorrow.

I smile and move forward. I'm glad I'm here. I remember what I missed, and I realize what I'm not.

I head south on the Bayshore Freeway toward San Jose, surrounded by an almost unbearable welter of traffic. I don't know where it's coming from, or why. This is only mid-afternoon; rush hour can't be starting yet. Maybe there's some big event at Candlestick or some giant accident down by the airport. Maybe the San Francisco equivalent of a sirocco or a Santa Ana is blowing through the air and making people crazy with the desire to move. Whatever it is, I'm flanked on all sides by walls of traffic, and we're not moving at all.

I sit thrumming my fingers on the dashboard. Guys on Harleys are roaring down the space between the lanes—an act that, though legal in California, I find dangerous and bizarre.

There's nothing to be done, so I occupy myself by reading bumper stickers.

There are the usual pushes for "Proposition this" and "Proposition that." But there is also this crypto-spiritual edge: "The mind is clear, open, infinite" and "Prayer creates abundance."

I think of the bumper stickers I see so often in Minnesota: "Keep honking. I've almost finished reloading," "My wife's car is a broom," and the endless "When guns are outlawed, only outlaws will have guns."

It's anecdotal sociology and not clear-cut, but there's an interesting dichotomy in the directions the sentiments lean. Out here, they seem to tend toward breathy glazed-eyed conviction; there, they tend toward moral and political outrage.

One is characterized by a disconnect, like the Mercedes in the next lane, with its perfectly spaced two bumper stickers: "Visualize world peace" and "I don't need to get it. I've already got it." The other exhibits a smoldering impotence and not very well-masked anger.

In their extremes, they explain why I've ping-ponged between the West and the Midwest. Too long listening to people in Mercedes' tell me to visualize world peace while Mexicans are sitting on the side of the road, and I'm likely to say, "Keep talking, I've almost finished reloading." Too long listening to people in smoke-belching pickups roar, "When guns are outlawed, only outlaws will have guns," and I'm likely to say, "Couldn't you just visualize world peace?"

But you can't have it both ways. There is always some chaff in the wheat. Sooner or later you have to choose.

Without warning, the traffic opens and begins to move. I look around, but can find no explanation—no chunks of headlights on the freeway, no tow trucks pulling wounded vehicles to the side of the road. Soon we're up to seventy, bumper to bumper, heading south toward San Jose.

I see the sign announcing the exit for Palo Alto, the home of Stanford. I'm sorely tempted to stop and visit the campus. In some ways, it's where this journey all began. And though I spent only a year there, it really was a major fork in the road of my life. Had I finished my Ph.D. there, a few phone calls from Professor A to Professor B at some distant, ivy-covered college would have greased my way into an academic appointment that would have been the beginning of a life-long career. Right now, I would probably be a full professor, wearing ratty tweed coats and giving lectures to groups of students rather than conversing with chicken-cut cap-shop girls and lost souls hanging out on the streets of Berkeley.

But I ran off to the woods and fell in love with sculpture and a life without square corners. Now I meet old schoolmates at gas stations and they're surprised I'm not dead. Ah, well, we all choose our park bench and do what we can.

No, I'll let Stanford be. One more road not taken, now as well as then.

I follow the lemming flow south on the Bayshore and lean left down U.S. 101 at San Jose. I've got twenty-four hours left before it's time to leave. I could go sit on the beaches at Santa Cruz and take in the first hints of southern California sun. But I've decided I want to visit Greenfield, the town the Mexican man at the canal left behind in search of riches in Marin and San Rafael. The old socialist in me still smolders; I want to see what it was that drove him north.

This stretch of 101 is a road I've never really driven. When I lived out here and had to travel south, I always used either the ruthlessly efficient and lethally boring I–5 fifty miles to the east, or the beautiful, winding U.S. 1 through Carmel and Big Sur a few miles to the west. Highway 101 was an afterthought, a residual roadway left over from California's simpler days. It never caught my fancy, and I left it to the locals.

101 deserves better. It's the true California road, the highway remnant of El Camino Real, the Royal Road, mapped out in the late 1700s by the Jesuits, and later the Franciscans, as a road between missions. In its original form it stretched from San Diego to San Rafael in what is now Marin, with the missions built a day's journey apart. Depending on your point of view, it was either the sword of God's truth or a Spanish dagger stuck into the heart of Native California. The missions that defined it now stand as roadside tourist attractions for travelers more inclined toward history and meditation than theme parks and water slides.

But 101 still represents the spiritual heartbeat of California. More than any other road, it is layered with ghosts. Their presence echoes on the hillsides.

And what echoes they are. There are the Ohlone and the Yakuts and the other Native people who first lived along this thirsty Salinas Valley. There are the Jesuits, who came to proselytize, and the Spanish soldiers, who accompanied them and looted and pillaged; there are the Franciscans, who built the missions and tried to leave the natives to their own ways as much as possible so long as they accepted the Gospel and lived in accordance with its dictates.

There are the Californios—wealthy landowners who came up from Alta California and established great feudal grazing empires. There are the eastern immigrants who poured in after the cry of "gold" in 1849. There are the water barons who built the canals and sluiceways that turned this from an arid desert to an oasis of crops, and the Okies and Arkies who came here during the dust bowl to harvest those crops.

There are the stars and starlets and seekers of fame and fortune who have driven this road by the thousands in their movement between L.A. and San Francisco. And there are the Mexican migrant workers who have, for the last half century, been giving their time and their families and their labor and their health to these now fertile fields in hopes of grasping a sliver of the American dream.

Ghosts, all of them, rising up from these hills. And they come across me like the warm wind that blows through this late November sky. I'm glad I chose to take 101. This may not be my land, with its unslakable desert thirst and rolling arid hills, but it's my kind of place, with spaces that echo and put distance in the imagination.

A Spanish moon is beginning to rise over the soft, feminine hills. It's still only a phantom, great and round and spectral. But in these unpeopled spaces, it holds its own with the landscape, and its arrival becomes an event. Soon it will take on the glow of the setting sun and hang heavy over this thirsty valley, and the ghosts will begin to speak in the imaginations of those who care to listen.

I will listen, as best I can. I am still here to learn. But each passing day has taught me, more and more, that the voices I hear best are those that rise from the fogs and the mists of my northern oxbow streams—the voices of the Ojibwe paddling in their sleek canoes made of birch and pitch, of the French Jesuits making their way down the rivers from the north, of the Finns and Norwegians and Germans dragging their meager possessions on sledges through the winter snow, of the men laboring in logging camps and women going slowly insane in sod huts during six-month winters, of Native children pulled sobbing from their parents to be taken off to boarding schools. These are the voices that speak to me most clearly; these are the spirits I was born to hear.

I may not always like the songs they sing or the stories they tell, but I can no more deny them than I can deny this moon by placing my hand over my eyes. They're the texture of my spirit, the color in my heart. Their lives, like mine, were shaped by the deep winters of snowy silence. Their spirits were formed in the brooding enclosure of forests, and by the endless turning of the prayer wheel of the seasons.

Does this make our spirits darker than those of the people who walked this western land? Of course it does. But that is the music the land has played on our souls. Loon calls, pine whispers, banshee winds, lapping waters, the thundering cracking of icebound lakes, close rustling in brittle grasses—life evolving, not transforming, with the heavy weight of the glacier's remembered presence carving patience into our spirits and our dreams. That's who we are; that's who we always will be.

And that's why I can't give myself over to trombones and buses and applause and motorcycles, no matter how joyful the cacophony. It's why I can't quite become one with the rhythmic exhalations of the pounding surf, and the great skyward whispers of the redwoods, and the drumbeat of steady winter rain, no matter how much I love their music. Given a decade, a generation, perhaps my mind would forget. But my blood would remember and would pass that memory along. My children would have to be born and reborn, formed from the dust of their grandfather's bones, to truly be set free.

No, ours is the dark music of the North, a song of life played in a minor key. When we look to the sky, we don't see a soaring seabird or a swooping raven, we see an eagle, distant, staring down—a watcher, building its nest in the highest and most distant tree—aware, but somehow uninvolved, staying put, not migrating, when the harsh winds of winter adversity begin to blow.

We are the human kin to that eagle—the watchers, the observers, seeing much, claiming little, keeping life at a distance and living out our days in a fierce and solitary rectitude.

As I drive along this California road, that life once again feels less like entrapment and more like possibility. What it lacks in celebration, it makes up for in honor. It embraces the world with a long patience, and offers temperance where one might wish for passion. But it has the virtue of humility, and that is what I'm missing most right now.

This western land has touched me deeply and has, once more, ignited my spirit with forgotten dreams. But it speaks to me more of mastery than humility. Rivers are dammed, their courses changed. Valleys are flooded, drowning cultures forever. Cities are built where no cities should be. And all in the name of growth and progress and unfettered dreams.

Just moments ago, I passed a housing development set off in the hills on the side of the highway. It spread up through the draws and over the promontories like some kind of verdant, alien plasma. I'm sure if I lived here, I'd think nothing of it. It would be but one more subdivision built to meet the needs of a growing population. But to my northern sensibilities, whelped in a place of almost more water than land, it seems a dangerous and fragile imposition. It exists only because there was space, not because this earth could support it. Its gracious houses and well-manicured lawns are made possible only by the importation of hundreds of thousands of gallons of water from distant mountain ice packs and flooded valleys. It's a technological wonder—a celebration of our capacity to translate ideas directly from a developer's drawing board to a template of raw land. But it's also, in some way, a statement of our own hubris that such transformations are praiseworthy for the simple fact that we're able to achieve them.

It is on the land, not of it, and I am still the man who believes God broke my ankle because I stole a basketball. How much more are the gods of the land likely to do if we steal water from distant mountains to support the frameworks of our dreams?

I guess I truly am a man of the North and the Midwest. The old dead farmer waving from the snowbank tells a cautionary tale I can't ignore. There is something about appropriateness and humility that must be served. The earth is patient, long-suffering, and, as much as possible, forgiving and healing. But she has her limits and her laws, and we transgress them at our own peril.

I want to call Louise one more time. I am feeling the pull of home and family. I yearn to be back among the crisp, bright sounds of boots breaking through winter snow.

Ahead I see the last vestiges of the housing development. A convenience store–cum–gas station stands near the freeway exit thrusting its neon insignia forty feet in the sky. I turn off the 101 flyway and head toward it. Above me, stretching up the hillside, are the curving asphalt streets and manicured, tended lawns.

My eye wanders to where the green ends abruptly at the dry and desiccated hillsides. On one side there are curbs and cul-de-sacs and basketball hoops and emerald green lawns. On the other, dry arroyos and gnarled, desiccated stumps, weathered silver grey from years in the relentless sun.

No, I could not make my peace with this life. Even if I got swept up in the tranquil and idyllic lifestyle, in some still, small corner of my being I would wait every day for the inevitable retribution. As Nick Collins said, "There are things we do not know." I would spend each day wondering when we would know them, and in what dark fashion we might find them out.

I drive into the service station parking lot. A group of boys goes by me on dirt bikes, heading home from play. They have on headphones and carry basketballs under their arms. Their laughter brings me back to the realm of the ordinary.

Would my Nick be among them if we lived here? Of course he would, or at least I hope he would. We would live in a house on one of the cul-de-sacs; he'd go out in the evening to shoot baskets in a neighbor's driveway or ride his bike down here to meet his buddies at the convenience store. They'd swap CDs, stay too long at the magazine rack until they were hied out by the clerk, maybe irritate a neighbor by cutting across the corner of his lawn as they raced home to beat their curfew. I'd be outside, watering the shrubbery, talking to the guy down the street, as Nick wheeled in, breathless, asking, "Did I make it in time?" Then he'd go up to his warm and comfortable bed and fall into a deep sleep as the Spanish moon passed overhead, casting long shadows across this quiet, ghost-filled land.

But what would he know of those ghosts? Would he understand this land in the way he understands our home on a lake in the northern woods? Or would his understanding stop at the ends of the cul-de-sacs and the aprons of the convenience stores? Would he hear the echoes of those who have walked this land before him or only the music in his headphones?

I watch the boys on their bikes as they cruise around the parking lot. These are good kids; I can see it in their smiles and guileless faces, and in the way they lean their bikes against the wall of the convenience store rather than dropping them in front of the door.

How deep are the roots of their lives? What voices are they hearing? It's hard to know the land when the world in which you're raised is an imposition. It's hard to hear the ghosts, or even want to hear them, when you drink from distant waters while the spirits walk a thirsty land.

Louise answers quickly. The kids on their bikes are doing pirouettes and wheelies in the parking lot. One of them has a skateboard, and the clacking of its wheels makes the conversation hard to hear.

"It's time," I say, pushing the receiver tight to my head and holding my hand over my other ear. "I'm coming home."

"And I'm waiting for you," she replies. "Both of us are. How's it been?"

"Strange," I say. "I've been surrounded by ghosts."

"I hope you didn't let any of them catch you," she says. Distance hasn't dimmed her sense of irony.

"Nope," I respond. "Let the dead bury the dead."

"I'm glad to hear that. But you're sure you're ready to stop? There's a lot of West Coast left."

"Nope. I'm ready. I've seen enough. Even Ernest Shackleton didn't make it all the way across the pole."

"Nick will be impressed at the parallels," she says dryly.

"By the way," she asks, "what was that postcard? The one with the log truck. And the writing on the back? A box of raisins? Diet Pepsi? A large bag of Fritos? Was that some kind of code?"

I had forgotten. "It's a long story," I say. "I'll tell you when I see you. Tomorrow night."

"Well, here's a little thought to hold you," she says. "You're coming back to a gingerbread house with ice crystals on the windowpanes and snow dripping like frosting from the roof. Today there were three deer in the yard, and Nick saw an otter sliding when he was out playing on the lake."

"'Three deer in the yard, life used to be so hard, now everything is easy 'cause of you,'" I sing in some vague approximation of a melody.

"Don't quit your day job," she laughs.

"I don't have one," I remind her. "Is Nick around?"

"No, he's at chess club. At school. I've got to pick him up in a bit. Then I've got to take him to . . . are you ready for this . . . 'curling.'"

"Curling? Scotsmen in kilts sliding stones down the ice?"

"You've got it."

"What sort of monster are we creating?"

"Your monster. He decided it sounded . . . interesting."

I look around at the kids on the dirt bikes and skateboards with their headphones and basketballs.

"Curling. Chess. Saxophone. Shackleton . . ."

"Don't forget Groucho Marx and Richard Nixon."

"Groucho Marx now?" I say incredulously.

"Things change rapidly," she laughs.

We talk a bit. I tell her of the bus fiasco and the trombone accompanist.

"Maybe they need a saxophonist," she offers. "A specialist in 'When the Saints Go Marching In.'"

I briefly recount my encounter with Marin Dave, the boy in Berkeley, the man on the bench in Oakland, the man at the canal in San Rafael.

"Sounds like you got what you wanted," she says.

"Almost," I answer. "I've got one final piece of business, then I'll be up in the ebony skies. I'll be in tomorrow night. On the late flight."

"We'll be there. And, speaking of business, some man from the bank called, said everything's in order."

"I'll deal with it when I get back. For now I'm thinking of otters and curling and patient wives and our little dark corner of the world."

"Well, they'll all be here waiting when you get home."

We say our good-byes. I hang up the phone and try to visualize Nick curling. The kids on the dirt bikes are still doing wheelies and pirouettes as I walk back to the Tuna.

"Say, do any of you guys know what curling is?" I ask.

"Sure. He's one of the Three Stooges," says the kid with the head-phones.

I smile and give him a "thumbs up."

The Spanish moon is growing rich and round and luscious above the shadowy missionary hills.

A few miles down the road I see the sign for Greenfield. This is the town I've been looking for. I'm curious to see what the man at the canal left when he came north to Marin to seek his fortune.

I turn off 101 and head into the business district. Though I'm only a few minutes removed from the curved hillside sanctuaries and cul-de-sac developments, I've entered into a different world.

The town sits in the flatlands in the middle of the valley. The wide, low, windswept main street—a segment of the actual El Camino

Real—is bordered by one-story storefronts with signs like "Taqueriá" and "Michoacán's Ristorante." Many buildings are boarded up.

A dusty wind, pungent with the smell of soil and pesticide, blows warm in the growing evening. Brown-skinned men in sleeveless undershirts stand talking in front of shops. Girls laugh and shout Spanish epithets as young, slicked-back men in low riders and chopped pickups rumble slowly down this only main drag in town. I wonder if the Marin man's son, Cruz, is among them.

The streetlights come on almost unnoticed. They glow like lanterns against the rosy twilight hills. It is warm, sensual, forlorn. There is too much space, too much yearning, too little to do. The boys are too well groomed, the cars too well waxed. Everyone is all dressed up with nowhere to go. The rumble of the cars' exhausts echoes off the concrete-block facade of the supermarket and the laundromat and rises round and hollow into the night.

There's poverty in the air, and a sense of distances that cannot be bridged. The town has the feel of Friday nights fueled by alcohol, and televisions blaring through open windows in suffocating trailer courts on sweltering summer evenings. There are no convenience stores, no cul-de-sacs, and almost no Anglos anywhere.

Though I don't feel welcome, I feel strangely at home. This town has an honesty about it that I find inviting. It is arid and minimal, befitting the barren thirstiness of the land. Dust rises up and softens the edges of the twilight.

I follow the road through the town, thinking of the man by the canal. How many nights did he spend staring into this dusky sky, pondering the decision to leave his family and head north to follow the dream? Was he, too, as unsure of his journey as I was of mine? How much of his quest was for his family and how much for himself? Hard questions—questions I know well—and able to be answered only in the deepest corners of a father's and a husband's heart.

Where the main street fades out and the rich crop fields begin, I see a small construction trailer. Next to it is a half-finished street laid out in an S curve. Curbs are in, and the pavement has that shiny newness of freshly laid asphalt. On either side of the street are boxy California ramblers with their exposed pressboard construction not yet covered with faux redwood or stucco or whatever masking the developer has chosen. The street trails off where the last of these unfinished houses is framed in. Beyond lies the field from which this development is being carved.

All is dark. No one lives here yet. These cubicles huddle, half completed, on their dirt lots, surrounded by piles of plywood and construction detritus.

Next to the trailer stands a billboard: "Coming Soon. 3–4–5 Bedroom Homes Starting at $119,000." Another announces, "2 Bedroom, 2 Bath Town Homes, Coming Soon." They're written in English; their audience is an unseen, perhaps not yet arrived, Anglo clientele that works in Salinas or Monterey or at the Soledad prison. It is not the workers and youths who lounge on the corners and benches several blocks back. It is not my friend by the canal in Marin.

"Coming Soon." "Coming Soon." Yes, more seekers will be coming soon. And soon the pipelines and sluiceways and reservoirs that bring the water down from the Sierras will be asked to deliver a few hundred thousand more gallons per year so the families who buy these houses can live their simple, earnest, American dreams.

The Mexican pickers with their casual evening promenades and trailer-court lives will be forced into more discreet and less visible corners of town. Their taquerias will be bulldozed and replaced by Taco Bells and Taco Johns. Their Spanish laughter will fade from the main street, replaced by the laughter of Anglo kids on their dirt bikes. The whispers of the ghosts will become even fainter on these valley hillsides.

I step out and pick up a piece of the pressboard that's lying in a pile of construction waste by the side of the street. It still smells of glue and formaldehyde. I sail it aimlessly in the direction of the house in front of me. It hits in the dirt and skitters to a stop near the foundation.

I get back in the Tuna and head out toward the distant freeway. Beyond the edge of town, where the lights have disappeared and the road cuts through darkening fields, I see the bobbing silhouette of a grasshopper oil derrick. It rises and falls in an eerie rhythmic silence, like a great insect pecking the ground in search of some nectar. Like the cul-de-sac developments, like the Mexican youth slouched against their fenders with their malt liquor bottles in paper bags, it too, is thirsty. It too, seeks its fortune in the gentle curves and folds of this arid land.

Above the hills, the now full moon hangs rich and ripe. A warm wind blows, warmer than the air itself, presaging change. The radio crackles with country-western songs; the oil derrick continues its rhythmic bobbing. Pickup trucks and Maseratis fly by me on Highway 101 on their way to King City or Santa Barbara or L.A.; this is still the Royal Road, transporting the dreams of civilization between north and south.

I look out at the passing landscape. In the twilight the hills are no more than silhouettes, the same shapes that greeted the Franciscan friars as they made their way north over two centuries ago. Yes, this road is layered with ghosts. The good padres, the less-good padrones, the Indians who have been all but forgotten, the workers and the laborers and the migrants and the serfs; the wealthy and the desperate, the starlets and the Okies, the families coming soon to their cul-de-sac lives.

All have traveled this road in search of their own private El Dorado. And now I too am among them, just one more sojourner searching for waters to slake my unquenchable American thirst.

FIFTEEN

HOLY SPACES

South on 101.

The night, now, is closing in. I must make time.

The mailman's image rises before me. I see his face—the square lantern jaw; the kind, almost sorrowful eyes; the greying flattop haircut with its proud echoes of his military past. I remember his stories of his dust-bowl parents and their search for a home here in this valley. Did he once ride on this road, a young man in the back of his family's old truck, heading toward dreams of a homestead in Oregon? Did his parents pick crops in these fields, now tended by Mexican migrants with dreams no less real than theirs? Now he rides with me, one more ghost in this spirit-laden land.

I should probably head back north, spend the night in Seaside or Monterey. There's no need to take this route. But the ghosts are strong, and I can feel the pull of the South, sense the lure of the soft air and lambent twilights of Santa Barbara, L.A., San Diego. Perhaps I should have continued on, giving myself to their velvet nights. But those places are not my home—never can be, never will be. I am not made for thirsty land.

Now that night is falling, I just want to drive, to feel, to think, to dream. I want to fly by these small islands of light in the great California darkness, giving myself to them as I gave myself to those radio signals so many years before. I want to hear the wheels singing beneath me, the wind roaring through open windows; I want to see the images, half imagined, rising in the darkness, then disappearing into the night.

How much I am still like the young man, thirty years ago, who drove, bleary-eyed, toward endless dawns, intoxicated by motion, music, the purr of the engine, the smells of the passing land.

I have not changed so much.

And yet, I have.

I need only think of the people I have met, and those among them who have touched me.

Was it the trucker with the gun butt protruding from his belt? No, his cowboy ways seemed distant and out of sorts.

Was it the man on the ferry selling dreams in a bottle? Or Dave in Marin with his perfect system of success? No, they were good men, both of them, but their lives were too neat, their worlds too bounded by the self.

No, it was the cap-shop girl, with her chicken cut and her silly dreams, and the Mexican man, with his vision of Jaguars and Mercedes. They're the ones who captured my heart. Perhaps their dreams will always elude them. But their search felt so much more honest than the closed and self-referential systems of Dave and the man on the ferry. They were, at least, still engaged in the messiness of the universe.

And then there was the croupier boy at the casino, staring at seabirds and listening to the cold rattle of coins on metal, so aware of the fragile nature of the world and the hollow end to which even the purest faith can come.

And the young man carefully constructing falafels at the food booth in Evergreen. And the forest ranger, performing his small unnoticed act of private courage. Two men driven by an inner integrity that needed no praise, no recognition.

Yes, I have changed. Years ago I would not have seen their quiet dignity, their willingness to live a life made whole by the small gesture well made. I would have been banging against the edges of the universe, shouting "Why?" like the boy in Berkeley, thinking that the world owed me more, that I should have a free lunch of my choosing, and that justice and fairness should take the shape of my own understanding.

I would have been railing at God for the good man's deafness; sleeping on floor space because I had not been granted a seaside cottage. Falling short of perfect love, I would have had no love at all, blind to the fact that the world grows in mystery, deaf to the cries of those who wanted only for me to sit with them a while.

But I am different now. I'm not Thom or Shawn, "banking my way across America," or the boy on Telegraph, or George in Eugene tilting at windmills in a fulminating rage.

I understand more of the small movements in life. I understand how hard it is for the woman in Crescent City to leave her home, how much she risks, how much she stands to lose. I understand the couple with their motel in Edmonds, trying to get their children out of the world of gangs and trouble. I understand Tarique's father, caught between fear and dreams and reducing life to a bullet dodged or a bullet taken. I even understand the logger with his egg sandwich, watching the world change around him and trying to argue it back into shape by bludgeoning everyone with his private point of view.

But most of all, I understand the man on the bench in Oakland, reaching out to a few struggling kids, saying, in his own quiet way, that his humble ministry is life enough. He knows he is but a flicker in the great eternal night. But instead of raging against the smallness of his light, he illuminates what he can with dignity and grace, because he knows that he, alone, is given the gift of that place and time in this mysterious and magical passage through life.

Road angels, all of them, but he most of all. He is the one who is leading me home.

The cities pass; the night grows deep. I roll down the windows, let the air roar in. The night is alive with the pungent richness of the passing fields.

Bradley. Paso Robles. Atascadero. Islands of cities flying by in the night.

All around me the ghosts are rising. Californios, conquistadores. Raiders and seekers, friars and dreamers. Old lovers, lost fathers, lost chances, lost dreams.

A battered car sits broken down on the side of the highway. I catch a glimpse of white Mexican license plates, of a man hunched over a jack changing a tire and children standing back by the mother, watching. They are wearing no shoes.

They disappear into the darkness, into the world of ghosts, one more family down on their luck but pushed forward by dreams, willing to trade the world they know for some hope and a promise and a place in a rich man's field.

I salute them privately and applaud their courage. Their lives will not be easy. But their hopes are no less real than mine, their dreams no less worthy of pursuing.

Soon the lights of San Luis Obispo rise in the distance. I stare at the glow and think of her tree-lined streets, the cool holy silence of her mission, the gracious hacienda reality she offers her inhabitants. She is a jewel, so civil, so genteel. One more beautiful city balanced fragilely on this beautiful western land.

And yes, this western land is beautiful. All of it, from the misted inlets of Puget Sound to these ghost-laden hillsides to the white-sail harbor of San Diego Bay. So beautiful, so alluring, and for that we have flocked to her and embraced her and loved her too well. Now she struggles to bear the burden of our dreams.

I'm glad I spent time here in my youth. It was good for me to test my dreams against these limitless vistas and holy spaces, to try to fly free from the shackles of my past. But I am a child of the seasons, and now is the season to claim and be claimed. I sing in my chains like the sea.

I head up Highway 1 past Morro Bay. The sea rolls, dark and restless on my left; the road cuts a channel through the night. I am heading north toward Big Sur. I want to get there before the sunrise. I want to stand, one more time, on those God-drenched cliffs and watch the sun spread like God's fingers over the waiting waters. I want to see the dawn come alive on those great swan's-neck hills, feel the warmth of the coming day move across the land's soft curves like the caress of a gentle lover. Soon enough I will be back in the dark regions of the North. I want to say my good-byes in a kyrie of light.

The lights of the dashboard glow before me. The moonlight dances on the midnight sea. I look at the shards of this journey that lie scattered on the Tuna's seat beside me. Road maps, brochures, a toll ticket from the erector-set version of the Bridge of the Gods. They are like my memories—fragmentary, selective—moments floating with me on this river through the night.

In the distance, now, I see the great SUR hills rising. They stand, Buddhist-still, against the darkness. I begin my ascent into their presence. Far ahead, cars move like fireflies on the tiny roadway that clings to their cliffsides hundreds of feet above the sea. There can be no land more peaceful, no land more holy. The sky, the earth, and the sea sit in perfect balance, without striving or contending, like placid gods gathered to discuss their separate domains. It is the land as chant—a few parts sung in absolute harmony, reaching always toward the sublime. We humans can only bow our heads and listen.

Higher and higher I climb on the flank of the chanting god, until I, too, am only a flicker in the darkness. The line of moonlight cuts across the waters and bathes me in light.

Off to the right I see a road cutting upward into the hills. It is narrow and unmarked, hardly more than a trail. On a whim, I turn the Tuna and begin to follow. The ascent is curving, vertiginous, a series of switchbacks moving skyward through the night.

Up, up I travel, hearing the crush of gravel beneath the Tuna's wheels.

The path narrows. There is no guardrail. To my left the land drops precipitously into darkness. When I dare drive no farther, I park the Tuna and continue my ascent on foot.

I have no destination, but I want some finality. I want to find a place that commands me to rest, that by the very force of its presence says, "This is it. You have gone far enough."

I make my way upward, breathing heavily. The voice of the great Pacific whispers in the distance. Ahead, a promontory thrusts prow-like out toward the sea. It has the feel of a site for ritual.

I climb until I reach it, then pause, winded, and stare out over this hallowed landscape. I am on a plateau, a small earthen altar of the gods. Far below me, I see the thin ribbon of highway, and far below that, the ghostly line of breakers that marks the edge of the sea. The great harmonics of the wind float among the vales and crevasses. The deep, dark-throated silence of the hills sings out to the sea. In the dim distance, the rhythmic susurrations of the surf breathe quiet in the night.

I am so tiny as to be invisible. This is the perfect place to stop. I close my eyes to await the coming of the dawn.

The sunrise begins like an unheard melody. It creeps across the edges of the chaparral that covers the hillside, tingeing it with life. Soon a far light rises on the open sea. A distant color limns the horizon and dawn crescendos, then spreads across the water like a blessing from God's hand. Suddenly, without warning, a symphony of light bursts forth behind me. It races down the canyons and hillsides and meets the sea in full embrace.

The sun surrounds me, and a million diamonds begin to dance on the glistening waters. I stand, enfolded in the brilliance, unable to hold back a growing flood of tears.

I drop to my knees on the hard, rocky earth. I raise my head toward the sky, let the sun touch my face. This is the end, the edge, the full dream of the West. I hold out my hands. The sun streams in on them, a stigmata of hope that cannot be erased.

I reach in my pocket, take out the envelope I have carried with me. Carefully, in as close to ritual as humility will allow, I remove the rubber band. There, before me, is the earth from the mailman's land. I hear his voice, coming at me over the echoing distance of thirty years: "Someday I'd like to get to Big Sur. It sounds like a hell of a place."

I open the envelope slowly and let the dirt fly free. The wind catches it, carries it, disperses it on the ground and carries it out over the sea.

I stay kneeling in silence, wishing I could do more. But there is no more to do, no more to say. I stand, brush the earth from my knees, and face out toward the sun.

The sea chants. The day lifts me. I take the empty envelope and fold it twice. Without thinking, I kiss it once, the way a priest kisses an alb, the way I used to kiss my tools before I carved.

I turn and begin my slow walk down the hill. I delivered the mail. Now I'm going home.

SIXTEEN

FINDING HOME

The plane wings downward through the darkness. It has been almost an hour since we rose up from that sea of lights that was Minneapolis, and almost six since I lifted off from the soft air of San Francisco.

The plane surges and yaws as it begins its descent. Below me is only darkness and an occasional dot of light of the isolated farmhouse or the huddled cluster of a small town in the north-woods winter night. I'm getting that familiar feeling in my stomach: one part fear, two parts excitement, and ten parts fond release of the traveler returning home.

Our town appears, a puddling of lights rising up from the darkness, bigger than the others over which we've been passing. We drop lower and closer until I can make out the roadways, the tops of familiar buildings, the dark outlines of familiar lakes. Then comes the disembodied thump of the descending landing gear, followed by the real thump of the plane touching down. The engines reverse, the plane exhales, and we begin our long, slow taxi to the terminal door.

I peer out the tiny window. I can see nothing but the silhouettes of pines and the clear, star-filled northern night.

The plane turns and lumbers toward the gate. Then I see them, standing with their faces pressed against the glass, waving—Louise and Nick. I try to wave back, knowing they can't see me, but hoping they can.

The woman in the earphones with the flashlights directs us forward. The plane stops, the turbines still, the door opens, and the stairs descend. I stand in the aisle, waiting my turn.

Every moment is excruciating. I can see Nick waiting at the entrance. He's wearing some kind of strange, tasseled cap that hangs almost to his waist. A wizard? A jester? As Louise said, he's "my monster," and I'll take him just the way he is. Louise is behind, holding a small bouquet of flowers.

I walk down the steps onto the tarmac. The air hits me, cold, dry, and bracing, causing me to shiver. In just a week my body has gotten used to the warmer winter climes of the West. I pull my thin jacket around me and race across to the terminal. Louise stands back so Nick can be the first to welcome me home.

He tries to mask his enthusiasm behind a manly reserve. I reach out my hand in a gesture of mock military decorum. "Commander Shackleton," I say, "I bring my report of the western regions."

He wrinkles his nose and grins. Under his arm I see a book of the collected sayings of Groucho Marx.

Louise comes up behind him and gives me a small kiss. The symbol is enough; it speaks its own quiet volumes. "Oh, I missed you," she says. We hug with him between us—a "Nick sandwich," as it's affectionately known.

"So, there was no wizard?" she says.

"Nope," I reply. "Only a man behind a curtain."

She gives me a knowing smile.

Nick extricates himself from between us. I grab the tassel of his hat as he squirms free. "This is my wizard," I say.

"And you didn't even have to leave Kansas to find him," she laughs.

I recognize some of the faces in the airport. It was a late flight, the last of the night, and it was only half full. There are about twenty people milling around waiting for passengers. We wave to various friends and acquaintances who have come to pick up arriving visitors.

One of our friends walks by. We share a quick greeting. We all know that airport times are private times, so we keep our social discourse to a minimum.

"Been gone long?" he asks.

"A week, going on thirty years," I say.

"Business or pleasure?"

"All business."

"Well, welcome back to the land of ice and snow."

"It's good to be home," I say. And I mean it.

Nick has run across the terminal to the polished aluminum ramp where our baggage will be deposited. He knows how things work here and, in his own way, he's taking charge. Louise and I follow behind, holding hands.

The luggage gate opens and the bags are slid out one by one. Nick watches diligently and grabs the now rattier aviator bag as soon as it appears.

"You should get a new bag, Dad," he says. "One with wheels."

"Nope," I say. "Old friends are the best friends."

He shakes his head like a frustrated parent and drags the bag out to the car. I can see the snow packed in the grill from when Louise was stuck in the ditch on the side of the driveway.

It's late November. The stars are bright. There's just the slightest hint of northern lights moving in the sky. It's good to be home.

Five forty-five A.M. The house is quiet except for our two cats, Dennis and Sally, rustling around in their food bowls.

Louise is breathing gently. As always, her sleep is deep. I run my hand through her hair. She makes a small sound and burrows her head further into the pillow. I kiss her softly on the cheek and step quietly from the bed. I grab the aviator bag, still unpacked, and carry it out to the living room.

Like a surreptitious Santa, I take out the Pacific sunset coat and the Shackleton book and lay them on the couch. They make a delicious contrast: the soft, sumptuous orange and magenta and sky blue fabric against the hard, tintype cover photograph of Shackleton standing next to the icebound *Endurance*. Maybe these are the extremes of our dreams. Maybe this is who we are when we let our hearts fly unfettered to the farthest reaches of our imaginations. But now they lie together on a well-worn couch in a warm familiar house, awaiting their discovery by the two people I love most in the world.

I make myself a cup of coffee. This is my time, and always has been—the silence before the coming of the dawn. Just yesterday, I was standing before a sea transfigured. Now I flop down in an old leather chair, worn to a misshapen comfort that fits only me.

Dennis crawls up on my lap and noses at my chin. He likes to be held like a baby, on his back in the crook of the arm, and he's letting me know that nothing less will do. I flip him over and stroke his belly. The coffee sits on the stained and scuffed arm of the chair, surrounding me with its familiar aroma. Out the window, over the lake, the shadowy line of the distant trees cuts a faint and ragged silhouette against the dark of the northern sky.

Outside the window a birch is brushing faintly against the glass. People have suggested I trim it. But I like to hear his playful scratchings in the mornings. Besides, he's always been a bit of a rogue of a tree—excitable, ready for action amidst the stolid nobility of the pines.

I watch him swing his branches against the glass, urged on by the promptings of the wind.

"Not yet," I think, as if he can hear me. "Give me a few minutes." But he's insistent. And he's right. I've been sitting long enough. I've got work to do.

I stand outside the door of Nick's room and call softly into the darkness.

"Nick. Nick. Wake up."

I hear his covers rustle, followed by a few groans.

"Come on," I say. "I need your help."

"It's still dark," he says groggily, his voice still heavy with sleep.

"And will be for six months," I answer. "Come on. I need you."

I hear the clump of his feet hitting the floor, a few more groans, then his door opens a crack. A disheveled boy in discount-store fatigue pants and an old T-shirt squints out at me. He must have fallen asleep in his clothes.

"Good," I say. "Get some boots on. I need your help."

He's too tired to protest, too bleary to wonder why. I hear the grunts and clunks of a half-conscious ten-year-old rummaging through the junk in his room, until he emerges, jacketed and booted, with a confused look on his face.

"Don't I have to get ready for school?"

"In a bit," I say, shoving a piece of toast into his hand. "But we've got some business first."

He pulls on his jester's cap and we head out together into the pink-tinged winter dawn.

Light is growing in the eastern sky as we drive around the edge of the lake. The car is still stiff; the windows are still frosted. I rub a small circle in the foggy windshield as I drive. Nick huddles in the passenger seat, chewing absently at his piece of toast, kept from sleep only by the cold and his curiosity.

"What are we doing, Dad?" he asks.

"You'll see," I answer. He settles back and stares at the remaining perimeter of crust in his hand.

We drive in silence. The cold clouds of our icy breath fill the car and frost over the small clearing I've made in the windshield. The tires crunch on the freshly packed snow.

We pass the swamp where Nick and I saw the giant snapping turtle last summer, go past the beaver dam, now frozen into the ice and snow. We proceed up the hill and turn into a small trackless path.

Nick is sitting up now. The heater has kicked in, and the warm blast of blowing air has brought him awake. He's staring curiously out the window.

I proceed cautiously. Though a wall of pines has protected the path from the full brunt of the early winter snows, I could easily get stuck. But this is no mountain pass; here I know what to do.

"Where are we going?" Nick asks. He is now as alert and vigilant as a terrier.

"We're there," I say, stopping the car and shutting off the engine. "Let's go. Bring that hammer."

We step out into the clear morning silence. Nick goes around to the back of the car and takes out the heavy sledgehammer I placed there before we left. I watch him struggle with its weight.

"Do you want me to carry it?" I ask.

He shakes his head vigorously. "It's not that heavy," he says.

"You're sure?"

"I'm sure."

"Okay," I say, and start through the woods.

The snow is deep for so early in the year. It comes almost to my knees. Light is slowly filling the eastern sky. A pale and muted lavender illuminates the sparks of ice on the crusted surface as we crunch our way forward. Only the sound of our footsteps crushing through the snow breaks the brittle frozen silence.

Nick has fallen behind. His shorter legs make passage more difficult.

I stop while he catches up. The great empty stillness of the winter North surrounds me. I feel the heavy drumbeat of winter pulsing down from the distant Canadian prairies. Behind me, I can sense the South whispering, with its promise of brightness and warmth. To the east, the voice of the eastern seaboard settlements calls, and, to the west, I feel the roll of the great Pacific and the lure of the pools of lights from which I've just returned. I am once again a man in the middle, hearing muted voices, feeling the sensations of great distances, like a child listening to a radio in the deep midwestern night.

Eventually, Nick catches up. His face is red and flushed from the cold, setting off the small scar on his forehead that he got when he rode his walker down the stairs years ago. He looks at me quizzically. I put my finger to my lips. He's a quiet boy by nature and needs no more explanation. We climb the hill, step by step, father and son.

We reach the top of a small rise. The frozen lake spreads out before us, still pristine in its first blanket of winter snow. Nick grabs me by the sleeve and points. A deer stands motionless in a thicket of trees. She turns her dark liquid eyes toward us, then crashes off through the underbrush.

I wish I had the Native songs and chants that could set her at peace. But I'm only a man in love with the land, not yet a man at one with it. Maybe someday Nick will know its secrets more deeply than I.

The pale morning is beginning to fill with light. The air is clear and dry against our skin—a northern air—singular, direct, without nuance or complexity.

"Bring me the sledge," I say to Nick.

He drags it over to me clumsily as I thrust a long, pointed stake into the snow.

"Here," I say. "Pound this."

He looks at me strangely, then does as I ask. The heavy thwok of metal on wood cuts through the morning silence.

"It's frozen," he says.

"I know. Keep trying."

"Why are we doing this, Dad?" he says. He pounds again. The stake breaks through and enters the earth, claiming it, being claimed.

"It's our new land," I say.

His face moves through expressions like shadows on a northern lake—confusion, curiosity, hope, doubt.

"Our new land? You mean we're not going to move?"

"You've got my word on it. And my word . . ."

". . . is a rock," he chimes in. "You can . . ."

"Build . . . your . . . house . . . on . . . it," we say in unison.

The light of understanding begins to dawn in his eyes. He breaks into a broad grin and starts to look around at the trees, the contours of the hillside, the distant vista of the pine-rimmed lake.

I stand quietly as he begins the long, slow process of making the land his own. Chickadees are hopping from branch to branch. A rabbit track curls off under a canopy of pine and birches. Below us, at water's edge, a deer trail curves around the margin of the lake.

"It's really neat here, Dad," he says.

"I know," I say quietly. "And, hey, even Shackleton had to have a home. Come on. Let's go make Mom some breakfast."

We do not transform in this northern land. We learn, instead, to listen. The rattle of a leaf, the winging of a sparrow, the cry of a rabbit, and the rustle of a deer. From here few things are possible, but much is knowable. Wisdom runs as quiet and deep as the silent winter snows.

It was good I had seen the ad for this land when I was waiting in the airport; good that the banker in San Francisco had been so willing to help; and good that Louise had told me, through her words and her silences, that she waited only for me to come home. Like the woman in the Polynesian shop, she had known, when I first began, what I had wanted. And, like the woman in the shop, she had waited patiently for me to find it out for myself.

Deep beneath us, now, in the frozen ground, the waters gather—flowing, coalescing, entwining, seeking each other. They come together, a thousand streams, a thousand sources, until suddenly there's a river. And in its patient wisdom, that river takes us home.

ACKNOWLEDGMENTS

A friend of mine once dubbed me, with fair accuracy, a guerrilla theologian, and I've happily worn that mantle ever since. But publishers have not been so happy to accept that designation. It means they have an author who is constantly changing outfits, blending in with one crowd or another, and resolutely resisting the categorizing and branding that are so much a part of successful book marketing these days.

Only a rare and exceedingly perspicacious publishing house is willing to see the spiritual core of a writer who is as likely to be found slogging though the swamps of irony and self deprecation as thundering from some righteous hortatory mountaintop. It is to their great credit that HarperSanFrancisco is such a house.

And so I would like to take this little unread corner of *Road Angels* to pay tribute to the people who believed in, fought for, and now stand by, this quirky, loose jointed, spiritual road book. They have more courage and vision than you can imagine.

First, to my dear friend and agent, Joe Durepos, who humped around like a desolate vacuum cleaner salesman, getting door after door slammed in his face as publishers wrinkled their noses and said, "What is that?" when he showed them the outlines of what would eventually become *Road Angels*.

To John Loudon, executive editor at HarperSanFrancisco, who has observed my work with a long patience, sensing what I'm about and quietly championing me within the context of the company mission.

To Steve Hanselman, Harper's publisher, who has created a climate of confidence and vision in HarperSanFrancisco that even a cloistered and overheated author two thousand miles away can sense in the voices and commitment of all those with whom he deals.

To Jim Warner, who caught the hundred countervailing and nuanced impulses in the book, and somehow evoked them all in his cover design.

To Terri Leonard and Chris Hafner, who looked at my obscure and illegible chicken scratchings and, with good humor and impeccable accuracy, turned out a clean and visually sparkling product on a schedule that, to this day, strikes me as manifestly impossible.

To Calla Devlin, who in her publicist's role, brought that rare and magical commodity of honest enthusiasm to the task of promoting and marketing this book.

And, lastly, to my editor, Gideon Weil, who in an instant saw through the veil of obliquity and metaphor in the manuscript and said, "Of course it's a spiritual book," and then, with an artist's touch, proceeded to guide, cajole, and direct it into a meaningful narrative form.

Beyond these front-line folk, there are those in the background who deserve my thanks—my wife, Louise, who kept saying, in amazement, "You're really having fun writing this book;" my son, Nick, whose interesting and idiosyncratic character provided me with constant direct and indirect inspiration, and Sid, our current orange cat, who willingly offered his belly in talismanic fashion whenever I needed solace and diversion during the long and lonely process of turning this book from idea into actuality.

Lastly, I wish to thank the Bemidji, Minnesota, Region Two Arts Council for giving me a McKnight Foundation individual artists grant at a point when my resources and resolve were at their lowest ebb. It was a small gift with a big heart, and it made an impact and a difference far beyond the realm of the financial.

All of these people, as well as the panoply of characters—mentioned and unmentioned—who informed the spirit of this book, have my deepest gratitude. What a long, fun, trip it's been.

Kent Nerburn
Bemidji, Minnesota 2001